"Now thus much without vanity may it be asserted . . .
that if all persons, both Ladies, much more Gentlemen,
would spend some of their tyme in Journeys to visit
their native Land, and . . . make observations of the
pleasant prospects, good buildings and different
produces and manufactures of each place . . . it would . . .
form such an *Idea of England*, add much to its Glory and
Esteem in our minds and cure the evil itch of over-
valueing foreign parts."

Celia Fiennes, *The Journeys* 1685–1712

RUSSELL CHAMBERLIN

The Idea of England

With 131 illustrations, 19 in color

THAMES AND HUDSON

Dedication

To my Scottish, Irish and Welsh compatriots
with relative apologies for use of the
universal adjective "English."

Half-title *The taming of the countryside: the park at Longleat, itself
the first of the architect-built great houses.*

Frontispiece *The Pilgrims' Way near Kemsing, Kent, still
functioning as a high road.*

This page *"Saving the toll," engraving by Thomas Bewick
(1753–1828).*

First published in the United States in 1986 by Thames and Hudson Inc.,
500 Fifth Avenue, New York, New York 10110

Library of Congress Catalog Card Number 85-50752

Printed and bound in Yugoslavia

Contents

First and last of England: the white cliffs at Birling Gap, Sussex.

Introduction

The Idea of England is an attempt to pick up Celia Fiennes's challenge, quoted on the first page. But the motive is different: not to 'cure the evil itch of over-valueing foreign parts', rather to show how this 'Idea of England' gradually emerged through the writings of those who, for whatever reason, travelled round the country or reported back its affairs to their readers in foreign parts.

At first sight, the sheer mass of material from the eighteenth century onwards seems daunting. As recounted in Chapter 7, Alison Lockwood lists over 400 books about England written and published by Americans in the nineteenth century alone, and native writers from the mid-eighteenth century onwards are scarcely less prolific. But, in the event, the books chosen as source material proved to be virtually self-selecting. Before the late seventeenth century their very rarity ensured inclusion, and thereafter the application of one overriding qualification provided a path through the luxuriant jungle: the writer of the book, whatever his or her literary quality, *must* be intent on providing a portrait, or a picture, or an 'idea' of the land and its people. This automatically weeded out all purely descriptive travel writing, a particularly important result when it came to dealing with the enormous output in the second half of the twentieth century.

The book is in three sections. The first, *They Set Out*, tries to convey something of the freshness, of the excitement, of people venturing out into what is still largely an unknown land. And what comes out very clearly, from Chaucer to William Cobbett, was that passionate love of country, and hope in its future, so well expressed by John Leland to his king (p. 20). The love continues, but the hope, alas, weakens as the writers approach our own time. In this first section, too, is included the salutary experience for the English of seeing themselves as others see them – specifically, the view of England retailed back to their countries by foreign visitors. They disclosed some odd aspects of the English character which have come as a surprise to at least one Englishman – in particular, the idea of the English as not simply a violent, but a ferocious people, tempering that ferocity with an equally passionate democracy. (Or was one, perhaps, the cause of the other?)

The second section, *The Imposition of Form*, shows the Englishman standing back from his country, as it were, trying to give shape and meaning to what he saw. Some of it was absurd, like William Gilpin's dismissal of Tintern Abbey as 'disgusting' because it did not conform to his artificial theory of the 'picturesque'. But it was here, in the England of the eighteenth century, that was born (or, at least, disseminated) the idea of natural beauty, the idea that the landscape existed in its own right regardless of economic potential, and should be protected.

The last section, *Brave New World*, brings the story down to our own time. Here is the idea of England as gained, and spread, by the close relatives overseas in the Americas and the Antipodes. Here, too, a place is found for one of the odder sidelights on English history, the description of destitution in the 1920s and 1930s. Curiously, although recent years have seen far higher numbers of unemployed, nothing has yet emerged, or seems likely to emerge, to rival these vivid, touching personal accounts of life in a parallel England, *Into the Abyss*.

The book ends on a disconcertingly pessimistic note, disconcerting because it was neither intended nor desired by the writer, but simply emerged as a result of the chronological arrangement of material. The pessimism is expressed here in the sense of ichabod conveyed by the sympathetic Indian and Israeli observers, the weary resignation of the two native English writers, or the onslaught of the American. Even J. B. Priestley, who not unfairly gained the sobriquet 'Jolly Jack' for his habitual optimism, strikes a sombre note – curiously at variance with that of his novels – in *English Journey*.

Yet there is no profession more hazardous than that of prophet. In discussing the 1983 television version of Priestley's book, John Cunningham remarked in *The Guardian*: 'the need for such literary forays in compact, homogenized Britain has gone'. Just two centuries earlier, in 1789, the Honourable John Byng said almost the same thing, 'because our Island is now so Explor'd, our roads in general are so fine, and our speed has reached the summit'. Between John Byng and John Cunningham appeared most of the books whose accounts form the substance of *The Idea of England*. It seems not unlikely that, in or about 2189, some writer will be lamenting the fact that there is no more to be said, no more exploring to be done, in England.

I

THEY SET OUT

'I was totally enflammid with a love to
see thoroughly all partes of this your opulente
and ample reaulme.'

John Leland to Henry VIII

CHAPTER ONE

Your Opulente and Ample Reaulme

They appear, briefly but brilliantly, from out of the darkness of the past, passing before us like a procession on a brightly lit stage before exiting again into darkness. A procession composed of thirty people of both sexes, mostly in early middle age and covering a wide social range. Most of their professions and trades are familiar to us: there is a miller and a lawyer, a university professor, a seaman, a civil servant, a farm labourer, a couple of nuns. But one or two of them follow trades or occupations that seem bizarre to our twentieth-century eyes: a man who sells religious pardons, another whose well-paid task it is to summon to court people who have broken ecclesiastical law.

They have come together quite by accident, 'a companye of sondry folk, by aventure y-falle', meeting in a large inn on the south bank of the Thames just outside London. But they all have the same destination, the city of Canterbury, and after discussion among themselves they agree that they should go as a group and to wile away the three-day journey they will tell each other stories. The one who tells the best story will have a dinner at the expense of the rest on their return to the inn at Southwark. The date is 7 April some time before the year 1387.

The individual characters in *The Canterbury Tales* are perfectly, unforgettably drawn – the broad-beamed, ineradicably vulgar, indestructible Wife of Bath; the painfully genteel Prioress who must have winced at every bawdy joke of her companion; the tough but gentle Knight; the crude, drunken Miller – but they belong not so much to the fourteenth century as to a gallery of immortal human portraits. It is for the priceless incidental details that historians trawl through the Tales – through the linking Prologues in particular – in search of material to bring to life that long-vanished century. How the pilgrims travelled, what they ate and drank, the arguments that sprang up between them on the road – all this helps to lift momentarily the veil imposed by time and death. And, in doing so, it points up how much our knowledge of the past is dependent upon accident – upon the accident of an observer not only being in a particular place at a particular time but also having both the desire and the ability to record.

So we see this chance-gathered group through the eyes of a civil servant in his late forties. He is a man running to fat, gentle by nature but well able to defend himself: rather withdrawn, but ready to respond to a friendly overture. When the Host chides him for his stand-offishness –

> What man artow?
> Thou lokest as thou wouldst finde an hare
> For ever up-on the ground I see thee stare
> Approche neer and loke up merily

– and demands a merry tale, he replies cheerfully enough that he has no great store of tales but will do his best. He then proceeds to tell the dullest tale of all, and amiably accepts being cut short by the Host's impatient cry, 'No more of this, for goddes dignitee'. A well-travelled man: not so widely travelled as some of his characters, perhaps – the Knight, for instance, who has fought from Eastern Europe to Turkey, or even the Wife of Bath who has been to Jerusalem three times – but who knows Italy and Spain and France well and so

'Then longen folk to go on pilgrimage'; portrait of Geoffrey Chaucer from the early fifteenth-century Ellesmere manuscript of The Canterbury Tales.

is able to place his own country in an international context. A man urban to the core, a member indeed of the court of King Edward III, living most of his life in London, courtly, sophisticated – but, like all his compatriots, drawn to the country and the things of the country.

In the *Canterbury Tales*, on the very threshold of English literature, Geoffrey Chaucer sounds that poignant love of nature which is to be a leitmotif of English life, century after century. This people who created some of the world's most superb urban architecture, who evolved perhaps the most just, flexible and practical form of government – of necessity rooted in urban life – has behaved throughout its history as though personally expelled from the Garden of Eden, ever seeking means of returning to it.

But the immortal opening lines of the great Prologue not only sound the leitmotif and set the scene, they also give the prime motivation for those particular travellers, in that particular segment of time, for going on their journey. In those few lines we see the delight of a northern people responding to the spring. For four months or more they have been cooped up in small smelly houses in an atmosphere compounded equally of stuffiness and icy draughts, living on dried and salted foods, their horizon shrunk to a few yards. Then, as the generous sun warms and thaws and dries, it also draws them out, filling them with the divine discontent:

> Then longen folk to go on pilgrimage
> And palmers for to seken straunge strondes.

It is worth following in some detail the departure of this, the first recorded tourist journey. For, despite the immense changes wrought on the south bank of the Thames in the nineteenth and twentieth centuries in particular, it is still surprisingly easy to follow the route of the pilgrims through the tangled traffic-choked modern streets, testimony to the powerful sense of identity of an urban community. We know exactly where the Tabard was, who built it, why it was built and when it was pulled down. The inn was originally the town house of the Abbot of Hyde in Winchester (the Palace of the Bishop of Winchester was not far away on what is now Winchester Walk) and was built in 1307, lasting almost into living memory for it was not demolished until 1875. Southwark was the natural starting point for any journey down to Kent. London's only bridge debouched here, and inns and taverns inevitably sprang up to cater for those wayfarers caught outside the city by nightfall, or reluctant to penetrate into it. We even know who ran the Tabard in Chaucer's day: a man called Harry Bailey. It must have been a big inn, to accommodate thirty chance-arrived travellers, and the inn-keeper of such a place would have been both tough and well known: the kind of man who appears in the Tales.

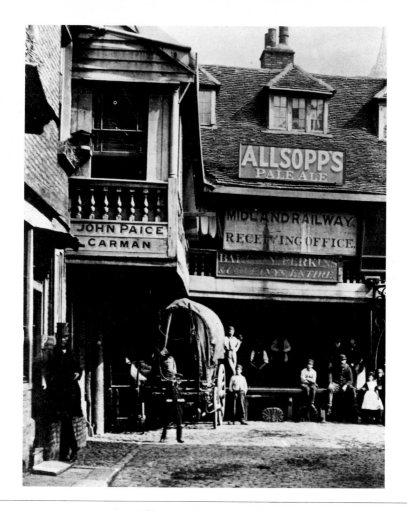

Bifel that in that seson on a day
In Southwerk at the Tabard as I lay . . .

Built in 1307, the great inn survived into the era of photography, and was not
demolished until 1875.

So, on an April morning the company leave in ones and twos, straggling
along, now meeting, now breaking up, passing down what is now Tabard
Street to St Thomas Street. Here was a stream, known as the Watering of St
Thomas, one of many such streams and wells dedicated to the saint, and there
Harry Bailey calls them together and supervises the cutting and drawing of
straws for the first tale. The lot falls to the Knight and he embarks on his story,
presumably riding in the centre of the party as they follow what is now the
Old Kent Road through Deptford Broadway and over Deptford Bridge. The
villages of Greenwich and Deptford come in sight at 7.30. The party must

have stopped to hear part of the Knight's Tale and were perhaps delayed by the quarrel which followed between the Reeve and the Miller, for even now they are only a little over two miles from Southwark. Harry Bailey firmly cuts the Reeve short:

> Say forth thy tale and tarry not the time
> Lo, Depeford and it is half way prime [7.30 a.m.]
> Lo, Greenwich ther many a shrew is in
> It were all time thy tale to begin

and obediently the Reeve begins. And after that they pass out of our ken for it is no longer possible to link time and place as they ride on to Canterbury, 'the holy blissful martir for to seke'.

One of the great myths of our time is the view of the entire medieval period as a static, inward-looking society engrossed with one abstract idea, the avoidance of Hell and the gaining of Heaven. Had this indeed been the case, then the Americas, the Far East and much of Africa would have remained undiscovered by Europeans and the world would have been a considerably quieter place in consequence. People travelled widely, if with considerable discomfort, throughout the European Middle Ages. From AD 800, when Charlemagne refounded the Roman Empire with the adjective Holy, until its apogee in the late sixteenth century, the Emperors ran their vast domain indifferently from Sicily, Spain, or Germany, making immense journeys along what were little more than forest tracks with astonishing celerity. In England, an indication of the rate and quantity of movement is provided by the fact that nearly a third of all English surnames are derived from place names. And one can only identify a man by his place of origin if he is no longer living there.

Serfs remained chained to their villages. But throughout the rest of society there was a continual and restless to-ing and fro-ing. At the top, the king and his court, the great nobles and retainers moved from estate to estate, from manor to manor, for the most elemental and pragmatic of reasons – hunger. It was easier and cheaper to bring mouths to food rather than food to mouths. The court would descend upon an estate, strip it of current produce, and move on to the next. The monarch, too, had the habit of descending upon some powerful subject, ostensibly to do him honour but not infrequently with the deliberate intent to impoverish him and so weaken a possible centre of disaffection. Elizabeth I was particularly fond of these raiding expeditions, conducted under the guise of a 'Progress', though her popularity took the sting out of them. 'God send us both long to enjoy her, for whom we both mean to exceed our purposes', Sir Christopher Hatton wrote to his friend

Lord Burghley on news that Elizabeth was preparing a state visit to him. A dexterous courtier could obtain solid returns in the form of sinecures as a result of a successful, if expensive, visit.

Below the level of the great, came the army of traders, ranging from such substantial men as Chaucer's Merchant, to Shakespeare's Autolycus two centuries later – 'a snapper up of unconsidered trifles', a pedlar by trade, but certainly not averse to stealing, much less swindling. Only the larger towns had shops, with the trader – who as often as not was also the manufacturer – living above or behind his stall. Elsewhere people were dependent upon one of the most ancient figures in civilization, the chapman or pedlar with his pack full of gewgaws, covering incredible miles each year, sometimes on foot, sometimes on horseback. He brought with him something far more valuable than the 'women's tryflinges' that filled his pack. They would pay gladly enough for his gloves and pins and thimbles and brooches and swatches of silk, but it was the news he brought from the great outside world that brought them flocking to him, garbled news, reaching them at seventh, eighth, or tenth hand, but linking them up with the society that existed beyond their fields and hedges.

And parallel to these figures who travelled for the pragmatic reasons of provender or trade were the conveyors of the abstract, all those whose functions are, in the twentieth century, covered by postal services or, increasingly, by electronic means – the messengers of the great. Edward II had a corps of twelve messengers accompanying him wherever he went, paying them threepence a day when they were actually on the road. They had absolute right of way on the road, with heavy fines for whoever dared to impede them. When the Constable of Roxburgh Castle was foolish enough to detain the messenger of Edward III's queen, he was not only fined the incredible sum of £10,000 for the offence but obliged to find £2,000 as indemnity for the messenger. With that kind of backing, these royal couriers covered immense distances in a short time: in 1316 the news of the election of Pope John XXII took ten days to travel from Lyon in France to York, where the king was in residence. The message was not always neatly written on parchment: sometimes couriers carried the hacked-up parts of a traitor to display around the kingdom as warning to others. One wonders how the messenger coped with his grisly burden in summer time.

Only the poorest went on foot. In the *Canterbury Tales* it is very evident that all, even the humble Ploughman, were on horseback. That casual fact gives us, incidentally, some indication of the size of the Tabard – an inn big enough to provide overnight stabling for thirty horses, as well as their fodder, and the quantity of dung to be removed would be reason enough to have an inn of this size on the outskirts, rather than in the centre, of London. The opening up of England was largely dependent upon a creature strong enough to carry a man, his arms, clothes and provisions hour after hour in every kind of weather, across every kind of surface, a creature docile in temperament, choosy in its diet – but that diet fortunately widely available. For at least four centuries before Chaucer, and as many afterwards, the man or woman on horseback was the prime means of communication. Kings and queens had their horse litters and their carriages as early as the fourteenth century, but these were strictly for show, costing almost literally a king's ransom. Edward III paid £1,000 for a carriage for his sister Eleanor, at a time when the average price of an ox was thirteen shillings. The Luttrell Psalter has a superb illustration of one of these land-galleons, an immense four-wheeled vehicle, elaborately carved and gilded, supplied with windows but apparently open at rear and front. Usually, they were for the ladies of the court: certainly, the passengers in the Luttrell Psalter carriage are all women. When John Paston fell ill in London in 1443 and had to return to his home in Norfolk, it never occurred to either him or his wife that he should use a carriage. 'I pray you,' writes Margaret Paston, 'if your sore be whole and so that ye may endure to ride that ye will ask leave and come home, when the horse shall be sent [back] again.' A quantity of stuffed silken cushions doubtless helped to reduce the bone-jarring motion of carriages, but travel in them could not have been other than an endurance test under the best of conditions. Even when properly swung vehicles arrived in the sixteenth century, relatively few preferred their

Great lords moved from place to place at the centre of immense entourages. Here the Dukes of Exeter and of Surrey are en route to Chester in 1399.

sickening motion and stuffy interiors to the freedom of horseback. As late as the nineteenth century, when metalled roads and efficiently sprung carriages brought some comfort to travellers, William Cobbett preferred to hoist his broad beam upon a horse's back, because it gave him the freedom of the byways. And the true rural life of England, he declared, was to be found away from the high roads.

The high road. It is difficult to transcend one's own time, particularly in the use of words. A century of efficient road transport conjures up for us an entirely different concept of the word 'road' than it would have meant for any of our forebears since the departure of the Romans. 'Road' today means a broad, hard, smooth surface moving in a purposive direction: for our ancestors, it meant simply a line along which it was theoretically possible to move, the English, indeed, deriving the word from *ridan*, 'to ride'. The condition of points along that line varied from a reasonably hard, open surface to actual swamps, churned up by traffic, where it was perfectly possible to drown, or deep pits, into which it was perfectly possible to tumble and break one's neck.

As it happens, there has survived in southern England a section of trackway, called the Pilgrims' Way, which is probably exemplary of most 'roads' until the nineteenth century. The name itself is a scholarly fiction, dreamed up by nineteenth-century antiquarians and given substance by the early editions of Ordnance Survey maps. It runs between Winchester and Canterbury (hence the 'Pilgrims'' Way), and of its total length of 112 miles about half remains

Slow, cumbersome, uncomfortable for passengers and easily bogged down, the carriage was mainly for show.

rural and unchanged. It follows an immense chalk ridge or spine, running about halfway up the flank, abandoning it for lower ground only if it becomes too steep or swings too far to the north. On the upper levels the rise and fall of human or animal feet over, perhaps, millennia, have compacted the chalk into a narrow terrace, the 'ridgeway'. On the softer, lower ground, those feet have gradually kicked the soil away, creating at last a 'hollow way' that is virtually now a tunnel with hawthorne and hazel arching overhead. Along most of its length, the direction of the track is clear enough, but at certain points it splits up for topographical reasons. Even today, some skill in orientation is required in order to decide which of the varying trackways will eventually become 'the' trackway, a graphic demonstration of the medieval traveller's nightmare of losing his way.

The term 'Pilgrims' Way' applied to a neolithic trackway is undoubtedly a misnomer, but an understandable one. Until 1555, when an act of Philip and Mary placed the responsibility of maintaining roads upon the parishes, the Church was the biggest single factor in maintaining land communication in Britain. The road hermit, sponsored and usually subsidized by the local bishop, combined the offices of warden, roadman and religious. In 1453 the Bishop of Ely, in appealing for funds for a certain William Green, specifically acknowledged his role: 'Since our church at Ely is surrounded by waters and marshes and the relics of the Holy Virgin lying in it can only be visited over bridges and causeys requiring daily repair, we commend to your charity William Green, hermit who at our command has undertaken the repair of the causeys and bridges.' Maintenance of the vital bridges, in particular, was both a matter of religious duty and civic patriotism: Stratford's great bridge, still carrying traffic today, was the gift of a wealthy son of the town, Hugh Clopton; in Birmingham the Gild of the Holy Cross 'mainteigned and kept in good reparaciouns two greate stone bridges and divers foule and daungerouse highways, the charge whereof the town hitsellfe ys not able to mainteign'. The great inns which, century after century down to our own times, have given refreshment and shelter to countless travellers were mostly offshoots of the monastic system. The George and Pilgrims at Glastonbury, the King's Head at Aylesbury, the Angel at Guildford, the Talbot at Oundle are among dozens which began life as the guest-house or hostel for a monastery.

And along these roads and over these bridges, gratefully taking shelter in the inns or less enthusiastically putting up at the wayside taverns, came, decade after decade and century after century, companies 'of sondry folk, by aventure y-falle' – the pilgrims. Until the first, tentative journeys of the antiquaries in the sixteenth century, these were the only people who took to the road for any other than the most pressing and practical of reasons. The religious objective

Pilgrims at a meal, probably in a monastic guesthouse. Those portrayed here are bound for Santiago de Compostela in the mid fifteenth century.

not only gave shape and meaning to the journey, it also provided justification. The towns and villages of medieval England did not welcome the stranger: to the contrary, the law specifically enjoined the apprehension of 'any straunger that pass by the country in the night'. The pilgrims' badge gave some protection, but even better was the company of one's fellows: those thirty people gathered in Southwark on the morning of 7 April were not only desirous of entertainment but, even more, of mutual protection.

Strictly speaking, pilgrims were supposed not only to have a badge but to wear a complete uniform – staff, long tunic, scrip and broad-brimmed hat. The fact that, by 1387, Chaucer's pilgrims were wearing their own clothes (the Merchant was even wearing motley) shows the extent to which the holiday atmosphere was gradually taking the place of the purely religious journey. The companions of the real-life Margery Kempe, who left King's Lynn for the Holy Land in 1453, were irritated by her admittedly ostentatious piety: 'Ye shall not speak of the Gospel,' they warned her, 'but shall sit still and be merry as we do.' The French moralist, Jacques de Vitry, spoke for all sober Christians everywhere when he inveighed against those 'light-minded and inquisitive persons who go on pilgrimage not out of devotion, but out of mere curiosity and love of novelty'. But though the sobersides might deplore the fact, in due course these light-minded and inquisitive persons would outnumber the rest, casting their bright and curious glances upon the land around them, embarking upon quite a different kind of pilgrimage.

And some time about the year 1535, one of these new. pilgrims began to record what he saw. His name was John Leland. We know little enough about this English Herodotus, this true founding father of English topographers. He was born about the year 1505 or 1506 and took his BA at Cambridge, in 1522, about the age of 17 or 18 – precocious enough even for his day. He then turns up in Paris, possibly as a King's Scholar. His great successor, William Camden, noted that 'until our times many of the most hopefull youths were chosen out of both the Universities and trained up in strange countries, for the better adorning and inabling of their minds'. The King whose Scholar he might have been was Henry VIII, for Henry, the killer-king of his maturity, the bigot who would burn a man (or a woman) alive for disagreeing on a point of interpretation, in his youth was a bright and cultured man, warmly responsive to the things of the mind and the spirit. He had come to the throne, at the age of 19, when Leland would have been about three years old. And when, in due course, the mature Leland returned to England in his mid-twenties in 1528 it was as a pensioner of the King's. How and where they met is unknown, but certainly two years later Henry, who already prided himself upon his love of learning, made Leland Keeper of the Royal Libraries. And there the young man plunged, with a dedication which amounted to an obsession, into the study of English history and it was as a result of this, he later told the King, as a result of the 'honest and profitable studies of these historiographers, I was totally enflammid with a love to see thoroughly all partes of this your opulente and ample reaulme'. And Henry agreed to underwrite his expenses during the five long years that his tours occupied.

Most of what we know about how and why Leland undertook this unprecedented action comes from an elaborate letter, 'The Laborious Journey and Serche for Englandes Antiquities', which he wrote to the king as a 'New Yeare's Gyfte' in the thirty-seventh years of Henry's reign, that is, in 1546. His long-term aim was a total description of England. According to tradition, the emperor Charlemagne 'had emonge his tresors thre large and notable tables [tablets] of silver richely enamelled, one of the site and description of Constantinople, another of the site and figure of the magnificent cite of Rome and the third of the description of the worlde. So shall yowr Majestie have this yowre worlde and impery of England so sette forthe yn a quadrate table of silver, if God send me life to accomplische my beginninges.'

According to his friend John Bale, Leland taught himself 'British, Saxon and Welsh' in order to quarry into the works of native historians and so prepare himself for his task. Certainly there was no lack of material from Julius Caesar onwards. The two monks, Matthew Paris and Ranulf Higden, Caxton's delightfully named assistant Wynkyn de Worde, Geoffrey of Monmouth, Pynson, Julian Notary – all had contributed to the history of the island kingdom. But if quantity was not lacking there was a certain dubiety about content to give so conscientious a historian as Leland pause. Even sober men like De Worde repeated legends and anecdotes quite uncritically, copying each other in blissful unawareness of or indifference to inherent accuracy or even possibility. Every chronicler worth his salt, for instance, solemnly informed his readers that fishwives would slit open the belly of a carp to demonstrate its fatness and if the purchaser did not buy the fish it was popped back into the tub no whit the worse, for the tenches placed with it would nibble away and soon cure the wound.

An extreme example of the problems facing any would-be historian of England is that provided by Geoffrey of Monmouth's amazing *History of the Kings of Britain*, written in the first half of the twelfth century. After the myths and legends of the Dark Ages one seems on solid ground as soon as one encounters his confident introduction. He tells us his source: 'Walter, archdeacon of Oxford, a man learned in the histories of foreign languages offered me a certain most ancient book in the British language that did set forth all in due success from Brute, the first king of the Britons onward.' He warns off his contemporary chroniclers William of Malmesbury and Henry of Huntingdon, who impertinently tried to trespass on his field, with the lofty injunction to 'be silent as to the Kings of the Britons for they do not have that book which Walter did convey out of Brittany', and off he goes on a farrago which for long was accepted as a true history. Brute, son of Aeneas, after leading his fellow Trojans to freedom obeys Diana's instructions and sails to the west. He and his company settle in Brittany but then decide to cross to the White Island and land 'at last in safety at Totnes' – the kind of precision that persuades throughout. At that time the name of the island was Albion and none of it was inhabited save by a few giants. The giants are defeated, the Trojans settle in the city called New Troy (later corrupted to London) and from there onwards the reader is taken through an intimate account of no less than ninety-nine kings, pride of place being given to Arthur.

Leland made no comment on the works of his predecessors, except the silent comment of rejecting their entire approach. He would go and see for

Matthew Paris's map of Britain, mid thirteenth century. The shape in this, the first map of the country, is just recognizable, with Hadrian's wall at the top and Dover at the bottom, but it is obviously useless for detailed information.

himself, ask questions in person, accepting nothing at second-hand if first-hand was available. Later he told the King that, 'sparing neither labor nor costes, by the space of these vi yeares paste that there is almost nother cape, nor bay, haven, creke, or peere, river or confluence of rivers, breches, washis, lakes, mere, fenny waters, montaynes, valleis, mores, hethes, forestes, woodes, cities, burges, castelles, principal manor places, but I have seene them; and notid in so doing a hole worlde of thinges very memorable'.

The great personal and historical tragedy is that Leland lost his reason, at the age of 42, and died shortly afterwards before he had a chance to turn his mountain of notes into that polished account which he had promised the King. Yet the tragedy has some value for posterity, for what we have here is 'work in progress' and it is possible to follow the working of the writer's mind as, day after day on horseback, he slowly covers the land of England. There are his injunctions to himself, the kind that every writer recognizes: 'Remember to ask Mr Batchelar'; 'take better heed' after a piece of carelessness; 'I have written in a small piece of paper', and the like. Evidently he worked from a series of centres, sometimes perhaps a town, riding out daily to cover the surrounding countryside, sometimes staying at the house of some great magnate industriously ferreting among family papers. 'Mr Brudenell of Dene' was particularly generous in this matter. He was one of the sons of Chief Justice Brudenell (and his distant descendant, still living at Dene Park, was to lead the Charge of the Light Brigade) and Leland refers several times to papers and rolls Brudenell had lent him, at the same time presumably providing him with hospitality.

Leland's style is staccato, stilted: one is left with the vivid impression that again and again a note was made *en route*, jotted down while his mount moved slowly along. But despite that terseness, Leland can encapsulate a place in a phrase. Droitwich is dismissed as a town famous for a single street: 'the towne itself is somewhat foule and dirty when any reyn falleth.' Wakefield's buildings 'are meately fair, most of tymbre but sum of stone'. He goes behind appearances to find causes. Noticing that the town of Bewdley 'att the rising of the sun glittereth, being all of new building, as it were of gold', he asked around and discovered that 'Bewdley is but a new towne, and that of old time there was but some poor hamlett and that upon the building of a bridge there, men began to inhabit there' – in other words, exactly as in the twentieth century, though on a smaller scale, a 'new town' had been grafted onto the nucleus of an old.

In 1536, just a year after Leland began his travels, the Act of Dissolution was passed and the great plundering of the monasteries was underway. The scholar, John Leland, must have looked on in horror as greedy, ignorant magnates took what could be turned into money and destroyed the rest. He contacted Thomas Cromwell, the King's chief adviser in this matter, complaining that foreigners were actually coming to England to carry off the contents of the monastic libraries. Even this was better than the wholesale destruction taking place, and he begged Cromwell's assistance to get the more valuable chronicles and records into the protection of the King's Library. Cromwell's response to this appeal can be judged by the bitter comment made by John Bale in 1549: 'If there had been in every shyre of Englande but one solempme library, to the preservacioun of those noble workes, and preferrment of good lernynges in oure posteryte, it had bene yet sumwhat. But to destroy all without consyderacyon, is an wyll be unto Englande for ever, a moste horryble infamy among the grave senyours of other nacyons. Yea, what maye bryng our realme to more shame and rebuke than to have it noysed abroad that we are despysers of learning.' There was an even more serious long-term effect than Bale could have possibly imagined. Major works of scholarship would have been preserved by somebody, somewhere: it was the local material – that relating to the little towns and villages for which the local monastery would have provided the natural home – that suffered. It is not too fanciful to see that here, at the very outset of English historiography, was born that contempt for 'local history', and the cause of its threadbareness, so painfully in contrast with that of most Continental countries, which has continued almost down to our own time.

John Leland died in 1552, his great work uncompleted. But his contemporaries realized its value: John Stow, who was to do for London what Leland had attempted for England, made a perfect copy of the *Itinerary*, as the work was now commonly known, and this found asylum in the Bodleian Library, Oxford, in due course furnishing the text for the first printed edition of 1710. But long before it entered print it had done its work, like a spring rising in a desert. One of those who saw Stow's copy of the *Itinerary* was William Camden, the Clarenceux King of Arms. And Camden's *Britannia* triumphantly achieved what Leland had planned, a combined historical and topographical picture of England in the sixteenth century.

Camden was born in London in 1551 and after a conventional education at St Paul's School and Oxford, became an usher, and finally headmaster, at Westminster School. His approach differed basically from Leland's, for where Leland had attempted to cram everything in five or six years travel – and doing it all singlehanded – Camden spread his travels over most of his life, and in later years did not disdain to use assistants. And where Leland began in the present and worked back into the past, Camden seems to have regarded the whole interim period since the departure of the Romans as a regrettable

'*Mr Camden came to see the church and particularly took notice of a little painted-glasse-windowe . . .*'. *William Camden, who presented accurate details within a broad picture.*

mistake. As a modern scholar, Professor Douglas, has put it: '*Britannia* is essentially Roman Britain as seen in relationship to its later growth.' Camden, with a fine disregard for chronology, based his picture of sixteenth-century England firmly on the tribal divisions of the first century A D. But it was still a personal, first-hand picture. Like Leland, he refused to retail shopworn descriptions: the England that appears in his pages is the England that he saw personally. In his *Brief Lives* John Aubrey has an anecdote pointing up Camden's care for the small and the local as well as the grand and the national: 'When my grand-father went to schoole at Yatton-Keynell (neer Easton-Piers) Mr Camden came to see the church and particularly took notice of a little painted-glasse-windowe in the chancell, which (ever since my remembrance) has been walled up, to save the parson the chardge of glazing it.' Nearly three centuries later Camden's most recent editor, G. J. Copley, noted in the 1977 edition of the *Britannia*: 'It is astonishing how much of what he described yet survives. Scratch the surface of twentieth-century England and there is a good chance that a fragment of Tudor England will show through. Go out into the countryside or into the country towns and the survivals are numerous' – although, inevitably, the editor must also enter a caveat: 'Camden's England is [now] being bulldozed into oblivion faster than at any time in the past.'

Camden's style has been unfavourably compared with Leland's: where Leland is staccato but lively, Camden is admittedly polished but dry. The probability is that Leland, too, would have been forced to adopt this style, to cut out the asides which make for liveliness but also clutter up the narrative. And Camden, too, can be lively enough when a subject takes his attention – in particular, anything associated with his beloved Romans. His description of the ford where Caesar was supposed to have crossed the Thames at Oatlands combines archaeology, personal observation, and historical deduction in a fascinating manner. He turns to the *Ecclesiastical History* of the Venerable Bede to find evidence for the stakes planted by the Britons in the river bed, 'each of them of the thickness of a man's thigh and covered with lead', as a defensive measure. Camden believed that he had identified the precise point of the crossing: 'I cannot be mistaken in this, the river being scarce six feet deep hereabouts, and the place now called from these stakes *Coway stakes*.' And proudly he goes on to say: 'I think I have now first revived the fleeting memorial' of the passage of the Thames. Modern investigative techniques have placed Caesar's crossing either at Brentford (where sharpened stakes have also been found), or London, and the probability is that the stakes which Camden undoubtedly discovered were part of a fish weir; but this does not detract from his unchallenged status as a historical detective, rather than yet another retailer of anecdotes.

The complaint of modern readers that Camden's approach is generalized was discreetly echoed by his contemporaries. William Lambarde, who had published the first county history, *The Perambulation of Kent* in 1576, and who generously referred to the younger man as 'Master Camden, the most lightsome [elegant] antiquarie of this age', obliquely criticized *Britannia*. After justly praising it as something that 'farr exceeded whatsoever hath been attempted in that kynd', he went on to say: 'Nevertheless, being assured that the Inwardes of each place may best be knowen by such as reside therein, I cannot but still encourage some one able man in each Shyre to undertake his own [shire history] whereby many good particularities will come to discoverie everywhere.' Lambarde's rather touching belief that local antiquaries were best in the position not only to ferret out, but also to present 'many good particularities' has not been, on the whole, justified, as any student who has had to plod through most local histories will feelingly admit. But in addition to his own epochal work, he doubtless had in mind the great *Survey of London* upon which his friend and contemporary John Stow was working throughout most of his adult life, and which was finally published in 1598, four years before Lambarde's death.

Stow himself, a Londoner through and through, says that he received the stimulus from Lambarde's book: 'I have heard of sundry other able persons to have (according to the desire of that author) essayed to do somewhat for the

John Stow, Londoner: from his portrait bust in St Andrew Undershaft. His meticulous Survey *can still be followed round the City.*

particular shires and counties where they were born or dwelt', an excellent example of the snowball effect of historiography. Born in Throgmorton Street about 1525, he was the son and the grandson of tallow chandlers, solid, established citizens. It is therefore curious that he seems never to have attended any of the free grammar schools available for the sons of freemen but appears to have been entirely self-taught. By the time he came to write the *Survey* he had a number of respectable publications behind him, but his supreme qualifications for writing this seminal book were good health and a sturdy pair of feet: at some time or other he must have walked down every street in London, already a sizeable city with a population of at least 200,000. His own trade was that of tailor, but gradually as his topographical work became an obsession with him his ostensible trade suffered. In the small world of literary England he was admired and respected by his peers: more than one of them, the great Camden among them, was to record their gratitude for unstinted access to the rich library that John Stow built up over the years. But neither libraries nor publications – not even the great edition of Chaucer which he brought out in 1561 – could provide a decent income. Faced with a penurious old age, and urged by his friends, in 1604 he applied to King James for a pension. His influential friends had done their work well: the king, so proud of his own learning and recognizing the value of Stow's antiquarian labours, generously granted him letters patent, permitting him or his representatives to

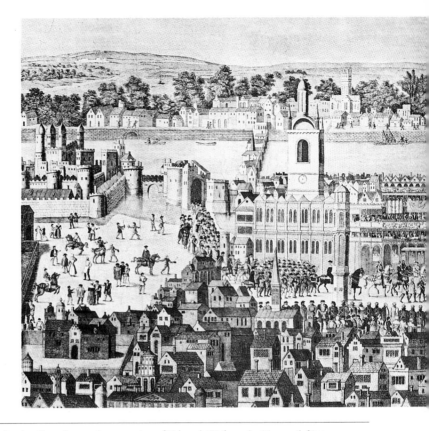

The London Stow knew: the procession of Edward VI from the Tower (left) to Westminster (right) in 1547. Other landmarks are London Bridge, the Cross in Cheapside, old St Paul's with Ludgate and Temple Bar.

obtain 'voluntary contributions and kind gratuities' from whomever was disposed to offer them. In other words, King James I kindly permitted him to beg.

Edmond Howes, Stow's friend and later literary executor, left a delightful portrait of him: 'He was tall of stature, lean of body and face, his eyes small and crystalline, of a pleasant and cheerful countenance; very sober, mild and courteous and retained the true use of all his senses until the day of his death. He could never ride, but travelled on foot unto divers cathedral churches and other chief places of the land to search records. He lived peacefully, and died of the stone colic, being four-score years of age.' Such a man, one feels, would simply have smiled wryly at his monarch's grotesque meanness, counted his small change and trudged off in quest of yet another monument, another scroll, another interview.

For he combined live interviews with topographical descriptions. With the *Survey* in hand today it is possible to follow him around central London, even after the vast changes that have taken place. He will list, painstakingly, the names of those buried in this or that church (providing a priceless record for posterity, for most of those churches were doomed to disappear by fire). He lists, under the title of 'temporal government', all the mayors and sheriffs of the City from the Conquest onward. But vital though these are, they would be dry stuff without the occasional personal comment that, with restraint, he permits himself. Like the marvellous story he tells about how his father and their immediate neighbours were robbed by Thomas Cromwell of a large portion of their gardens in Throgmorton Street. Cromwell had built himself a splendid mansion there, and decided he wanted a garden big enough to set it off. The house of Stow senior was in the way. 'This house they loosed from the ground and bare upon rollers into my father's garden twentytwo feet ere my father heard thereof. No warning was given him, nor other answer when he spake to the surveyors of that work, but that their master Sir Thomas commanded them to do so: no man durst go to argue the matter, but each man lost his land and my father paid his whole rent, which was 6s 6d the year, for that half which was left.' But the gentle old man could not bring himself to condemn even this except in the mildest terms: 'Thus much of mine own knowledge have I thought good to note, that the sudden rising of some men causeth them to forget themselves.'

Among those who made full and good use of Stow's library was an Essex clergyman, William Harrison, who, commissioned by Raphael Holinshed to write a *Description* of England, turned to his old friend for help and gracefully acknowledged it. 'I have borrowed them [law terms] from my frend John Stow whose studie is the onlie storehouse of antiquities in my time, and he worthie therefore to be had in reputation and honour.' Strictly speaking, Harrison does not belong in the company of Leland and Camden and Stow, men who rode or walked out in all weathers, covering immense distances to glean just that little more of knowledge. As he himself cheerfully admitted to his patron, Lord Cobham: 'I must needs confesse, that untill now of late, except it were from the parish where I dwell unto your Honour in Kent, or out of London where I was born unto Oxford or Cambridge where I was brought up, I never travelled forty miles forthright and at one journey in all my life.' Nevertheless, though sedentary compared to the great travelling antiquaries, his cast of mind was such as to make him yet worthy to be ranked with them. Curiosity was his distinguishing characteristic, whether observing how an adder carried its young in its mouth, or the nature of modern architecture compared with that in Henry VIII's day, or types of armour, or the layout of gardens, or modern furniture, or the laws of England – all was grist that came to his mill. The raw material was turned into a sprightly, quirky prose which despite its casual style – that of a man discoursing before his fireside – succeeds in covering a remarkable area of ground, presenting a lively and fresh picture of Shakespeare's England.

He came to write his book almost accidentally. Reginald Wolfe, the Queen's Printer, with that splendid world-view which characterized the Elizabethans, proposed to publish 'a universall Cosmographie of the whole world', and hired Raphael Holinshed to collate the histories of the separate nations. Wolfe died before the immense project got off the ground, Holinshed cannily cut back the scheme to cover the histories of England, Scotland and Ireland and commissioned Harrison to cover England. In an uncharacteristically modest dedication to his patron, Lord Cobham, Harrison deprecated his own talents and gave some idea as to how he went about his task, smaller than that originally envisaged but still an immense work for one unaided man. 'One help, and none of the smallest that I obtained herein, was by such commentaries as Leland had collected of the state of Britain. Secondlie, I gat some knowledge of things by letters and pamphlets from sundrie places and shires of England. The third aid did grow by conference with divers either at the table, or secretly alone wherein I marked in what things the talkers did agree, and wherein they impugned each other'. In other words, though much of his text was the product of the study, much too came to him first-hand from those who sat down at his hospitable table, giving him their own impression of the 'state of Britain'.

Harrison's point of departure is a passionate patriotism, coupled with a good, sturdy xenophobia. Italy comes in for a particular drubbing from this Protestant parson. England is being ruined by the snobbish practice of sending the sons of noblemen into that sink of iniquity, he protests, 'from whence they bring home nothing but meere atheism, infidelitie, vicious conversation and ambitious and proud behaviour'. The honest English workman, by contrast, 'is merie without malice and plain without inward Italian or French craft or subtiltie'. Even criminals are praised: 'our condemned persons doo go cheerfully to their deaths, for our nation is free, stout, hautie, prodigal of life and blood.'

He is fond of legends and anecdotes, but by no means blindly credulous. Relating the tale of how an ancient book in the British language was supposed to have been discovered in the walls of St Albans, he adds in a marginal comment (and these comments of his are a delight throughout), 'I doo believe this to be a lie.' He devotes an entire chapter on 'Apparel and attire of the English', much of it an invective against empty-headed fashion. He declares that it is quite impossible to describe an 'Englishman's' dress, for it is first Spanish, then French, then German, then Turkish, 'except it were a dog in a doublet you shall not see anie so disguised as are my countrymen of England'. He is one of the first to be fascinated by that class distinction which will preoccupy his compatriots over the following centuries, meticulously dividing them into four main classes – 'gentlemen, citizens, yeomen and labourers' – and minutely subdividing the divisions with instructions on how to address whom. Labourers, for instance, are not to be called masters, but goodmen, 'as goodman Smith, goodman Cockswet etc.' He is very good on food and drink, excusing what appears to be the gluttony of the English with the explanation: 'The situation of our region, lieng neere unto the north, dooth cause the heate of our stomaches to be of somewhat greater force; therefore our bodies doo crave a little more ample nourishment than the inhabitants of the hotter regions are accustomed withall.' This dispensation does not, however, apply to the Scots, whom he dismisses as gross gluttons, 'unapt to anie other purpose than to spend their times in large tabling and bellie cheere'. All in all, from the comfort of his study in Radwinter, Essex, Parson Harrison turned as bright a light upon his fellows as if he had, in person, passed through all the shires.

CHAPTER TWO

Entry of the Clowns

Shortly before seven o'clock on an overcast morning in early spring, 1599, a boisterous crowd began to assemble in front of the Lord Mayor's residence in London. They were joined by four men, one of whom carried a pipe and drum, but it was for his companion – a man about thirty-five years old, short of stature but compact and obviously well-muscled and sporting the fashionable forked beard – that the crowd reserved their most tumultuous welcome. They knew him well, an actor called Will Kemp, a member of Shakespeare's company at the Globe Theatre. Usually he played the part of the clown and specialized in the jig – an extempore interlude usually accompanied by music and dancing. It was in his capacity as dancer that he was here now, for he had announced his intention of morris-dancing the entire way from London to Norwich, taking the compliments of one mayor to the other. His three companions were his taberer, Tom Slye (who certainly deserved recognition on his own account for he improvised music for Kemp for nine solid days); his servant William Bee; and a man called George Sprat, who was to accompany him as referee. Kemp achieved his feat, but it aroused so much interest, creating such preposterous reports (so he claimed) that he was obliged to publish an account of it. Dedicated to Anne Fitton, one of the Queen's Maids of Honour, it came out the following year under the title of *Kemps nine daies wonder*. It is a small pamphlet of just twenty-two pages, but it was the forerunner of an immensely popular genre that has flowered in our own time: the 'travel book'.

Despite its title, Kemp's journey to Norwich took twenty-three days. The days of actual dancing were meticulously recorded – that was the purpose of George Sprat's presence – and Kemp seems to have averaged around three miles an hour. He was free to 'bank' any part of the distance he wished: arriving at Chelmsford, for example, and finding himself still fresh, he danced on another three miles, returned on horseback and when he set out on the next stage of the journey from Chelmsford he rode out to the point where he had

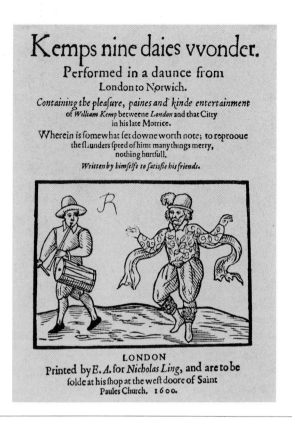

Title-page from Kemps nine daies wonder, *probably with Kemp himself depicted. The journey actually took over three weeks.*

ceased dancing. Alternatively, he was given a lift on horseback when just a quarter of a mile from Romford and therefore returned to the point where he was picked up when departing on the next stage.

He danced only as far as Mile End on that first day, mostly, he claimed, because of the crowds. But the fact that money was pressed upon him almost certainly was a factor in the delay; the *Nine Days Wonder*, like most other such travels, was undertaken with the financial aspect very much in view. At Mile End he encountered a hazard which beset him all the way: being pressed to drink, he wisely turned it down: 'It stands not with the congruity of my health.' At Ilford he was offered the traditional 'carowses in the great spoon', a famous and immense spoon holding about a quart. 'One whole draught being able at that time to have drawne my little wit drye', he observed feelingly, 'I soberly gave my boone Companyons the slip.'

He seems to have been followed from town to town by considerable crowds, certainly of not less than a hundred people sometimes. The crowds were big enough, and well-heeled enough, to attract thieves: four London cutpurses mingled with them, following the star attraction as far as Brentwood before they were detected and arrested. Kemp knew one of them, 'a noted Cut-purse, such a one as we tye to a poast on our stage for all people to wonder at, when at a play they are taken pilfering'.

Will Kemp was no writer, but a clown and a dancer. Nevertheless, he had the Elizabethan's gift for words, the ability to draw a vivid little pen picture like the delightful vignette he sketched of the 'lusty Country lass' outside Sudbury. He had been challenged by a butcher, who swore to accompany him morris-dancing for at least a mile, but gave up after half a mile, unable to keep pace. 'As he and I were parting a lusty Country lass being among the people called him a faint-hearted lout, saying "If I had begun to daunce, I would have held out one myle though it cost me my lyfe."' She was mocked at but insisted that she would accompany Kent in the dance if he would lend her a 'leash' of bells. 'I looked upon her, saw mirth in her eies, heard boldness in her words and beheld her ready to tuck up her russet petticoate. I fitted her with bels which she merrily taking, garnisht her thicke, short legs and with a smooth brow bad the Tabrer begin. The Drum strucke, forward marcht my merry Maydnemarian, who shook her fat sides and footed it merrily to Melfoord, being a long myle. There parting with her, I gave her (besides her skinfull of drinke) an English crowne to buy more drinke for, good wench, she was in a pitious heat.' Near Braintree he had an experience which demonstrates, in the most graphic manner, that a sixteenth-century 'road' was an idea rather than a structure. Coming to a broad 'plash' of mud and water, and finding that he could not go round it, he attempted to jump it, just clearing the main pool but going in up to his ankles. A country lad who was following him tried to do the same, but fell in the middle and was wholly unable to extricate himself until his companion cautiously waded in and helped him: 'I could not chuse but lough to see how like two frogges they laboured'.

Will Kemp, with his faithful taberer and closely watched by George Sprat, arrived outside Norwich on the twenty-third evening of his journey, a Wednesday. He put off his formal entry until the Saturday, so that good notice could be given to the local gentry. The city gave him an astonishing welcome, preceding him by the mayor's whifflers, and serenading him with the city waites: 'few citties in our realme have the like, non better.' There was a tremendous press of people in the market place, one poor lass being pushed so close that inadvertently he stepped on her long skirt: 'Off fell her petticoat from her waste but as chance was, though her smock was coarse, it was cleane. Yet the poore wench was so ashamed (the rather for she could hardly recover her coat again from unruly boies) had she her cheeks all coloured with scarlet.'

Kemp finished his epic dance with a great leap over the churchyard wall of St John Maddermarket. To his considerable annoyance, Sprat had lost sight of him in the crush and insisted on him repeating the dance across the city. He did this on the following Tuesday, 'and I must confess that I did not wel, for the Cittizens had caused all the turne-pikes to be taken up on Satterday that I might not be hindred.' But all ended happily and Kemp presented his buskins to the city: they were solemnly nailed up in the Guildhall, for the instruction and wonderment of posterity, together with the measurement of the mighty leap which had taken him over the churchyard wall.

Financially, Kemp did very well out of his feat for, in addition to the spontaneously offered sums collected *en route*, the Mayor of Norwich not only gave him five pounds but also (Kemp claims, though there is no record of this) a pension for life of forty shillings a year. He was, however, already a well-established figure and the main purpose of making both journey and pamphlet was self-advertisement. By contrast, John Taylor, the self-styled 'water poet', made his lengthy and leisurely journeys up and down the kingdom entirely for the money he earned by selling pamphlets on his feats:

> This long journey (first and last) I undertook
> On purpose to get money by my book.

He also expected to be well entertained by those he met on his journeys, repaying the hospitality by favourable mention in his pamphlets. If Leland was the founding father of the great school of topographers, John Taylor was undoubtedly the founding father of the modern school of travel journalists.

Taylor had a crowded and adventurous youth. Born in Gloucester in 1580 of poor parents, he received a grammar-school education which was very considerably widened when he was pressed into the Navy. According to his own account (and admittedly one has to treat whatever he says about himself with considerable reservation), before he was twenty-three years old he had made sixteen voyages in the Queen's ships and was present both at the siege of Cadiz in 1596 and Flores the following year. Retiring from service with a lame leg, he became a Thames waterman.

He had joined a brutal, self-sufficient society of hard-living men. Execrations of the Thames watermen echo down the decades until they were largely put out of business by a combination of the growth of hackney-carriages ('hell-carts' in Taylor's words) and the increased number of bridges across the river. The Thames was a major highway, quicker, safer, marginally

'Row, row, row a pox on you row'. Thames watermen labouring, with old London Bridge in the background.

more pleasant than travel by road. A public barge, rowed by four men and carrying about twenty-four passengers, went regularly between London and Gravesend and London and Windsor, but rapidly stealing traffic from this cheap but tedious and lumbering 'Long Ferry' were the tilt-boats. They derived their names from the canopy or 'tilt' which protected the passengers from the weather, were also rowed by four men and, charging ten or fifteen shillings a boat load, as against the barge's twopence a head or four shillings a load, made more frequent, faster journeys. Fighting among themselves to get custom, bullying and blackmailing passengers once in their power, the watermen were universally disliked. But Taylor gave the other side of the picture: how a waterman could row 'till his heart ake' and sweat 'till he hath not a dry thread about him' and receive at the end the statutory twopence and not a farthing more. He leaves, too, an unforgettable picture of the man-about-town using the waterman like a beast of burden, the 'Roaring boy who must be shipped in a pair of oares at least. His gay slop [breeches] hath no sooner kist the cushions but with a volley of new coyned oathes he hath never left roaring row, row, row a pox on you row', and trying to cheat the oarsmen at the end.

Taylor rapidly found that his skill as pamphleteer and rhymester brought him in as much money as the back-breaking work of a waterman. He could, and did, turn his pen to anything: a marriage ode, a piece of invective, a funeral elegy, a mocking caricature. And at an early stage he tapped a useful seam – his fellow countrymen's passionate fondness for vicarious travel. He possessed the travel-writer's two vital skills: the ability to distil a lengthy journey into a few pages of racy prose, and the ability to find someone to pay for his jaunts. Before starting a journey he printed and distributed hundreds of prospectuses, which he called 'Taylor's bills', describing the planned journey and inviting subscriptions. He claimed that sometimes 3,000 people and more would promise to buy his pamphlet when produced, though he probably expended as much energy in persuading these subscribers to honour their promise as he did in the journey itself. But he undoubtedly had a persuasive tongue: his very last prospectus, issued at the age of seventy-five just three months before his death in December 1653, was for a journey to be undertaken 'I know not when, I know not where'. Nevertheless, he received subscriptions.

On the journey itself he expected, as a matter of course, to be fed and lodged free, returning the courtesy by 'writing up' the donor. At Petworth, a gentleman

> paid the chinque and freely gave me drink
> And I return my gratitude in Ink

while at Hull

> Thanks Mr Mayor for my bacon gammon
> Thanks Roger Parker for my small fresh salmon

Undoubtedly, his cheerful, swaggering, rollicking manner (a manner which, in fact, hid a deep melancholy) made him a welcome guest in remote, dull little country towns and villages. And even important gentry – people like Francis Godolphin in Cornwall and the Archbishop of York at Bishopthorpe – gladly had him at their table and sent him on his way with food and drink in his belly and cash in his pockets. And if the gentry did not so respond, or he did not receive the hospitality he expected as of right, then he had the scribbler's ultimate weapon, the printed page to pillory them for their stinginess. The Mayor of Bath (a baker) was held up to public, national mockery: 'Mr Mayor was pleased to entertain me most kindly (with both hands in his pockets) and like a man of few words, forebore to say welcome to the town. So we parting drily, I left him in his shop, Lord Baron of the brown loaves. There is no doubt but the man may live a fair age and die in his bed – if he escape the unfortunate destiny of Pharaoh's baker.' In York, he gave the Mayor 'a well bound book of all my works', but received 'not a pint in exchange'. At Hull a pompous merchant complained that, although only a waterman, he had been placed in a 'towns-man's pew' in church:

> His character I finely will contrive
> He's scornful proud, and talking talkative
> A great ingrosser of strange speech and news.

He knew all about the device later to be described as the newspaper stunt which would attract potential subscribers. (Taylor would, one feels, have been extremely successful as a features editor for a twentieth-century tabloid.) Thus he announced, and embarked upon, a journey between London and Queensborough in Kent in a boat made of brown paper and rowed by stockfish tied to canes as oars and, indeed, travelled a good three miles before the inevitable happened and the boat fell to pieces. But he was also skilled at organizing public events, arranging a major pageant on the Thames to mark the marriage of the Princess Elizabeth and another for the Lord Mayor in 1634. Grandly he styled himself the 'king's water-poet' and 'the queen's waterman' with no authority whatever, but with sufficient bounce to attract the amused admiration of such fellow scribblers as Ben Jonson and Thomas Dekker.

The magisterial *Dictionary of National Biography* haughtily dismisses Taylor's literary works as 'contemptible' – but devotes ten columns to listing them, so prolific was he as a writer. Certainly he had the most cavalier way with verse, not hesitating to rhyme 'Northampton' with 'my horse stamped on' and 'Hockley' with 'like a block lie'. But at his best (and there is much of it) he shows a skill with the mechanical rhymed couplet reminiscent of the great Pope himself. His highly mannered prose set-pieces, with their laboured classical allusions, simply irritate today's reader, but were immensely popular with his contemporaries – particularly those pieces in which he lambasted his great rival Thomas Coryat.

But it is John Taylor's worm's-eye view of England that makes him a priceless mirror of his day. He was no learned scholar, backed by a royal or ecclesiastical purse, nor was he an aristocrat, enduring only a temporary discomfort for the sake of novelty. He was an ordinary working man with a saleable skill of writing which he was turning to what advantage he could. One gets the very strong impression, indeed, that he did not like travelling and endured it only for the sake of the money it might earn him through his pamphlets:

> Thus have I brought to end a work of pain
> I wish it may requite me with some gain.

Sometimes the mask of jollity slips and we see through his weary, ageing eyes the endless road ahead: 'a tedious way for a crazy, old, lame, bad-foundered waterman.' He was not only observing and recording as he went, but actually selling his books as he travelled, carrying them on horseback:

> Like to the stone of Sisyphus I roll
> From place to place through weather fair and foul
> Yet I every day must wander still
> To vent my books and gather friends' good will.

The England, then, that he was seeing and experiencing was the England seen and experienced by the ordinary man: the filthy rooms of an inn 'besprinkled and strewed with excrements of pigs and children'; fleas 'so plump and mellow that they would squash to pieces like young boiled peas'; the evening meal consisting of a piece of bread and butter. It was an England where roads were still so uncertain that this man, who literally counted every penny, was at times obliged to pay out the immense sum of three shillings a day for a guide from one town to the next.

This was, above all, a land where the traveller was still viewed with the utmost suspicion on the reasonable assumption that no man travelled for the fun of it and, if the object of his travel were not evident, then he was certainly up to no good. Taylor illustrates this with a story partly ludicrous, partly frightening, which he tells in a poem with the excruciating (and singularly inappropriate) title of *A Very Merry Wherry-Ferry Voyage*. He and a crew of four were travelling by wherry from London to York by way of the coast when they met with a sudden storm off Cromer. On his coastal journeys he never ventured more than a mile or two from the coast and they were able to beat into Cromer. But, he adds in one of his notes, 'We were like Flounders alive in a frying pan that leaped into a fire to save themselves.' They were seen by some women who, far from coming to their aid, rushed to turn out the watch ('forty men with rusty bills'). In vain Taylor protested his *bona fides*:

> I was John Taylor and a waterman
> And that my honest fellow Job and I
> Were servants to King James his Majesty
> I freely opened my trunks and bade them view
> I showed them books of Chronicles and King's . . .

But all in vain. It was undoubtedly the most exciting thing that had happened to Cromer for years. People hurried from far and near, pouring into the town to view these dangerous prisoners, who were probably pirates or thieves or both. Some, to Taylor's extreme annoyance, ordered beer and subsequently left him to pay for it. Others turned the boat upside down, badly damaging it in search of they knew not what. All this, as the irritated waterman remarked, over

> Five unarmed men in a wherry boat
> Naught to defend, or offend with stripes
> But one old sword . . .

And, he adds in a note, 'the sword was rusty with salt water that it had need of a quarter's warning ere it would come out'. Eventually he was hauled before two local magistrates who, fortunately for him, were well acquainted with his work. Not only did they order his release but actually contributed to his slender funds and entertained him to dinner. Or so he said, and as he identified both gentlemen it seems likely that the Taylor charm prevailed even in these unlikely circumstances.

The Water-poet settled down as an inn-keeper in Long Acre in London, but continued still to travel and scribble and publish up to a few weeks before his death at the age of seventy-five. He was an anomaly, the travel writer pure and simple two hundred years before his time. He specifically disclaimed any intention of making exact descriptions of cities and towns, urging those of his readers who wanted such hard facts to turn to Camden or Speed. His only real rival was Tom Coryat, but while Coryat was dashing around Europe, Taylor, after one or two brief trips on the Continent, was far more interested in noting the absurdities and customs and quirks of his fellow countrymen in their natural habitat: the hideous guillotine at Halifax, operated by the thief's victim or not at all; the people of Mevagissey who stared at him 'as if I had been some strange beast or monster brought out of Africa' and declined to give him shelter; the extraordinary potion known as 'Eastbourne Rug', a drink so potent as to render him almost incomprehensible for a page and a half; the fact that there were no privies in Rye and that in Nottingham a poor man could get a house for his family, free, by simply carving a hole in the castle mound.

I The Pilgrims' Way near Charing, Kent. Most medieval 'roads' would have resembled this.

THE SPAS

*II–IV The formality of the spa towns
represents one particular 'idea of
England'. Lansdowne Crescent, Bath
(right); Buxton, from the town hall
(opposite); and Tunbridge Wells's
Pantiles (below right).*

Overleaf
*V The Wye Valley: first goal of the
seekers after the 'picturesque'. William
Gilpin started the cult – and also
helped to change his compatriots view
of nature – with the publication of his*
Picturesque Observations *in 1782.*

CHAPTER THREE

The Idea of England

The mapping of England had begun, on a reasonably scientific basis, as early as the 1570s when Christopher Saxton made his survey. His map was admirable, showing town sites, bridges, even hillocks (for which he seemed to have a passion) – but no roads. John Norden, who followed him, produced his ambitious *Speculum Britanniae* – the Glass or Mirror of Britain – in which roads were indeed shown but so hesitantly as to be little more than conventions. The greatest of these early cartographers was a man who came to the craft only in his seventies. He was the Scotsman John Ogilby, who was born in Edinburgh in 1600 and died not long after giving his great gift to travellers in Britain in 1676. He took the map out of the gentleman's study and out of the antiquary's hands and placed it firmly in those of the traveller. His maps were meant to be used on the road, for they were in the form of 'imaginary scrolls, whence your road ascends to the top of the said Scroll then down to the bottom of the said Scroll'. His details for main roads are quite astonishing: they all start from the Standard Inn, Cornhill in London and each mile is marked with a high degree of accuracy.

But even Ogilby's maps are concerned only with the main roads. The byroads of England were still as impenetrable a maze as they were a century before, and as they would continue to be for at least another century. And it was along those byroads, a few years after Ogilby's death, that perhaps the most remarkable traveller of all – a woman who would be as outstanding in our own time as she was in the 1680s – took her way. A spinster in her mid-thirties, prim, rather sharp-tongued though generous enough, religious, and incredibly observant: Celia Fiennes, who braved the very real dangers and the very considerable discomforts of seventeenth-century travel for one reason only:

Now thus much without vanity may it be asserted of the subject that if all persons, both Ladies, much more Gentlemen, would spend some of their tyme in Journeys to visit their native Land, and to be curious to inform themselves and make observations

The romantic title-page of John Ogilby's severely practical wayfarers' guide.

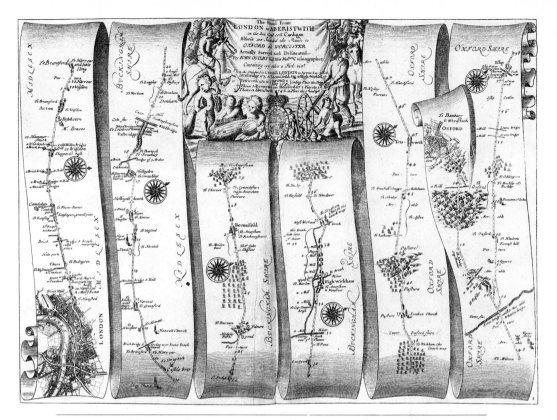

A detail showing Ogilby's remarkably clear and accurate map. Starting with London (bottom left) it takes the traveller with precision to Oxford (top right).

of the pleasant prospects, good buildings and different produces and manufactures of each place . . . it would be a souveraign remedy to cure or preserve from these epidemick diseases of vapours, should I add Laziness? It would also form such an *Idea of England*, add much to its Glory and Esteem in our minds and cure the evil itch of over-valueing foreign parts.

In other words, Celia Fiennes was the archetypal 'tourist', a species which would come to fruition in the late eighteenth century, enjoying travel for its own sake but, because the Puritan work ethic was strong, justifying that travel by copious recording.

Celia was born in 1662 at Saham Toney, near Salisbury. Her father was the second son of Viscount Saye and Sele of Broughton Castle near Banbury – that devious man known as 'Old Subtley' in whose home the rebellion against Charles I was plotted. Celia came to know the Castle well, although she did not think much of it – 'it's an old house moted round and a parke and gardens

Broughton Castle, Oxfordshire, seat of Celia Fiennes' family. She thought little of it, but today it houses her precious manuscripts.

but are much left to decay and ruin when my brother came to it'. By one of the quirks of history, that 'old house moted round' was to provide a permanent home for her Journals, now firmly in the custody of the present Lord Saye and Sele.

The *Journals* consist of two notebooks. The smaller is in her own handwriting and, in its cramped and headlong style, is probably the book she actually had with her on her travels. The larger volume is in another hand, probably that of an amanuensis, but with sufficient of Celia's own emendations and notes to establish its provenance. Although she claims she is writing for her own amusement, internal evidence leaves the strongest suspicion that she expected – or, at least, hoped – for wide circulation if not publication. Her writing is by no means easy to read, and her modern editor Christopher Morris compares it feelingly with Molly Bloom's soliloquy. Even with the addition of punctuation – something she seems to avoid at all costs – it is a headlong, tumbling, breathless style. But, for that very reason, it is a living style and, once the reader has caught the rhythm, her personal voice comes through loud and clear. It is a very modern voice: the kind of architecture of which she approves is that which is going up in London in her own day. She is indifferent – virtually contemptuous – of all aspects of antiquity, Camden being one of the very few writers to whom she refers. The new industrial processes fascinate her but she has only a passing interest in human beings and their motivations. An extreme example of both aspects of her character is provided by the occasion when she called on the Earl of Chesterfield at his seat, Bretby Park, to find that a great social event was being celebrated – nothing less than the marriage of his daughter. She dismisses this glittering, very feminine occasion in a single sentence – 'There was companye to wish her joy' – but then goes on to give a lengthy, precise and ecstatic description of the newly installed waterworks in the gardens.

Between 1685 and 1712 Celia travelled England in a series of journeys which eventually covered the entire country from Newcastle in the north to Penzance in the south-west, and from Chester in the west to Norwich in the east. In what she calls her 'Great Tour' of 1698 she made an incredible circular tour from London to the Scottish border via East Anglia, then south to Cornwall before turning north again to London. In her day there was still no general agreement as to what constituted the distance of a mile. In Lincolnshire she says, 'I went 8 mile to Ely which were as long as the 12 I came from St Edmundsberry' in Suffolk; altogether, however, she could not have covered less than 3,000 miles in a decade. She is very sparse in giving dates and times. One of the rare occasions when she does so was in 1697 when she left London in May and, after an immense journey north during which she passed through Cambridge, Lincoln, Tadcaster, York, Scarborough and back down through Derbyshire, 'I returned to London, in all our companye very well without any dissaster in 7 weeks tyme.'

Her lack of interest in human beings extends not only to herself (we get no impression at all of her physical appearance) but also to her companions. On that journey in 1697 she seems to have been accompanied by two female cousins, relatives by marriage, but most of her journeys were apparently undertaken in the company of only one or two male servants. Unlike most male travellers, who were for ever inveighing against the condition of the roads, she is stoical, only referring to them when conditions made them all but impassable. When, therefore, she says almost casually how near she came to death when travelling in the Fenland one is disposed to accept the truth of what she describes, even though it seems barely possible. The causeway to Ely had been covered by heavy rainfall. 'My horse, ernest to drink ran to get more depth of water than the Causey had, was on the brink of one of these [water-filled] dikes but by a special providence which I desire never to forget and allways to be thankful for, escaped.' Near Peterborough, 'the road was so full of holes and quick sands I durst not venture, the water covering them over and a stranger then cannot easily escape the danger.' On her Great Tour she notes, as a novelty, the first appearance of signposts in Lancashire: 'at all cross ways there are Posts with Hands pointing to each road with the names of the great town or market town it leads to.' This simple but immensely effective aid to travellers had been introduced by statute only in the previous year of 1697.

The dangers of the road included human as well as natural menaces. Celia describes, with quite extraordinary insouciance, an encounter with highwaymen near Chester: '2 fellows all of a suddain from the wood fell into the road, they look'd truss'd up with great coates and as it were bundles about them which I believe was pistolls, but they doggd me, one before the other behind, and would often look back to each other and frequently justle my horse out of the way to get between one of my servants' horses and mine.'

Celia disliked York, as she did most old towns. In her time, however, the Shambles (shown here as it is today) would have been a mean and evil-smelling little street.

Norwich Castle. Although not refaced until the nineteenth century, the ruins of the vast keep would have been clearly visible in the seventeenth. How did Celia come to miss it?

Fortunately, they came up to a large party of male haymakers and the highwaymen – for such they undoubtedly were – made off.

Celia is weak in describing general views, using the usual stereotypes, and for towns she employs again and again the same adjective 'neat' if the town described deserved such a compliment. Nottingham earned such an accolade – 'the neatest town I have ever seen' – because its houses were in the modern style, 'much like London'. York delighted her not at all: 'The Pavement which is esteemed the Chief parte of the town . . . is so mean that Southwark is much before it.' She disapproved of Chester's Rows as she disapproved of most antique buildings. She must have been among the very last writers to observe that the City of London and the City of Westminster were two separate entities. But she was also among the first to observe a modern phenomenon, the growth of suburbs: 'Most of the great towns and cittys have about them little villages as attendants or appendix's unto them which are a sort of subburbs, there being straggling houses for the most part all the way between that and the gates.' In general, she was extremely accurate, though with the occasional odd error. Speaking of Norwich castle she says, 'Nothing of the castle remains but a green space.' How could she possibly have missed the enormous bulk of the keep, ruinous but still lowering over the town, high on its immense mound?

Celia Fiennes liked 'Spaws' and was particularly fond of Tunbridge Wells, shown here in 1748 at its heyday.

Like most of her class she was a connoisseur of 'Spaws' and her lengthy, detailed description of taking the waters at Bath has now become a classic: the description of the baths themselves, the elaborate means of preserving modesty by wearing a stiff canvas garment 'so that your shape is not seen', the technical means of filling and emptying the baths – but only the briefest description of the social life that attracted most people. She prefers Tunbridge Wells by far, giving quite a lengthy and lively description of the social round: 'The Post comes every day and returns every day all the while the season of drinking the waters is: you pay a penny Extraordinary for being brought from Tunbridge Town which is 4 mile distance, that being a post town.'

Little enough of her personal preferences and prejudices comes through. She certainly liked her drink. At Rye she enjoyed fine French white wine, almost certainly smuggled in: at Nottingham the strongest, clearest ale she had ever encountered. She notices the Yorkshire custom of charging a groat for a tankard of ale – 'the only deare thing in Yorkshire' – but this also included the price of a substantial meat or cheese dish with it. The claret in Scotland was 'the best and truest French wine I have drunk this seven year' – virtually the only good thing she has to say about the country whose poverty and savagery appalled her. She was scornful of Dissenters. She went to a Quakers' meeting at Scarborough, 'but it seemed such a confusion and so incoherent that it moved my compassion and pitty to see their delusion and ignorance', though she was as contemptuous of 'the superstitious papists of Holywell'.

It was, however, in her description of industrial processes that Celia Fiennes excelled, and to record them she penetrated with zest into the most insalubrious places, despite her delicate upbringing and supposedly frailer sex. At Exeter, she was fascinated by the technique of producing serge, disregarding the stench of the operation to make copious notes. 'They lay them [strips of serge] in soack in urine, then they soape them and soe put them into the fulling-mills . . . the mill does draw out and gather in the serges, its a pretty divertion to see it, a sort of huge notched timbers like great teeth, the mill draws in with such violence that if one stands neere it, and it catch a bitt of your garments it would be ready to draw in the person even in a trice.' Allowing for her eccentric dislike of punctuation, her description of paper-making at Canterbury is clear and succinct, an invaluable historical record. At Nottingham, she made a glass swan for herself in the glassworks; at York stamped a half-crown in the Mint.

Mines, in particular, fascinated her, from the tin mines of Cornwall to the lead mines of Derbyshire, where she described how the wretched miners, yellow from lead poisoning, were let down into their deep, dark holes. On Brownsea Island she saw how they prepared copperas, the stone used in

One of the industrial processes that fascinated both Celia Fiennes and Daniel Defoe. This is the Backbarrow Furnace in Lancashire, an early ironworks, burning charcoal.

dyeing and ink-making. 'They place iron spikes in the panns full of branches and so as the liquor boyles to a candy it hangs on those branches: I saw some taken up it look'd like a vast bunch of grapes, the coullor of the Copperas not being so much differing, it looks cleare like sugar-candy.'

Celia describes in some detail twenty-five different industries, some traditional as brick-making, others employing new techniques as in iron-founding. Her preoccupation with these industrial processes makes her paradoxically an anomaly and an exemplar at the same time. An anomaly, for where others of her sex would be spending their time enthusing over ribbons and gossiping over beaux and queening it at balls, she was enthusiastically poking around smelly fulling-mills, scrambling through the frightening peaks of Derbyshire to visit a lead mine, ignoring the social life of Canterbury in favour of seeing how the paper-makers went about their trade. But she was an exemplar, too, in that she was unconsciously responding to the deep subtle changes of rhythm in society which, in under a century, would burst into the Industrial Revolution.

Celia Fiennes died, at the age of 79 still a spinster, in 1741. And by as neat an example of historical serendipity as one could wish, one of the witnesses to her will, dated 1738, was a Daniel Defoe. It was not the great man himself, who had died seven years earlier, but his eldest son, a more successful merchant than his accident-prone father had ever been. But a Defoe signature on a Fiennes will established a human link between two of the liveliest observers of England of their age.

On the face of it, there could not be a greater difference between the two people. Celia, despite her Puritan and republican background, was indubitably blue-blooded: a fifteenth-century ancestor had been beheaded by Jack Cade. Defoe, despite that aristocratic 'de', was a man of the people. Celia never had to worry about money: it was the major preoccupation of Defoe's life. As he put it feelingly:

> No man has tasted different fortunes more
> And 13 times I have been rich and poor.

There seems, too, to be a basic difference in their styles. Although Defoe was only a year older than Celia, and died ten years before she did, his great survey of England, *A Tour through the Whole Island of Great Britain*, seems incomparably more modern – it is certainly much easier for the modern reader. The difference, however, is mostly orthographical, a simple matter of punctuation and spelling, understandable enough since Defoe earned his living by writing – the 'father of modern journalism', as he has been called with an accuracy usually lacking these glib labels. But all their differences of

Daniel Defoe: rogue or honest man? He obtained most of the material for his great Tour *while acting as a government spy.*

class disappear as irrelevances when compared with the field in which they resembled each other, their admiration for the present and indifference – contempt – for the past, their awareness that England was trembling on the brink of immense change. Defoe makes explicit what in Celia is only implicit. As each of his three volumes appeared, he found it necessary to add an Appendix to bring things up to date: 'The improvements that increase, the new Buildings erected, the Old Buildings taken down, New Discoveries in Metals, Mines, Manufactures in a Nation. These Things open new scenes every day and make England especially shew a new and different face in many places.'

Born in 1660 – the very year of the Restoration of the Monarchy – Defoe was the son of a tallow chandler or butcher in Stoke Newington, just outside London. He was a Londoner through and through: where others saw the explosive growth of the capital as a danger and a monstrosity, a wen on the face of England in William Cobbett's vivid words a century later, Defoe saw London as a great dynamo drawing in raw material from the provinces and converting it into wealth for the good of all. He was, pre-eminently, a trader. His Dissenting parents had wanted him to be a butcher, but he became a merchant – buying and selling anything that made a profit – and flourished at it. Then, in 1692, he crashed, owing the immense sum of £17,000: to his credit, he somehow contrived to pay off £12,000 over the next decade and, typically, got some profit out of it all by writing a lively pamphlet advocating reform in the bankruptcy laws. Trade attracted him again and again, but again and again he burnt his fingers and it was as scribbling pamphleteer that he made a living.

Bad luck followed him even in this trade. His pamphlet *The Shortest Way with the Dissenters* was so brilliant an exercise in irony that it fooled many leading Tories, who ached to adopt its supposedly bloodthirsty measures. Their rage on discovering their mistake brought about his imprisonment in 1702. But it was to have a long-term effect that was curiously beneficial both for Defoe and for English literature. He gained his release on agreeing to become a government spy and it was during his travels round the country in this unsavoury capacity that he gained much of the material for his *Tour*. Defoe's best and most sympathetic editor, G. D. H. Cole, raises but does not answer the question: 'Was he a rogue, or an honest man?' Cole, securely settled in a profession with a comfortable regular income, did not, perhaps, appreciate the terrible pressures on a Grub Street hack, the need to earn something to keep his ever-growing family while yet retaining an inner core of integrity.

A Tour through the Whole Island of Great Britain was written (or, at least, published) during the remarkable last ten years of Defoe's life which saw the production of all those works upon which his literary fame rests, *Robinson Crusoe* among them. He claims that he made seventeen separate tours or circuits, publishing the results in three successive volumes in 1724, 1725 and 1727. He goes out of his way to give the impression that he is describing everything at first-hand – 'I copy nothing from books but where I quote the books and refer to them' – but the reader has to take this with a very large pinch of salt. Even when he is indubitably describing something he has personally experienced, the experience may have happened ten, fifteen or twenty years before. Sometimes he makes explicit use of this fact, for instance comparing the growth of Liverpool between 1680, his first visit, 1690, his second, and his third visit around 1710, but he does this for a particular reason, to demonstrate the marvellous effect industry is having on our towns.

Defoe views England essentially as a trader – a failed trader, perhaps, but an extremely observant one. His first objective in every new town is the market place – who is selling what and for how much. In the hands of a lesser writer this could become deadly boring but, with Defoe, it is an exciting new view of an ancient country changing its pattern of life. Just occasionally, indeed, the novelist will take over from the observer and the statistician and the economist: his lengthy, touching description of the use of decoy ducks by fowlers in Lincolnshire has all the poignancy of a Hans Andersen story. Like Celia Fiennes before him he is indifferent, if not downright contemptuous, of that antiquity which the following generations will venerate. Cathedral cities usually come in for a drubbing. Worcester is 'closed and old, the houses standing too thick'; the Chester Rows are 'dark, dirty, uneven'; Lincoln is 'an ancient, ragged decay'd and still decaying city'. He gives all honour to Camden, referring the reader to the great *Britannia* when it is necessary to understand the history of a place. (Celia Fiennes, too, invariably fell back on Camden where necessary, ignoring all others.) He was very much a man of his time in his attitude to some of England's most famous historical episodes. Talking of the '*most noble* Order of the Garter', he remarks: 'What honour redounds to that Most Noble Order from its being so derived from the garter of a . . . . For 'tis generally agreed she was the King's Mistress, I will not enquire.' In Worcester cathedral he recounts the story that King John is buried between two saints who will help him up at the Last Day. 'I can hardly think the King himself so ignorant, whatever the People might be in those Days of Superstition . . . They may all three go together at last and yet, without being assistant to, or acquainted with one another at all.'

Defoe's low opinion of antiquity is qualified by one outstanding exception, his veneration for the Romans. He even contemplated walking along their 'Pictish Wall' but changed his mind because 'antiquity is not my business'. His admiration for the Romans was based on their administrative skills and, above all, their skill as roadmakers. Again and again he complains of the appalling condition of modern roads, comparing them with those of the Romans many hundreds of years before: 'The Streetways of the Romans were perfect solid buildings, the foundations were laid so deep and the Materials so good, however far they were obliged to fetch them that if they had been vaulted and arched they could not have been more solid.' It was not a blind adulation: with considerable acumen he argued that the reason why the Romans were able to cover the land with these superb structures was because they were using virtually slave labour: 'But now the case is alter'd, Labour is dear, Wages high, no man works for bread and water now.' He returns again and again to the theme that trade was England's lifeblood, that roads were the arteries along which that blood travelled, and unreservedly praises the new system of turnpikes that was opening up the country.

Defoe had the popular journalist's eye for the startling or the macabre. Like John Taylor before him, he was fascinated by the horrid Halifax guillotine. The instrument itself had disappeared since Taylor's time, but the stone shed was still there to attract the attention of the morbid. Celia Fiennes had actually declined to go to Halifax, because of its reputation, but Defoe industriously ferreted out all the gruesome details for his readers. The wonders of nature meant little to him: he was particularly caustic about the famous Seven Wonders of the Peaks. Of the Peak District in general he said: 'Travel with me through this howling wilderness and you shall soon find all that is wonderful about it.' His curiosity, however, was aroused by one of the Wonders, the

According to Celia Fiennes, 'by reason of the Steepness and Hazard of the Wayes you are forced to have a guide in all parts of Derbyshire'. Sensible travellers avoided these 'horrid wastes' which, today, have become popular tourist spots.

Eldon Hole. Celia Fiennes had made a special journey to see this supposedly bottomless chasm and had made the commonsense remark that the reason why it could not be plumbed was probably because 'the hole runs aslant so the plummet and line could not pass'. Defoe, to the contrary, confidently stated that it was over a mile deep. Two years later its depth was, finally, established as being seventy-six feet! Travel in these regions presented dangers quite unknown to the softer south. Crossing Blackstone Edge in August Defoe and his companions were blinded by a snowstorm and considered themselves lucky to escape with their lives.

Despite his extrovert appearance, Defoe was as reticent about his private affairs as was Celia. Very rarely does he refer to his companions even indirectly and certainly never identifies them. In Yorkshire there were apparently three in the company, with two servants, and in Nottingham some of them got drunk on the very strong local ale.

It was industry in all its forms, from the cottage industries of Derbyshire to the booming cities of Lancashire, that took his attention. The modern reader, accustomed to think of the Industrial Revolution as being, at earliest, a late eighteenth-century phenomenon, encounters with something of a sense of shock the evidence of an exploding economy that Defoe presents almost casually in the opening years of the century. Even the detritus of industry has virtue in his fond eyes. Regarding the stinking water, 'tinged with the drugs of the Dying Fat and with the Oil, the Soap, the Tallow and other ingredients used by the Clothiers' that was allowed to run freely, he remarks: 'the Water so tinged and so fatten'd enriches the land they run through.' Like Celia Fiennes, he was fascinated with mines, and in his description of the lead mines of Derbyshire again the novelist took over from the economist, leaving an unforgettable picture of the terrible lives of the lead miners. He describes how

Blackstone Edge. Defoe was caught in a snowstorm – in August – while crossing this moor. In the foreground is one of the Roman roads he so admired.

he was following a guide through the rough countryside when, abruptly, a hand, then an arm followed by a head emerged from the ground at their very feet:

The man was a most uncouth spectacle: he was cloathed al in leather, had a Cap of the same without Brims, some tools in a little basket which he drew up with him, not one of the names of which we could understand but by the help of an interpreter. Nor indeed could we understand any of the man's Discourse so as to make out a whole sentence. For his Person, he was as lean as a Skeleton, pale as a dead Corps, his Hair and Beard a deep Black, his Flesh lank and, as we thought, something of the colour of lead itself.

The miner dragged up with him about a hundredweight of ore, and Defoe and his companions bought some of it as a souvenir. Shortly afterwards, they met him in an alehouse where he was turning the money into 'good Pale Derby'. Instead of upbraiding him, Defoe paid for the ale and insisted on the man taking his money home to his family.

It was in this same locality that Defoe met a lead miner's wife and subjected her to the same kind of inquisition that Henry Mayhew was to make famous over a century later, drawing out from her a terrible tale of poverty and deprivation which he presented with precision and compassion.

I asked her how much he [her husband] earned. She said, if he had good luck he could earn fivepence a day . . . I then asked what she did. She said, when she was able to work she washed the Oar: But, looking down on her children, and shaking her Head, she intimated that they found her so much Business she could do but little, which I easily granted must be true. But what can you get when washing the oar, said I, when you can work? She said, if she work'd hard she could gain Three-pence a day. So that, in short, here was but Eightpence a day when they both worked hard and that not always, and perhaps not often, and all this to maintain a Man, his Wife, and five small children . . . The Woman was tall, well shap'd, clean and (for the Place) a very well looking, comely woman nor was there anything look'd like the Dirt and Nastiness of the miserable cottages of the Poor . . . This moving sight so affected us all that, upon a short conference at the Door, we made up a little lump of money, and I had the honour to be almoner for the Company and though the sum was not great, being at most something within a Crown, as I told it into the poor Woman's Hand I could perceive such a surprise in her Face that, had she not given vent to her joy by a sudden flux of tears, I found she would have fainted away.

With that lively awareness of his for market values, Defoe had a keen sense of topography, an awareness of the relationship of a town to its surrounding country and the effect that relationship will have upon its trade. He was certainly not always right: of Yarmouth in Norfolk he thought that, while it was a 'beautiful town encreasing in wealth and trade', it would be unable to expand physically because of its position. Modern Yarmouth sprawls hideously up and down the coast and deep inland. On the other hand, he was probably the first writer to raise that problem regarding the different identities of 'villages', 'towns' and 'cities' which has bedevilled English topographers to this day. 'We have no Authority, but ancient Usage and Custom for the distinguishing Places by the names of Towns and Cities', he remarks. Places like Wells and Ely which used to be of great importance and truly deserved the style of 'city' had, in fact, now shrunk almost to nothing, while others – like Plymouth, Portsmouth and Manchester – whose population and wealth had increased spectacularly still bore the humbler styles: 'these retain but the name towns, nay even of Villages in some of which the chiefest magistrate is but a Constable, as in Manchester for example.'

Defoe, like Celia Fiennes, was pleasantly tolerant of the foibles of his fellow-countrymen, but where Celia vented her scorn upon canting Dissenters, Defoe reserved his for the social whirl of Assemblies. With tongue in cheek he denies the foul accusation that the pretty ladies of Suffolk hasten to the assemblies at Bury St Edmunds as to a market, and rarely loses an opportunity to lambast that immoral and undignified innovation of gathering women together in chattering packs in assembly rooms in order to grab husbands for themselves or their daughters. Specifically, he praises the old-fashioned customs in Dorset. 'The Ladies here do not want the help of Assemblies to assist in match-making, or half-pay Officers to run away with their daughters which the meeting, called Assemblies, in other parts of England are recommended for. Here's no Bury Fair, where the women are scandalously said to carry themselves to market and where every night they meet at the Play or the Assembly for intreague'; and yet, he muses, there are no more spinsters and nuns in Dorset than anywhere else. He describes, with a good journalist's pen, the goings on at the fashionable spas of Bath and Buxton and Tunbridge Wells; but, without condemning outright, he gives a vivid picture of the pointlessness of the activities of the 'fashionable' world, the sheer ennui that must develop as they shuffle from tea room to card room, from assembly room to ballroom to bedroom, starting the whole process over and over again with no end in view beyond that of killing time.

As he travelled round the country amassing his statistics (he had a very twentieth-century fondness for figures and the story they could be made to tell), recording local customs and, above all, reporting on markets and trades, Defoe was very much aware of breaking new ground. Despite the increasing number of travellers on the road, he says, no one else has bothered to record the burgeoning new world around them but all are content to follow in each other's footsteps. 'None of the pretended Travel-writers and Journeyers through England have yet thought this most remarkable part of our country [industrial Yorkshire] worth speaking of, or knew not how to go about it.' He sneers at the typical tour-writing traveller's method of laborious note-taking, in which he tells you what he had to eat and drink where, and when, and contrasts it unfavourably with what was evidently his own decidedly slap-dash technique – relying almost entirely upon memory, backed up with a few insignificant notes.

Defoe returns again and again to the paucity of good travel writing: had he but known it, the country was about to be overwhelmed with a flood of *Memoirs* and *Journals*, of *Journeys*, *Travels* and *Tours*. Writing in the 1780s, the Honourable John Byng noted wryly: 'Tour-writing is the very rage of the times. Everyone now describes the manners and customs of every county through which they pass and new Yoricks monthly improve our minds with their sentimental effusions.' In his superb anthology, *Journeys in England*, Jack Simmons noted that more than half of his passages came from works published between 1760 and 1860. After Defoe had left the road, scores seem to have taken his place, everyone who could ride a horse or sit in a carriage and jot down a few hundred words daily, hastening to do so. In 1736 five young men take themselves off for a *Five Days Peregrination*. They seem to have spent most of their time lurching from inn to inn, stuffing themselves with enormous meals (at Rochester they dined off soles and flounders, a stuffed calf's heart, a roast leg of mutton and green peas, topping the whole off with prodigious quantities of beer and port) and in between playing puerile pranks on the locals. The *Peregrination* would be scarcely worth recording or recalling, were it not for the identities of the five: William Hogarth and Samuel Scott, artists, John Thornhill (Hogarth's brother-in-law), and a merchant and an attorney. John Gay makes a five-day journey to Exeter, and promptly turns the experience into verse. In the 1740s Thomas Pennant is totting up his *Tours* from one part of the country to another, leaving some lively descriptions of the perils of coach travel: at Meriden it took eight horses to get them out of a slough: 'We were constantly out two hours before day and as late at night: and in the depths of winter proportionately later.'

The new-born race of novelists joins in the fashion, subjecting their heroes to the vicissitudes of the road. Smollett's Roderick Random experiences the contempt which the quality – i.e. those who travelled by coach or private conveyance – felt for humble wagon folk. 'While we were about to sit down to dinner, the inn-keeper came and told us that three gentlemen, just arrived, had ordered the victuals to be carried to their apartment, although he had informed them that they were bespoke by the passengers in the waggon. To which information they had replied, "The passengers in the waggon might be damned – their betters must be served before them."' Fielding's Tom Jones has the alarming experience of being benighted on the road: they are almost within sight of Gloucester, but might as well be in the Himalayas for all the chance they have of food and shelter for the night. Fielding, too, emphasizes the strong class-consciousness of roadside inns. Mrs Abigail finds that she has to dine in the kitchen: 'Turning to the post-boys, she asked them Why they were not in the stables with their horses: "If I must eat my hard fare here, madam" says she to the landlady "I beg the kitchen may be kept clear, that I may not be surrounded with all the blackguards in town. As for you, sir" says she to Partridge "you look somewhat like a gentleman and may sit still if you please: I don't desire to disturb any but mob."' John Wesley is making his immense journeys, covering thousands of miles saving souls for God: at one stage he calculated that he had travelled 2,400 miles in seven months. His *Journal* is mostly concerned with his high mission, but vivid vignettes of life on the road point up – but only incidentally – the dangers and discomforts he cheerfully endured.

There is no lack of material, but these journals or memoirs of tours are, for the most part, either incidental (the writer undertaking the journey for a purpose other than its own sake) or scrappy and ephemeral. Towering above them all, both in style and consistency of purpose, are the so-called 'Torrington Diaries' recording the tours of the Hon. John Byng between 1781 and 1794.

Byng became Viscount Torrington on the death of his brother only in the last fortnight of his life. He was born of an illustrious naval family in 1742 – an uncle was that unfortunate admiral who was shot 'to encourage the others', in Voltaire's sardonic phrase. He served in the army himself as a lieutenant-colonel and when he actually began his Diaries in 1781 at the age of thirty-nine he was a civil servant in the not very exciting Commission of Stamps. As he dryly summed up his life in two lines of doggerel:

> His early life was spent in Camps
> His latter days were pass'd at stamps

(doggerel which, incidentally, was by no means his normal standard. As well as being quite a good artist with a sketch-block, he was a poet of some skill and sensitivity). Looking at England with the same pride and affection as did Celia Fiennes and Defoe, he was diametrically opposite in his approach. The Industrial Revolution was some fifty years closer to him, its harbingers clearer, and he hated what he saw. He loathed the increased pace of enclosures, loathed the ruthless destruction of woodlands to feed insatiable factories, loathed the

Tyburn, or Oxford Street Turnpike, London. Although travellers hated paying tolls, the turnpike system provided the best roads between the departure of the Romans and the coming of Telford and McAdam in the eighteenth century.

cotton-mills that were swamping the valleys of Yorkshire and Lancashire and Derbyshire. He records, hiding horror with sarcasm, the first intimations of that child labour which spread a horrid blot over the nineteenth century. In 1792, a merchant in Manchester tells him of the 'wonderful importation of Children purchased in London at so much the half-score (nine sound and one cripple) by those merchants, the most forward against the Slave Trade'. And where Defoe specifically hailed the coming of the turnpikes as the advance of civilization, Byng turned his scorn and mockery upon them: 'I wish with all my heart that half the turnpike roads of the Kingdom were ploughed up, which have imported London manners and depopulated the country. I meet milkmaids on the road with the dress and looks of Strand misses.'

Despite his diatribe against the turnpikes, Byng would never have covered the remarkable distance he did without their aid. He was the straightforward holiday tourist, each year leaving his home some time in July or August, travelling for a month or so and then returning home to write up his journal. Most of the time he was on horseback, but occasionally travelled by coach, phaeton or chaise, though he disliked wheeled transport. 'One of the very many bad things is the endurance of heat during the day without perspiration and the endurance of cold afterwards without exercise.' In general, he averaged between twenty and thirty miles a day – during his tour in South Wales in 1787 he covered 530 miles in twenty-nine days.

One of the attractions of Byng's Diaries is their honesty. Again and again he puts to himself the question that every traveller does at some time or other: why on earth have I abandoned a comfortable home for the discomforts of movement? 'The imposition of travelling is abominable: the innkeepers are insolent, the hostlers are sulky, the chambermaids are pert, and the waiters are impertinent. The meat is tough, the wine is foul, the beer is hard, the sheets are wet, the linen is dirty and the knives are never clean'd!! Every home is better than this.'

He invariably travelled with a servant 'to attend my horse, make my bed and give me consequence'. Baggage was sent on ahead and, usually, the servant would accompany it, awaiting his master at a pre-selected inn. Corn and hay for horses overnight frequently cost more than food for the humans and it was primarily to ensure the wellbeing of his mount that a servant was included. Sometimes Byng would travel with a friend and they would take it in turns to ride the one in a chaise, the other on horseback. The usual pattern was to spend a day or so riding alone (for Byng certainly did not count a servant as company) and eventually meet his wife and her friends at some pre-arranged resort. There he might spend anything up to a week, riding out to explore the surrounding countryside during the day and taking part in common activities at night.

And pretty dismal is the picture he paints of these pleasure resorts, even after making allowance for the fact that the Honourable John Byng was very much a loner. Of Weymouth he says unequivocally: 'That the infirm and the upstart should resort to these fishing holes may perhaps be accounted for. But that the healthy owners of parks, good houses and good beds should quit them for confinement, dirt and misery appears to me to be downright madness.' He is even more damning of Cheltenham. He had joined his wife and friends there and at first quite enjoyed the public breakfasts: 'The women are in their natural looks, not disfigured by over-dress and paint and the men are civil – and sober.' But gradually, as the days of tea-drinking and card-playing and play-going slide one into the other, so there emerges an almost overwhelming feeling of the ennui endured by those who did not have to work for their living in provincial towns. Cheltenham was particularly subject to the most bitter rivalries and factions, no less vicious because they were rooted in the most petty of reasons. Feelingly, he observes: 'After some stay in one of these

Cheltenham, the Old Wells and Pump Room. The Hon. John Byng was contemptuous of the vapid, backbiting life led by habitués of such places.

places there is nothing left to say, see, or do . . . Cheltenham, I quit thee with pleasure and hope never more to revisit thee.'

One receives the undoubted impression from the Diaries that it was only because of his wife, the sprightly Bridget, that Byng entered, much less stayed in, these resorts of vacuous pleasure. His own preference was for such places as Tintern Abbey, or the New Forest, places which either conformed to the newly burgeoning cult of the 'picturesque' or were remote or, alternatively, offered interest to his speculative, questing mind. He was very much a man of his time and place, in particular having a generous share of the national xenophobia. At Woodstock, he abandoned his breakfast to show a non-English-speaking Frenchman the way to Blenheim and was very smug and complacent about it all. 'Like other Frenchmen he commented upon he knew not what and only looking for glare, is ignorant of the cleanliness and real comfort that we possess . . . We like to enjoy our comfort and our own societies, not to be eternally jabbering and living in public, and the French are so forward and obtrusive that they wear us out.' But he was no bigot. His dislike of the growing effects of the new industrialism did not prevent him admiring some of its products, such as the Iron Bridge over the Severn: 'the

Tintern Abbey. The romantic John Byng responded warmly to these great ruins, unlike the 'scientific' John Gilpin who thought the gables 'disgusting'.

Despite his profound dislike of industrial processes, Byng was much impressed by the Ironbridge of Coalbrookdale, one of the first great artefacts of the new age.

admiration and one of the wonders of the world'. He shared in the growing interest in antiquity, recording his disgust at the act of the Duke of Marlborough in pulling down the old abbey gateway at Eynsham 'for some business at Blenheim. I should like him to read this page, to feel ashamed and to know that such pieces of antiquity are as enviable gems as any he possesses.' But neither did he scruple to take part in that universal plundering of antiquities which was the hallmark of the 'cultivated' tourist. At Stratford-on-Avon he acquired a couple of pieces of Shakespeare's chair (which were afterwards framed and hung up in his home), while in Stratford church itself, during the absence of the caretaker, 'I pilfered (in common with other collectors) from the Roman pavement at the head of Shakespeare's grave, a tesselated tile which I hid in my pocket.'

Byng was undoubtedly writing with an eye to posterity, if not specifically with a view to eventual publication. At one point he remarks that: 'If my Journals should remain legible or be perused at the end of 200 years there will, even then, be little curious [i.e., of interest] in them relating to travell. Because our Island is now so Explor'd, our roads in general are so fine and our speed has reached the summit.' For the edification of that posterity he includes the ephemera collected by all tourists: the hotel bills (which, in his case, show charges for food, drink and horse fodder – but never for accommodation);

posters of local events, such as the Weymouth Grand Regatta for cutters and luggers; and picturesque views, including his own sketches. What, in his day, would be trivialities become priceless historical clues in the twentieth century. That deceptively casual, civilized glance of his noticed that country-women wore red cloaks on going to market; that a 'painted window' in Bolingbroke church in Lincolnshire had been 'all thrown away, or broken by the Boys'; that Dorchester 'has a shady walk round the town on the old embankments', and that North Leach, otherwise 'a poor, dismal place', has 'a very ancient cross in the market place and a very large (unfrequented) pillory'. The Honourable John Byng, jogging round England in the last summer months of the eighteenth century with no other object in view but to entertain himself, left a better record than many a formal antiquary, devotedly but blindly moling away.

Byng's attitude would have appeared a mere frivolity to his contemporary, Arthur Young, had Byng's *Diaries* been given to the public in their day. For Young, there was only one reason for travelling around England, and that was to inspect her farms. So obsessed was he with the life of the land that the best tribute he could pay his wife, who died in 1815, was to record on her tombstone that she was 'the grand-daughter of John Allen, esq of Lyng House in the county of Norfolk, the first person who there used marl'. Nevertheless, his obsession – which might fairly be described as magnificent – provides for posterity a significant change of direction: for the first time the land itself was the subject of interest – its form and structure, above all its capacity to provide food. Looking at the vast, uncultivated width of Salisbury Plain, Young could only hold up his hands in horror at so grotesque a waste of space: 'all the corn exported from England would annually grow in such a square'.

Young was himself a member of the landed gentry: his father was the rector of Bradfield in Suffolk, where he was born in 1741 and whose manor and lands the Youngs had held for nearly a century. Arthur seems to have been an ebullient young man of immense confidence: he began to write a history of England while still at school and at the age of twenty-two launched his own monthly magazine, *The Universal Museum*, which had the distinction of not providing a platform for Samuel Johnson. The good doctor sensibly declined Young's invitation to write for it and warned him that it could not possibly succeed without capital. Johnson was right: the magazine failed with impressive debts and Young had no choice but to accept his mother's invitation to run one of her farms which she held as dowry. He had no experience whatever of agriculture but not only threw himself into farming but promptly began to pontificate upon the subject, publishing a collection of essays in 1767 under the resounding title of *Sylvae: or occasional tracts on*

Husbandry and Rural Economics. Later, he deeply regretted that impetuousness 'in publishing the result of my experience during these four years which, speaking as a farmer, was nothing but ignorance, folly, rascality and presumption'. He did himself an injustice but, by then, farming was to him an all but sacred occupation worthy only of the highest thought and most undivided attention.

Young's failure as a practical farmer no more stopped him writing on agriculture than Defoe's failure as a merchant inhibited him from writing on trade and industry. In both cases, the personal experience gave insight into a general trend and Young brought to agriculture the alertness to change, and the ability to record the process of that change, which Defoe brought to industry. And rarely has a style more exactly reflected the man. The author of a terse, sinewy, energetic prose was a tall, slim, wiry man with thin features and restless, hawk-like eyes. Even in his old age he rose at around 5 a.m. and in his maturity invariably bathed in the open air – on one occasion not only breaking the ice on the lake but actually rolling in the snow to find out the effect on his body.

He planned his *Tours* in a thoroughly modern manner, first advertising his route and then collating the replies from farmers who had invited him to visit them. Like Defoe, he claims to write only of what he has personally seen: unlike Defoe this is almost certainly true. 'Registering minutes on the spot was a new undertaking, having never before been executed either in this country or any other country in Europe.' His three *Tours* present a remarkable medley of material. Here he will be giving a precise list of labourers' wages and local prices: elsewhere he will provide almost Virgilian instructions on how to set corn and assess the condition of soil. Abruptly, he will turn to an appraisal of the pictures at Holkham or describe Walpole's splendid new house at Houghton. Like others of his class, he moved from country house to country house during his travels, yet his descriptions of them are, for the most part, again a matter of statistics and meticulous measurements.

But it is to the land that he turns again and again and the England that is gradually unfolded to the reader is neither a stage for antiquities, nor a playground, nor a setting for industry. It is the vast larder without which that epochal revolution could never have taken place. He looks with approval on those enclosures which so offended John Byng, for the disappearance of the old wasteful strip farming could only result in greater efficiency, more and cheaper food. He praises those farmers who are experimenting, mocks those who stick blindly to the old wasteful ways, acting as a kind of benevolent bacillus in infecting the country with the excitement of a new approach to the oldest of all crafts. Yet he was not blind either to natural or architectural

For both Young and Cobbett, trees were regarded, essentially, as a crop. Here are shown the results of good and bad husbandry.

beauty. It seems, indeed, as though he sternly refuses to be diverted from his mission but frequently succumbs to record the beauty of a hillside curve in Kent perhaps, or the splendour of the country around Barnard Castle, or the nobility of the Chapter House of York Minster.

There was one subject which Arthur Young made all his own, and that was the abysmal state of the so-called high roads of England. What he describes presents a most remarkable historical asymmetry. A century after Christopher Wren had raised the miracle of St Pauls, and about the time that the Woods were laying out the classical perfection of Bath and Birmingham was launched upon its vast industrial role, the English were attempting to maintain communication with each other along roads which would have aroused the incredulous mockery of the Incas. Other writers were to complain occasionally: Young kept up a detailed and bitter lament which posterity would be tempted to dismiss as exaggeration were it not for the veracity of the body of his work. Of Norfolk, which he knew well, 'I know not one mile of excellent road in the whole country.' Outside Chepstow he complains of 'the turnpikes! as they have the assurance to call them and the hardiness to make one pay for it . . . they continue mere rocky lanes, full of hugeous stones as big as one's horse and abominable holes.' Matters were no better nearer the capital. 'Of all the cursed roads that ever disgraced this kingdom none ever equals that from Billericay to the King's Head at Tilbury . . . I saw a fellow creep under his wagon to assist me to lift, if possible, my chaise over a hedge. The ruts are of incredible depth.' He describes the extraordinary traffic jams along this infamous road where wagons carrying chalk would pile up, stuck so

deep in the mud and ruts that 'twenty or thirty horses may be tacked to each, to draw them out one by one'.

Small wonder, therefore, that when the greatest rural traveller of them all began to explore England in October 1821, he avoided the high roads but stuck to the byways, where the true rural life of England flourished.

On a June morning in the year 1777, a fourteen-year-old boy set out to walk the eighteen-odd miles from his home in Farnham in Surrey to Kew. A countryman's son, he had heard tales of the fabulous new gardens established at Kew and determined to find work there. He was a solid lad, high coloured, fair-haired with small, grey twinkling eyes. He was wearing a blue linen smock and cross garters of scarlet. He had sixpence halfpenny upon him, of which he spent threepence for his midday meal of bread, cheese and beer, and then lost the odd halfpenny. The remaining threepence, intended for his evening meal, was spent on impulse on a copy of Swift's *Tale of a Tub* which he found in a bookshop in Richmond. He went supperless, but cheerful, to bed in a haystack and, on the following morning, walked to Kew. There the Scottish gardener gladly gave the sturdy lad a job and he worked contentedly and efficiently in the Gardens until his father came to take him home.

The boy was William Cobbett and it is possible to give such a remarkably detailed account of one day in his life because he was one of the most prolific

The fame of Kew Gardens inspired the farmer's boy, William Cobbett, to make the long walk from Farnham to Kew to get a job there in 1777. The view opposite was engraved in 1763, the year of Cobbett's birth.

Portrait of 'Peter Porcupine' or 'Old Mutton-chop'. William Cobbett: MP, journalist, polemicist and – above all – farmer.

self-revealers ever to put pen to paper. He published his first identifiable work in 1792: he died in 1835 and he scarcely ever ceased writing during those forty-three years. Technically, what he produced was journalism, for it was all written at high speed, published in mostly ephemeral media and was intended for immediate effect. He was totally blind to much of what passes for culture: music was for him songs in an alehouse or a fiddler on the green; he was contemptuous alike of William Shakespeare and Samuel Johnson. But by virtue of an eye for living detail and a plain but polished and vigorous prose style he was to join their company as one of the grand masters of English prose – a fact which would have amused him enormously.

Cobbett thought of himself as a working farmer – yet, like Defoe and Young before, it is unlikely that the bulk of his income came from his preferred trade. He joined the army at the age of twenty-one and while in it he taught himself to read and write: 'I learned grammar when I was a private soldier on the pay of sixpence a day. The edge of my berth, or that of my guard bed, was my seat to study in; my knapsack was my bookcase, a bit of board lying on my bed was my writing table. To buy pen or a sheet of paper I was compelled to forego some portion of my food, though in a state of semi starvation.'

After his discharge in 1791 he entered on his first brush with authority when he attempted to have his late officers court-martialled on a charge of corruption. Fearful of authority's revenge, he fled the country, first to France, then to America, where he earned his living teaching English to French immigrants – the ideal way of learning one's own language. Meanwhile, he threw himself into the bitter polemics of the day, gaining such a reputation that, on his return to England in 1797, he was invited by leading members of the Government to discuss how his pen could best be employed. It was a signal honour and he basked in it: a few days later, riding back to his old home in Farnham, he mused on all that had happened since he left seventeen years before. 'What scenes I had gone through, how altered my state. I had dined the day before at the Secretary of State's [William Windham – incidentally one of the sprightly Bridget Byng's passionate admirers] in the company of Mr Pitt and had been waited on by men in gaudy livery. I had had no one to assist me in the world. I felt proud. And from that moment, less than a month after my arrival in England,' he concluded, 'I resolved never to bend before rank and wealth.'

His honeymoon with the Establishment did not last long. In vain, Cobbett waited for the promised attack on corruption, on the complex, tottering, self-supporting system of placemen and sinecures and pensioners, above all on the paper currency which was inflating prices grievously to the harm of the ordinary man. In 1815, the long-drawn-out war which had created the system came to an end – but the system continued. Discharged soldiers flooded the market: farm prices – Cobbett's particular interest – tumbled. In a well-meaning attempt to alleviate distress, the magistrates of Speenhamland pegged the level of relief to the price of the gallon loaf. In effect, the poor laws subsidized the farmers: they could reduce wages, confident that the parish would make them up. But Cobbett put his finger on the glaring weakness of the system: again and again he describes situations where able-bodied men were improving roads in order to allow the hated 'jews and jobbers' to travel comfortably in their carriages while the fields lay untilled. In the country the mythical 'Captain Swing' copied the activities of the Luddites in the towns with rick burnings and destruction of threshing machines.

So, on that foggy October morning in 1821, William Cobbett, a hale and hearty yeoman farmer not quite sixty years old, hoisted his massive body – 'just the weight of a four bushel sack of good wheat' – on horseback and set out on his *Rural Rides* to see how the countryman fared. The Rides were undertaken in a series of tours, in all seasons and in all kinds of weather, between 1821 and 1832. He penetrated into Scotland and Ireland but in the main it was England south of the Wash that engrossed him, in particular his own country of Hampshire and Surrey. His usual technique was to write his essays while actually travelling and send them off to London for publication in the weekly *Register*, his own, highly idiosyncratic newspaper. They therefore have all the defects, and all the virtues, of instant reporting.

Sometimes he would be accompanied by a friend or a servant, or his little son Richard whose brother, James, would in due course edit the *Rides* and give them to a larger public even than those thousands who subscribed to the *Register*. One can only marvel at the man's sure powers of endurance. After a ride of perhaps thirty or forty miles, sustained by nothing more than a hunk of bread and cheese bought from a cottager, as often as not soaking wet from rain and mist, he will pick up pen and paper and dash off several hundred words of invective or observation or reminiscence while waiting for his mutton chop.

He is a violent, intemperate writer. 'People have about Cobbett as substantial an idea as they have of Cribb,' William Hazlitt noted. 'His blows are as hard, and he himself as impenetrable. One has no notion of him making use of a fine pen but a great mutton fist. His style stuns his readers.' Certain key words and phrases appear again and again as a leitmotif. Predominant is THE THING, the Pitt system of government with its swarm of pensioned hangers-on. Repeated as counterpoint to this motif are the endless litanies of hatred directed against Jews, loan-jobbers, stock-jobbers – all those who derived a living other than from the land or manufactures. He might fairly be called a professional John Bull; in his description of the market place in Norwich, he compares the trim, neat Norfolk women and their wholesome produce with the French, whose 'meat is lean and bloody and nasty and the people snuffy and grimy in hands and face'. There was, however, another side to the man – the side portrayed by Miss Mitford when she left a charming picture of a happy household, presided over by a loving husband and wife. Or by his contemporary biographer, Edward Smith, who provides a delightful vignette of him and his men one Sunday. Cobbett had arranged with them to work for double pay on the farm that day and gave them a good dinner at the end of the day, putting each man's pay before him: 'Now, if you go to hell for working on Sunday, don't you go and say you b'ent been paid!'

But it was the land that William Cobbett truly loved. He 'reads' it as a geologist reads strata or an archaeologist reads deposits. He is aware, and makes the reader aware, of the bones and structure underfoot: that the soil, being like this, will produce such and such a crop and will look in this or that manner after winter's rains, after summer's drought. He describes trees not in the vague way of the urban nature lover, nor the precise manner of the botanist, but in terms of the working farmer – this kind of tree, planted in that kind of place, will yield so much timber for such and such a purpose.

He is aware, too, of natural beauty, as in one entry where he graduates from a prosaic consideration of woodland technique to a passage of considerable

Blickling Hall, Norfolk: 'the birthplace, they say, of Anne de Boleyn', observed Cobbett in Rural Rides. *'She married the king while his real wife was still alive. I could have excused her if there had been no marriage.'*

poetic power. He appraises a town as he would a good dinner: 'solid, substantial, clean, neat' – these are his words of praise. He has an eye always for pretty young women, seeming to regard them as though they were a particularly attractive and valuable crop. History, English history, is for him a real and living – though thoroughly garbled – presence. Passing Blickling Hall in Norfolk he is moved to speculate on Anne Boleyn, then by natural association to Catherine of Aragon, thence to Cranmer and Foxe's *Book of Martyrs*, commiserating the one and trouncing the other with gusto. England before the Reformation is, for him, the Golden Age and again and again he compares the kindly monks and friars of that mythical age of piety with the greedy, lazy, degenerate parsons of his own time. He has a fixed idea that the population of England had declined disastrously since the Middle Ages, repeatedly citing as evidence the vast size of churches in tiny villages.

It is this last attitude which makes William Cobbett at once a fascinating and a dangerous guide to the rural life of early nineteenth-century England. He knew, none better, that he was viewing a world on the brink of immense change, but where people like Defoe and Young welcomed that change, he abhorred it. He anticipated William Morris, and in a different setting, by half a century. Happiness, true happiness, lay in the virtues of the past: in working with one's own hands on one's own land, eating the bacon produced by oneself (he had an almost mystical reverence for bacon as an index of an

76

independent peasantry, contrasting it scornfully with the growing use of potatoes, 'Ireland's lazy root').

In all the hundreds of thousands of words that flowed so easily from Cobbett's pen, perhaps none so clearly sum up his viewpoint, and point the way that England was going, as his description of a farmhouse sale in Surrey in October 1825. He mourns the fact that once 'Everything about this farm-house was formerly the scene of *plain manners* and *plentiful living*. Oak clothes-chests, oak bed-steads, oak chests and drawers and oak tables to eat on, long, strong and well supplied with joint stools . . . . Now, there was a *parlour*. Aye, and a *carpet*, and a *bell-pull* too. One end of the front of this plain and substantial house had been moulded into a *parlour*, and there was a mahogany table, and the fine chairs and the fine glass and all as barefaced upstart as any stock-jobber in the kingdom can boast of. And there were the decanters, and the glasses, and the "dinner-set" of crockery ware, and all just in the true stock-jobber style.' Above all, he mourned the break-up of the old system where the farmer would lodge his men 'and sit at the head of the oak-table with his men, say grace to them and cut up the meat and the pudding. He might take a cup of strong beer to himself when they had none, but that was pretty nearly all the difference in their manner of living.' Small wonder that in the 1930s G. K. Chesterton, himself wistfully hankering after a mythical Merry England, should turn Farmer William Cobbett into a species of folk hero.

In the 1690s Celia Fiennes remarked scathingly that 'the common people know not above two or three miles from their homes': even 130 years later Cobbett encountered a woman who had never travelled more than two-and-a-half miles from her home in Ludgershall, Bucks. Being Cobbett, he thoroughly approved of her. 'Let no one laugh at her [for] the facilities which now exist of moving human bodies from place to place are amongst the curses of the country, the destroyers of industry, of morals and, of course of happiness.' Cobbett was thinking simply of accelerated road transport: of the mail coaches which stopped for no man; of the stage coaches which had shaved off the times at stage post inns so finely that the unfortunate traveller barely had time to swallow a hot drink before being hurtled off again into the dark and cold. Around the turn of the century the Englishman Thomas Telford and the Scotsman John McAdam had between them given Britain the first advance in a road system since the Romans had left. By 1803 it was possible to travel from London to Edinburgh in three days; by 1815 the Norwich *Times* was regularly doing the 112 miles from Norwich to London in a day with ample time at each end.

The road beneath might be vastly improved, but the motive power was still that provided immemorially by the horse, moving at a maximum speed of around eight miles an hour. In 1830, however, just four years after Cobbett had bemoaned the existing 'facilities for moving human bodies about' and barely a generation since Byng had opined that there would be no further point of exploration because 'our speed has reached the summit', the railway between Manchester and Liverpool carried 445,000 passengers in its first twelve months, at a speed of around fifty miles an hour. The railway had arrived and, like a knife shearing across a sheet of parchment, brought to an end a pattern of travel which had existed since man first hoisted a pack on to his back, or clambered on to the back of a quadruped. Not all were by any means pleased. The Duke of Wellington unconsciously echoed the plebeian William Cobbett when he snarled, 'It will encourage the lower classes to move about.' De Quincey made the point which occurs even more forcefully

The end of an era: opening of the Shoreham line in 1840. The depth of the still-raw cutting through the chalk shows the scale of the enterprise.

to modern users of air transport – that speed kills the sense of movement. 'They boast of more velocity, not, however, as a consciousness but as a fact of our lifeless knowledge, resting upon alien evidence; as, for instance, because somebody *says* that we have gone fifty miles in the hour, though we are far from feeling it as a personal experience. Seated on an old mailcoach we needed no evidence out of our selves to indicate the velocity. We heard our speed: we saw it; we felt it as a thrilling, incarnated in the fiery eyeballs of the noblest among brutes, in his dilated nostril, spasmodic muscles and thunder-beating hoofs.' But whatever the protests of poets and aristocrats and proto-sociologists, the railway had arrived, thrusting the road back into the obscurity from which it had begun to emerge. And as the twin, gleaming rails spread like a net over the ancient landscape, so England stepped, finally, into the technological age.

CHAPTER FOUR

The Ambassadors

Ay, marry, why was he sent into England?
  Why, because he was mad: he shall recover his wits there; or, if he do not, it's no
great matter there.
  Why?
  'Twill not be seen in him there; there the men are as mad as he.

Thus the gravedigger in *Hamlet*, Shakespeare neatly pandering both to his
fellow-countrymen's complacent view of themselves and their cheerful
acceptance of insult in preference to being ignored. Insult from foreigners, in
any case, scarcely counts. Four centuries later the Hungarian, George Mikes,
tapped that same vein, at first accidentally, in puzzlement and irritation, later
to his amusement and profit. His amiably corrosive portrait of the English
character in his book *How to Be an Alien*, first published in 1946, was promptly
pounced on by Rumanian Radio and serialized (without permission) as anti-
British propaganda. But, at the same time, the British Central Office of
Information sought permission from Mikes to translate the book into Polish as
a guide for the thousands of Poles newly resident in the country.

  In the 1890s a complete series of books, 'As Others See Us', was launched by
the publisher William Allen. The series editor deliberately left in any errors
because 'It is just these that are instructive.' He, too, sounds the warning of
change, that the world will never be the same, which afflicts all writers dealing
with current affairs. 'It is possible that the present [nineteenth] century will be
the last in the world's history during which national types will remain distinct
. . . Closer communication corrupts national peculiarities and already
national dress has practically disappeared in Western Europe.'

  At about the same time, the magisterial London Library created an entire
classification of books, 'Foreign Views of England', adding to it year by year,
decade by decade. They stretch now in serried ranks from the sombre green
and brown and dark blue buckram of the early nineteenth century to the gay
photographic colours of the late twentieth, testimony to the frequently

exasperated, often superficial, but never diminishing interest expressed by Continentals in the hybrids behind their twenty miles of water. Mr Pickwick meets one of these chroniclers, Count Smorltork, at the garden party in Eatanswill, and sets the ball rolling with the standard question: 'Have you been long in England?'

'Long – ver long time – fortnight – more.'
'Do you stay here long?'
'One week.'
'You will have enough to do,' said Mr Pickwick smiling, 'to gather all the materials you want in that time.'

. . . . .

'They are here,' added the count, tapping his forehead significantly. 'Large book at home – full of notes – music, picture, science, potry, poltic; all tings.'
'The word politics, sir,' said Mr Pickwick, 'comprises in itself, a difficult study of no inconsiderable magnitude.'
'Ah!' said the Count, drawing out the tablets again, 'ver good – fine words to begin a chapter. Chapter forty-seven. Poltics. The word poltic surprises by himself – ' And down went Mr Pickwick's remark, in Count Smorltork's tablets, with such variations and additions as the Count's exuberant fancy suggested, or his imperfect knowledge of the language occasioned.

Dickens's Count Smorltork is undoubtedly a caricature, but one not too far removed from the reality either of the nineteenth or the twentieth century. And even the most informed foreigner remains – a foreigner, liable to misinterpret subtle commonplaces. Yet, also, because he is a foreigner he can not only be objective but can highlight subjects which the native takes for granted, often with very surprising results. The self-portrait which a modern Englishman would give of his race would probably include the element of docility, a readiness to obey the law. George Orwell remarked that the English were the easiest people in the world to shoulder off a pavement. To read the memoirs of foreign visitors over the centuries is to encounter a rather different picture. The concept which occurs again and again is not simply that the English are a violent people, but a ferocious one. Italians who had experienced centuries of urban battle; Germans who had known the horrors of the Thirty Years War, and Frenchmen who had endured the terrors of the Revolution remarked upon the appalling ferocity of the London mob. Voltaire, caught up in one such, forgot all his wit, forgot all the sardonic weapons at his command, and came as near to grovelling as such a man could: 'Good people, am I not unhappy enough not to have been born among you?' Foreigners were shocked and sickened both by such sports as cock-fighting and bear-baiting and, above all, by the public executions.

Another part of a modern self-portrait would undoubtedly include the concept of being restrained, undemonstrative, unlike excitable Latins. Yet the sixteenth-century Italian Cardano 'completely thought myself to be among Italians: they were like in figure, manners, dress, gesture, colour'. Other key words applied by visitors to the English over the centuries are their hypocrisy, their cleanliness, their undoubted democracy. More than one foreigner recorded amazement at the way the classes mixed in the streets, jostling each other regardless of rank. The Frenchman, Jean Grosley, noticed this happening on London Bridge. One would never see such a sight in Paris, he declared. Another Frenchman, Misson de Valbourg, was astonished to see the Duke of Grafton engaged in fisticuffs with a coachman over a disputed fare. The Duke won, but Valbourg was still shocked: 'In France we punish such rascals with our cane.' Yet Valbourg also noticed that, no matter how violent a quarrel, an Englishman never drew a sword or dagger against an unarmed man, no matter what his class. It was, perhaps, a ferocious species' instinct for survival, like that of wolves who never fight to the death between themselves.

The fact that the traveller to England is approaching an island was always evident until the mid-twentieth century. In the Middle Ages and the Renaissance, the approach was exclusively cross Channel, usually to Dover. It was here that the pedantic German Thomas Platter saw the remains of wrecked Armada ships still visible a year after the defeat of the great fleet. In the early nineteenth century, the west coast opens up with Americans making landfall at Liverpool, moving on to Chester and so getting their first taste of antiquity before going on to London. In the 1920s the scene moves back to the Channel ports, for now it is the Antipodean visitors coming up Channel, usually after having made the passage of the Mediterranean. Their first glimpse of England is of the headlands of Devon and Dorset, their landfall Southampton. In 1958, the Indian Nirad Chaudhuri briefly has the best of both worlds, coming in by air but at so low an altitude that the beautiful island opens up beneath him, marvellously, from the chalk cliffs of Dover to Windsor Castle and Eton College Chapel. 'I thought it was a good omen that the first historic buildings to catch my eyes should be these renowned symbols of English life.' But that is only a brief-lived phase. From the 1970s onward the traveller is subject to the universal disorientation of stratospheric flight, the great jets thundering down from five miles up to give him only a photo-flash of the landscape before he enters the anonymous steel and glass and electronics world of an international airport. The first he will experience of England is the chaos of London, as happened to the Israeli Hannoch Bartov in 1968. 'These are the first moments, the first riddles we try to solve. All the streets, houses,

The gateway to England: picture map of Dover probably drawn to illustrate harbour works about 1543.

signposts that keep coming inexorably towards us are identical. How does a person know if he is coming or going? Where is north?'

But still those twenty miles of salt water, sometimes glittering, more often leaden, which the English impudently call the English Channel and the French, with uncharacteristic modesty, style the Sleeve, still act not so much as barrier as punctuation point. 'Up to here are these kinds of people, this kind of life: beyond is that.' Italians and Germans, French, Dutch, Swedes, Danes, Spanish, though they might cordially loathe each other, though each might be tightly wrapped in his own national mores, yet also know one another, moving backwards and forwards across mutual frontiers, sharing many of the same ideas, much the same religion. The twenty miles of water seemed to act for them (as well as for the inhabitants of the island) not only as punctuation point but as distorting mirror. As late as 1579 the Frenchman Jean Bernard was saying confidently that 'great and learned persons versed in the knowledge of history and foreign lands, each contributes his share of what he has seen and experienced, treating however mostly of Spain, Italy, Germany, Piedmont or the Netherlands but rarely of our English and Scottish neighbours'. He exaggerated: by 1579, certainly, the Venetian Senate had a very good idea indeed of what was going on in England through the copious reports of its ambassadors. That hearty bon vivant, Aeneas Sylvius Piccolomini, later Pope Pius II, left a friendly enough account of his travels in the White Island during the 1430s. Polydore Vergil, yet another Italian, tried to correct the myths which the English took for their history and got small thanks for his pains. But in general, Bernard was right: Continental travellers were more interested in each other than in the curious folk across the water. And it was long before any but the most pressing business would persuade a Continental to entrust himself to those twenty miles of water and the even more unpredictable people whom it screened.

But at about the time that the Canterbury Pilgrims were returning to their homes, picking up again the humdrum threads of life, a white-bearded, white-haired Frenchman, Jean Froissart, made a return visit to the land he had come to love as his own. Froissart first came to England as a young man of twenty in order to get over an unhappy love affair. Or so he said, and produced reams of poetry to prove it. But whatever the reason for his visit, he was fortunate enough to be taken into the entourage of Philippa, queen to Edward III, and it was from that comfortable position that he viewed the island race. Twenty-eight years later, in 1395, he took advantage of a brief truce in the long-drawn war between France and England to cross the Channel and present his credentials to the new king, Richard II. Like any other elderly man revisiting the scenes of his youth, Froissart was disconcerted to find no familiar faces. 'The inns were all kept by new people and the children of my former acquaintance were become men and women.' But it is to be doubted if Jean Froissart regarded himself as being in any sense in a 'foreign' country – certainly no more foreign than some parts of France, Burgundy or Aquitaine, would be to him, a man from the north-west. He regarded England horizontally, not vertically, that is, in terms of class, not nationality. By now, the court was speaking English as its first language, but virtually everybody there spoke French quite instinctively. The international code of chivalry ironed out most national distinctions. In his great *Chronicles*, Froissart moves quite casually between discussion of English and French affairs, drawing no real distinction between them: indeed, the first twenty books of the *Chronicles* are exclusively devoted to England and, unless he is following very closely, at times the reader might well be uncertain about just who is fighting whom, whether the writer is chronicling yet another battle in the long Anglo-French war – or a battle between French dissidents.

In this view, England is the furthest point of civilization, a last great bastion of at least partially Latin culture in a sea of Celtic barbarism. One can see the good canon listening open-mouthed to Henry Cassid's lurid description of the Irish: 'They never consider their enemies as dead until they have cut their throats like sheep, opened their bellies and taken out their hearts that they devour as delicious morsels.' The Scots are scarcely better: 'their habits of sobriety are such that they will live for a long time on flesh half sodden, without bread, and drink the river water without wine.' And he does not even mention the Welsh, long since conquered by his heroes.

Although these are English knights, they would have differed not at all from French knights in Froissart's eyes. His world was divided by class, not by nation. Illustration from his Chronicles.

Nevertheless, the *Chronicles* of Jean Froissart, 'treasurer and canon of Chimay in the county of Hainault and the diocese of Liège', provides the first clear indication that England is separating from the Continent. He is made aware that, outside the royal court, the English regard everybody on the other side of the Channel as a parcel of damned foreigners. Wryly he remarked upon the provincial knight who regarded him as 'a foreigner and a Frenchman (for all who speak the language of Oil are by the English considered as Frenchmen, whatever country they may come from)'. And he shows his awareness of the coming break, the fact that nationality will triumph over class and over chivalry, by the close attention he pays to the form of homage that Edward III paid to Philip IV for the duchy of Guienne. He describes carefully the physical act – the fact that Edward made only verbal homage 'without placing his hands in the hands of the king of France or any prince, prelate, or deputy doing it for him'. Later there was much anguished discussion amongst the lawyers 'by what means a king of England was a vassal to the king of France'. There was, of course, no means whatsoever by which one sovereign ruler could ever be the vassal of another and Froissart's *Chronicles* is largely an account of the opening of that so-called Hundred Years War which was to bedevil Anglo-French relations for centuries thereafter. Not until the nineteenth century would French and English troops stand shoulder to shoulder, instead of face to face, on a battlefield, and no such chronicler as Froissart would try to explain English to French for nearly two hundred years after he left.

Nevertheless, the island was emerging from its Channel mists as the stability of its monarchy, the tenacity of its traders and the ferocity of its soldiers made it a force in Europe. The Venetians with that cold, clear eye of theirs made haste to establish a permanent embassy, drawing England into the great communication network which made the Serenissima Republica the best-informed government in the world. Ambassadors reported back to their government through two clearly different media, *dispacci* and *relazione*. The *dispacci* were the formal letters emanating from the man on the spot more or less at the same time as the incidents reported. *Relazione* were more informal and, in the long run, probably more valuable. The returning diplomat would render a word-of-mouth report to his peers in council, filling in the details that he had only sketched in the *dispacci*, answering the probing questions of other, veteran diplomats, comparing his experience with theirs, building up a comprehensive, complex picture of the country he had just left. The four years which Sebastian Giustinian spent at the court of Henry VIII provided British posterity with one of the clearest of all pictures of the operations of that lethal monarch.

It is these Venetians who provide, among much else, the first clear indications of two dominant characteristics of the English, to be repeated again and again over the centuries: their xenophobia and their ferocity. Giustinian describes that London revolt against the presence of foreigners which took place on May Day 1517, a revolt so violent and widespread that it took the name of the Evil May Day. One can all but hear the note of resignation in the voice of this civilized, cosmopolitan man, inhabitant of a country which accepted the passage and presence of foreigners as a matter of course. A preacher had stirred up the mob, he said, 'and they commenced abusing the strangers in the town, alleging that they not only deprived them of their industry, and of the emoluments derivable thence, but disgraced their dwellings taking their wives and their daughters'. And Andrea Trevisano, ambassador to Henry VIII's father, referred not only to the English feats of arms ('They have a high reputation in arms, and from the great fear the French entertain of them, one must believe it to be justly acquired'), but also to the coldness and callousness of their nature, manifested in their treatment of their children: 'at the age of seven or eight years at the most, they put them out to hard service in the houses of other people'. In the years to come, other foreigners, Latins in particular, would refer to the dislike that the islanders apparently had for their offspring.

These early chroniclers paint with a very broad brush for the most part. They are concerned with the king and his court and there they do indeed paint in the minutest detail, telling us what he ate and drank, how he behaved in his cups, the degree of his veracity or otherwise, for the king, in this society, was all important. It was his likely motivations and reactions that interested their distant governments, not the everyday activities of ordinary people. It is not until the very end of the sixteenth century that the first true tourist, the man who has crossed the Channel just to look around and record what he sees, arrives. In the shape, unfortunately, of the German student Thomas Platter.

Unfortunately, because his journey in 1599 was, in the unkind but exact words of his English translator, 'The Pedant's Progress'. What could we have had if only Thomas Platter had been a Venetian or a Florentine or even a Parisian, what lively anecdotes, what insights into the life-style of these strange people? Instead, we have what amounts to a series of lists. One can see him taking out his tablets, solemnly jotting down whatever lies before him. At Whitehall Palace, where we long for a description of that vanished monster, he gives us a detailed list (with translations) of the Latin mottoes that proliferate in its chambers. He visits Mr Cope's house in 'Snecgas' – probably Snow Hill in London – and gives us another list, this time of the curios that Walter Cope collected on his lengthy travels. There is, admittedly, a certain charm about them, for they include a 'flying rhinoceros', a 'small bone implement used in India for scratching oneself', and a 'sea-halcyon's nest, sign of a calm sea', but one would rather have known more about this remarkable traveller himself.

However, for good or ill, Thomas Platter is our first true tourist and it is worth following his *Travels* in some little detail for they foreshadow and sum up many of the opinions and actions of the tens of thousands of foreigners who will come to England over the following centuries.

And the first test to endure is the Channel crossing. Today, hardly an hour by ferry or minutes by plane, the crossing of those twenty miles is barely a hiatus. For Platter, and all those down to the invention of the steamship in the nineteenth century, that narrow strip of salt water looms like an Atlantic: the days spent waiting for a favourable wind, the violence of the crossing itself. Platter's ship was still in sight of land when the seamen began desperately pumping ship, so old and crazy was it. Platter and his companions were so terrified that they begged to be taken back, offering to pay full fare, but the captain had other ideas. On arrival they upbraided him, and to their horror he admitted that he himself had had no idea that the boat was so bad and he intended to burn it.

From Dover Platter goes on to Canterbury, 'where, if I remember, St Thomas the Scotchman lies interred'; through Rochester, where he marvels at the monstrous warships that serve her majesty, and so to London. There, he enunciates a belief which generations of travellers will hold: 'He who sightsees London and the royal courts in its immediate vicinity, may assert without impertinence that he is properly acquainted with England.' During the five weeks of his stay, he leaves London only to make a quick circuit of the royal palaces at Windsor, Richmond, Greenwich and Nonsuch and a foray to Oxford. That circuit will, in fact, hold good for centuries. In 1984, the British Tourist Authority could in effect add only Stratford-on-Avon, the Lake District and, occasionally, Cornwall as places on the tourist circuit – that is, as places which tourists *wanted* to visit.

London overwhelms him, as it does all visitors, and through his stilted words one clearly gets a picture which time and the growth of other cities has blurred: that this is a maritime city and, effortlessly, the largest in Europe. He is invited to dinner with the Lord Mayor and he describes the vast meal with the same awe that the New Zealander Ian Donnelly will record in the 1930s when he, too, dines with City worthies. Platter falls into one of those traps which lie in wait for the hasty tourist engaged in extrapolating the general from the particular. The Lord Mayor of London, says he, 'must daily hold an open board to which inhabitants and strangers, men and women, may go unbidden'. One would like to have had the reaction of His Worship if several hundred hungry Londoners had turned up every day at his luncheon table.

Platter throws himself into the arduous business of sightseeing the enormous city. First to London Bridge, where he sees the skulls of thirty

One of the tourist attractions of London: 'traitors'' heads on the gateway to London Bridge.

The Globe

The Globe Theatre, Southwark. It is the foreign tourist, Thomas Platter, who leaves the first description of Shakespeare's theatre – and, perhaps, of Shakespeare acting there.

'traitors' decorating the upper works, and is told that their descendants actually boast of them, as evidence that their forebears were exalted enough to challenge the throne. Then on to the Tower of London, where he is shown the block and axe that separated those heads from their bodies. During his lengthy tour of the Tower he and his party are mulcted for tips no less than eight times, one of the less attractive traits of the English which will again and again be commented upon most unfavourably. He is agog to discover that 'London has two, sometimes three plays running in different places' and, quite casually, this stolid young German earns himself a glittering place in English dramatic history by describing the first performance of 'the tragedy of the first Emperor Julius Caesar' in what is, quite evidently, the Globe Theatre on the South Bank. 'There was a cast of some fifteen people [of whom one was very probably William Shakespeare taking a small part in his own play], and when the play was over they danced very marvellously and gracefully together as is their wont, two dressed as men and two as women.'

High on the list of tourist attractions is Gloriana herself. The Queen was staying in Nonsuch Palace, and again the reader is subjected to a frustrating experience, for Thomas Platter dismisses the palace itself (of which there was 'none such' in the world) with a cursory description. It stands isolated; visitors who are not actually accommodated in it must put up in tents; it is composed of a series of courts, the inner court of which 'has a handsome and elaborate snow-white fountain showing a griffin angrily spewing water with great violence'. But the reader is disposed to forgive Platter, for he makes up for this lack of architectural description with page upon page about the extraordinary ceremony that attended Queen Elizabeth's public appearances. He saw her in

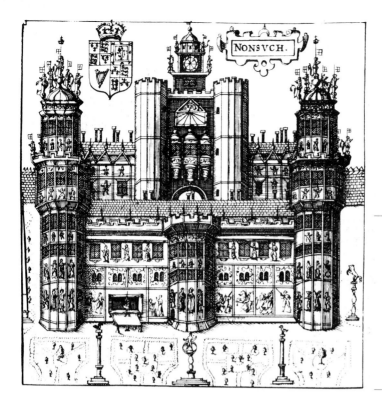

The south front of the extraordinary Nonsuch (left). Platter was among those who saw the Queen dining there.

(Opposite) The remains of Woodstock Palace, with Fair Rosamond's bower. All was swept away during the building of Blenheim Palace.

The coach Platter describes may well have been as ornate as this, for noblemen were prepared to hire out their coaches. The leather straps made for a smoother ride, but imparted a swinging motion many people found sickening.

person attending a church service ('just as in the Roman church', the good Protestant Platter notes disapprovingly) and afterwards enjoyed a privilege which seems curious to modern eyes – watching the monarch eat. In Elizabeth's case it was even more curious, for the food was served, with immense ceremony, to a completely empty table and then taken from there to an inner chamber where the queen ate in privacy.

Platter and his party went on to Windsor and Eton, where he was astonished to find that not one of the so-called scholars could speak Latin but

'pointed to their mouths with their fingers and shook their heads'. At Oxford they had an experience which vividly illustrates both the discomforts of road travel and the remarkable power of the University Chancellor. They were travelling by a hired coach, having contracted with the coachman to go from London to Oxford and thence to Cambridge for the very substantial sum of sixteen shillings daily. The coachman declined to go on to Cambridge because it had recently been raining and the road was very bad: 'He added that the coach was very expensive and he had hired it from a great lord to whom it belonged, and that he had newly set up house and should the coach get stuck in the mud he would be a broken man for life.' Platter took their grievance to the Chancellor who, having heard both sides and having had the coach inspected, came down partly in favour of the coachman. The road to Cambridge was indeed far too bad, he ruled, but it was perfectly possible to go back to London via Woodstock; and so it was decided, Platter contenting himself with seeing the palace where Elizabeth had been imprisoned and the secret bower that had been the home of the Fair Rosamond, 'concubine of King Henry II of England'. They had one more opportunity of seeing the Queen, this time in Richmond. She came to a window overlooking a courtyard where there was a great crowd, 'and she spoke in English "God bless mi piple" and they all cried in unison "God save the Queen" and they remained kneeling until she made them a sign with her hand to rise'. Platter says the English regarded her as a god, and three things were prohibited under pain of death: that her virginity should be questioned, her government questioned or her successor named.

On 20 October, furnished with a passport by milord Cobham, 'Jean Joachim Stuber, Petrus Julius, Andreas Pucher, Paulus Holtzbecher, Martinus Pissetius, Thomas Platerus, high Almaynes gentilmen and schollers come latelie over with a desier to see her Mayeste and the countrey, and noue disirous to passe over into frannce' again took ship from Dover. And again encountered the perils that wrapped round the island kingdom, for they sighted a Spanish ship that would undoubtedly have done them harm, though they managed to evade it. 'And God be praised we arrived safe and sound at Calais port towards dawn, where we made merry until daybreak in a fisherman's hut, as is the case with those who land happily in port after a great peril.'

Platter's *Travels* is the forerunner of a host of *Journeys, Diaries, Letters,* all purporting to describe the islanders. On their side, the islanders constructed a kind of league table of the foreigners. All were to be pitied or patronized for being foreign but some more, or less, than others. Long after the threat from Spain had evaporated, Spaniards continued to be best-hated. Orazio Busino, chaplain to the Venetian ambassador in the early seventeenth century, remarks how the Spaniards arrogantly – and foolishly – dressed in the Spanish manner. One such, he says, nearly paid for his arrogance with his life when a woman began belabouring him with a cabbage stalk, attracting a large crowd. He saved himself only by dashing into a shop.

It was Busino's opinion that had the Spaniard only dressed in the French manner, he would have been ignored. Relations between English and French waxed and waned according partly to pressures of Continental adventures, but partly also to deep cultural differences. The wounds of the Hundred Years War took long to heal, and even when they had passed into history the French tended to regard their neighbours, the 'goddams', as barbarians who either killed each other in civil wars, or cut off the heads of their kings, while the English returned the compliment by seeing the 'frogs' as essentially comic or frivolous or both. Yet the powerful cultural bond forged so long ago could not be entirely eroded: France was instinctively regarded as the fashion-setter, England as a place where 'liberty' really was something more than a catchword. The career of Charles St Evremond admirably summed up their curious relationship. Fleeing for his life from an enraged Cardinal Mazarin in 1661, he made his home in England for forty years and the English gave him not only a pension but also the signal honour of burying him in Westminster Abbey. Although he never actually got round to learning English, St

Evremond was an admirable and sympathetic observer not only of English life and manners, but of the foreigners who flocked to them. In his play *Sir Politick Would-be* he guys the archetypal tourist, in this case a German who does indeed bear a distinct resemblance to Thomas Platter, with his notebook in which everything is solemnly jotted down, the guidebook swotted up beforehand, the endless lists recording how long, how old, how high. Cross-examined on the sights he has seen, he comes up with a list very like Platter's: Westminster Abbey, the Tower, Whitehall Palace. The Italian, Giuseppe Baretti, swore that the English believed that there were indeed only two races, the French and the English. 'They know something about a sea-faring people called the Dutch, for whom they have the greatest contempt. They assume that Italians are French.'

On their side, the visitors frequently commented on how little love was lost between the inhabitants of the British Isles. Frederick Wendeborne, a German who knew England really very well in the eighteenth century (he was for many years pastor of a German church in London), noted: 'It is curious that the English, who pride themselves on the name of Britons which they bear in common with the Scotch, are notwithstanding rather more averse to them than even to a foreigner.' They refer to their Hibernian compatriots as 'Irish bog-trotter or fortune hunter and they are not seldom ridiculed in the public prints and on the stage.' Karl Marx was convinced that the only way the English upper classes could be dislodged was by a blow coming from Ireland: hence Irish independence was a prerequisite for revolution.

At the very core of the English character, behind the eccentricity and the casualness and the good-natured patronization, most writers detected a kind of cold steeliness which found expression sometimes in mob ferocity, sometimes in martial valour, sometimes in a stoic indifference to pain, or a refusal to go with the crowd, or a callous indifference to the wellbeing of the weak. In 1844 Frederick Engels describes walking through Manchester with a prosperous merchant, expatiating on the appalling conditions of the poor. 'The man listened to the end and said at the corner where we parted "And yet there is a great deal of money made here. Good morning sir".' It comes as a distinct surprise to discover that the English, who were almost to make a religion out of their love for animals, were renowned for a sickening cruelty towards them from the sixteenth century onward. Thomas Platter follows most of his fellow writers in describing, at fascinated length, the activities of a cockfight and, later, the baiting of bulls and bears in Southwark. Quite casually, he brings out the fact that it was cruelty for its own sake that attracted the crowd, not simply the matching of one animal against another. After a bear and a bull had been matched with mastiffs, each giving a very good

The Englishman's sport:
1 – *bear baiting in the mid nineteenth century.*

(Opposite)
The Englishman's sport:
2 – *watching public executions.*

account of itself, 'They brought on an old, blind bear which the boys hit with canes and sticks' until it ran away.

The public executions attracted the horrified attention of all visitors down to the nineteenth century, the detailed descriptions arguing that the writers had experienced nothing like it in their own countries. The account of Orazio Busino, chaplain to the Venetian ambassador in 1616, can stand as model for the rest. He combines in it everything which so surprised and disgusted the foreigner: the holiday-like atmosphere in which the condemned took part; their insouciance; and, above all, what might be called the mass-production techniques involved.

They take them [the condemned] five and twenty at a time, every month, besides sudden and extraordinary executions in the course of the week, on a large cart like a high scaffold. They go along quite jollily, holding their sprigs of rosemary, and singing songs, accompanied by their friends and a multitude of people. On reaching the gallows, one of the party acts as spokesman, saying fifty words or so. Then the music, which they had learned at their leisure in the prisons, being repeated, the executioner hastens about the business and beginning at one end, fastens each man's halter to the gibbet. They are so closely packed that they touch each other with their hands tied in front of them, wrist to wrist, so as to leave them the option of taking off their hats and saluting the bystanders. One careless fellow availed himself of this facility to shield his face from the sun. Finally, the executioner having come down from the scaffold has the whip applied to the cart horses and thus the culprits remain dangling in the air precisely like a bunch of fat thrushes. They are hard to die of themselves and unless their own relations or friends pulled their feet or pelted them with brickbats in the breast as they do, it would fare badly with them. The proceeding is really barbarous and strikes those who witness it with horror.

Busino undoubtedly means that it is the foreigners who are shocked, for commentator after commentator echoes, in some degree, Misson de Valbourg's comment in 1690: 'The English laugh at the delicacy of other nations who make it such a mighty matter to be hanged. Their extraordinary courage looks upon it as a trifle' – thus bearing out William Harrison's proud boast, 'our condemned persons doo goe cheerfully to their deaths', full of English valour. Yet there is a reverse to this picture: more than one writer refers to the English tendency to suicide, born not of melancholy but of passion. And despite their courage, their ferocity, their delight alike in fisticuffs and bloodshed, they have a thoroughgoing contempt for militarism. Most Englishmen would have heartily agreed with the Quaker who described armies to Voltaire as 'murtherers cloath'd in scarlet and wearing caps two feet high [who] enlist citizens by a noise made with two little sticks on an ass's skin distended'.

The real democracy which could have coal-heavers and noblemen crossing London Bridge shoulder to shoulder did not prevent the English practising that class distinction which they themselves recognized as characteristic. Pastor Moritz, travelling around England in 1782, discovered that in addition to the 'vertical' distinction they drew between themselves and foreigners, was the 'horizontal' difference they drew amongst themselves in terms of class. Moritz made this painful discovery because he was travelling on foot – partly to save money, but also because he believed it the best way to get to know the country. Very rapidly he found that 'a traveller on foot in this country seems to be considered a sort of wild man, shunned by everybody who meets him'. Servants in inns addressed him by the casual, almost contemptuous term 'master', instead of the formal 'Sir' they used towards coach passengers.

Innkeepers usually refused him a bed: on one occasion, having been given a bed before it was known that he was on foot, he was summarily evicted. He was the mildest and gentlest of men, but even he could revolt – though he unwisely chose the question of 'tipping' as the issue on which to make a stand. After having had a bad supper, contemptuously served, and a worse bedroom in which he was disturbed by a drunk, he encountered the usual outstretched palms in the morning. The waiter who had served him so ill the night before was waiting at the foot of the stairs. 'I gave him three half-pence, on which he saluted me with the heartiest *G–d d–m you*, Sir I have ever heard.' Further on was the slattern who had so signally failed to make him comfortable. She, too, was waiting with the traditional, 'Pray remember the chambermaid'. 'Yes, yes, said I, I shall long remember your most ill-mannered behaviour and shameful incivility.' But if he expected so to quash a sturdy English chambermaid he was much mistaken, for her response was simply 'a contemptuous, loud horse laugh'.

Yet what followed afterwards was pure magic, the kind that waits for all travellers and one of the reasons why Moritz looked back on his brief sojourn in England as one of the happiest periods of his life. On the road to Oxford late at night he fell in with an Englishman who was a fellow clergyman and they beguiled the journey with pleasant discourse in a mixture of Latin, German and English. They arrived at one end of Oxford's immensely long High Street sometime about midnight and Moritz's companion, aglow with patriotic pride, was anxious to show him the delights of 'one of the finest, longest, and most beautiful streets not only in this city but in England and, I may safely add, in all Europe'. Poor Moritz, utterly fatigued and with no prospect of a bed that night, was in no mood for admiring architecture but nevertheless politely dragged himself along until he collapsed on a stone bench, probably near Carfax. There, he said, he would stay the night, but his companion would not hear of it. Despite the lateness of the hour, he knocked up an alehouse and they were promptly admitted.

What follows is best told in Moritz's own words. 'How great was my astonishment when on being shown into a room, I saw a great number of clergymen all with their gowns and bands on, sitting round a large table, each with his pot of beer before him. My travelling companion introduced me as a German clergyman whom he could not sufficiently praise for my correct [i.e. English] pronunciation of Latin, my orthodoxy and my good walking.' Moritz was immediately made welcome and furnished with beer. He described his own university background, 'neither denying or concealing that now and then we had riots and disturbances. "O, we are very unruly here, too," said one of the clergymen as he took a hearty draught out of his pot of

High Street, Oxford. The fatigued Pastor Moritz dragged himself along here after his marathon walk.

beer and knocked on the table with his hand.' The pots were refilled, the night wore on with arguments on biblical meanings and dawn was breaking when one of the clergy said suddenly, 'd–nme, I must read prayers at All Souls this morning', and so broke up the session.

Although most visitors were deeply impressed by London, nearly all agreed that people were much more pleasant in the provinces. Baretti noticed that the further he went from London, the more sociable were the ordinary people: 'I never was honoured once with the pretty appellation of *French dog* so liberally bestowed by the London rabble.' Frederick Wendeborne thought how delightful was the family circle in Bristol, unlike London where card tables were automatically brought out after supper 'to conceal the fact that the company was incapable of rational conversation'. He also noticed that they went to bed at 11 p.m., at about the time when a London host would be putting supper before his guests.

In view of the virtually universal praise for the English sense of hygiene, Erasmus's stricture comes as something of a puzzle. Writing to Cardinal Wolsey's physician he raises the problem of the 'sweating sickness' which had been scourging England for many years. He puts the pestilence down to the English dislike of fresh air and, above all, their filthy habits. 'The floors [of their houses] are generally strewed with clay, and that covered with rushes which are now and then removed, but so as not to disturb the foundation, which sometimes remains for twenty years nursing a collection of spittle, vomits, excrements of dogs and human beings, spilt beer and fishes bones and other filth that I need not mention.' He seems to have been particularly unfortunate in the houses he visited, for all other visitors give a quite different impression. His fellow Dutchman, Levinus Lemnius, particularly praises 'the neat cleanliness [with] their chambers and parlours strewed with sweet herbs'. The Swiss César de Saussure remarked that, 'though they are not slaves to cleanliness like the Dutch, still they are very remarkable for this virtue'. Pastor Moritz, obliged to wear a shirt two days running, heard two women criticizing him in the street for wearing a dirty shirt.

What did arouse the disgust of all, from the early seventeenth century onwards, was the English addiction to smoking. Busino reported, doubtfully, the English claim that it cleared the head, and remarked that even decent women smoked, though in privacy. He calculated that the tax on tobacco yielded the king (James I) 40,000 gold crowns annually. Nevertheless, 'His Majesty Abhors it'. Samuel de Sorbière ascribed the badness of English trade to the merchant's addiction to tobacco smoking. Reading some of these accounts, one wonders whether the writers might not have stumbled upon some drug rather stronger than tobacco. Both Platter, in 1599, and Sorbière, in 1663, though describing what they said was tobacco smoking say that the smokers acted as though drunk. 'They perform queer antics when they take it', was Platter's comment.

Sorbière evidently found little to please him in England, his *Voyage en Angleterre* containing contemptuous comments on language, literature, food,

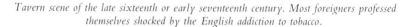

Tavern scene of the late sixteenth or early seventeenth century. Most foreigners professed themselves shocked by the English addiction to tobacco.

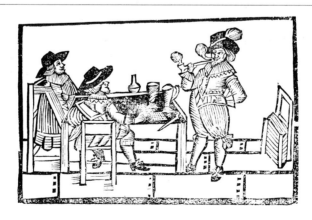

A London coffee house about the year 1705.

table manners. But other writers, both French and Dutch, though in general well disposed to the English, shared his opinion of their indolence. It is perhaps understandable that an industrious Dutchman like Emanuel van Meteren should accuse the English of exploiting their rich fishing grounds so idly that they actually had to buy fish from their neighbours. Jean Grosley, who came to London in 1765, and who was greatly impressed by English democracy, was considerably less impressed by the merchants: 'They rise late and pass an hour at home drinking tea with their families. About ten they go to the coffee house where they spend another hour. Then they go home or meet people about business. At two o'clock they go to 'Change. On their return they lounge a little at the coffee house and they dine about four.'

But the otherwise perspicacious and observant Grosley seems to have misinterpreted that 'lounging' in the coffee houses. As much work was done there as in formal offices. A potent factor in amassing the great wealth which made London a megalopolis was information: and a prime medium of information was the newspaper. The passion for print spread down into the labouring classes. 'All Englishmen are great newsmongers', the Swiss César de Saussure noted. 'Workmen habitually begin the day by going to coffee rooms in order to read the latest news. I have often seen shoeblacks and other persons of that class club together to purchase a farthing newspaper.' That was in the 1730s when the coffee house was at its height, but even when it was eclipsed by the tavern the newspaper habit continued. The Italian Count Pecchio, in the early nineteenth century, described the London tavern as the 'forum of the English' and explained how Sunday papers, carrying abridgement of the week's news, were available there, making the English working class one of the best informed in Europe. The passion for print even extended to the classics. Pastor Moritz's landlady was well acquainted with Milton and claimed that her husband courted her because of her skill in reading the great poet aloud. You wouldn't get anything like that in Germany, was Moritz's opinion. But few Continentals thought much of English literature, in particular the drama upon which the English so prided themselves. Remarking that most English tragedies are taken from history, Grosley says roundly: 'Most of their ancient kings act the part of fools, madmen or idiots.' Wendeborne was amused by the way in which the audience at a Shakespearean play seemed to think that the absurd ghosts and witches were real, reacting with surprise, fear or even horror at their appearance. Voltaire allowed that Shakespeare was a transcendent poet, but argued that this was, in fact, the ruin of the English stage: 'There are such beautiful, such noble, such dreadful scenes in this writer's monstrous farces, to which the name of tragedy is given, that they have always been exhibited with great success.' Inevitably, he said, other writers copied, and failed without the poetry.

The extraordinary English attitude to the Sabbath day was a preoccupation with foreigners from the Reformation onward. In the eighteenth century Casanova was astonished to discover that a citizen could be arrested in his own house for playing music or cards on a Sunday, but pointed out that an Englishman was perfectly at liberty to spend the holy day in tavern or brothel. (Two centuries later J. B. Priestley was making the identical point on a wet Sunday night in Bradford when only the pubs were open: 'I cannot see why playgoers, listening to music, watching films, even dancing should be considered so much worse than sitting and boozing with prostitutes.') Jean Grosley remarked how Londoners spent the day in an agony of boredom, waiting till the day is over, gazing 'in a melancholy mood at those who pass to and fro in the streets'. But it is Hippolyte Taine, the French historian who came to England in the 1860s, who leaves the most imperishable description of a Victorian Sunday: 'Sunday in London in the rain: the shops are shut, the streets almost deserted: the aspect is that of an immense and a well ordered cemetery. The few passers by under their umbrellas have the look of uneasy spirits who have risen from the grave: it is appalling. A yellow, dense fog fills the air . . . one meditates suicide . . . the lofty lines of fronts are of sombre brick . . . the mind quits the without to retire within . . . What is to be done on the day of rest? There is the church or the pothouse, intoxication or a sermon. . . .' – so on and on, a very threnody of despair. His compatriot, Paul Blouett, who wrote a bestseller in the 1870s called *John Bull and his island* under the name of Max O'Rell, gave it as his opinion that, Sunday being so awful, the English invented bank holidays as antidote. He gives a vivid picture of the saturnalia on Hampstead Heath, then makes the engaging comment that: 'The lower classes in England alone preserve the tradition of Merry England. Regardless of the future, living from hand to mouth, noisy and coarse, they form a most striking contrast to the rest of this nation of ants, morose, frigid and still preserving the same dread of happiness and joy as in the days of John Knox. . . .'

Throughout these centuries, from the third Edward to Victoria, the majority of articulate visitors to England came from the Continent, different indeed from the islanders but sharing the same culture and religion, and at much the same stage of technological development and social change. In 1836, however, there arrived three young Persian princes, brothers, one of whom – Najaf Koolee Merza – kept a journal. It was later privately printed and through its artless pages appears the England that would be seen by the increasing number of Africans and Orientals who, for whatever personal reason, were drawn to the heartland of a world empire.

The translator of the Journal is a Christian Syrian, a certain Assaad Kayat, who gives what must be the most unusual excuse ever made by an author for an incomplete manuscript. He was crossing the desert on a camel, he says, when he was stopped by a gang of Bedouins who rifled his pack. They came across the Journal in its original Farsi; he tried to protect it by saying that it was the Koran but they, saying that their mullah needed the Holy Book, helped themselves to the last dozen or so pages.

The three princes, of the royal house of Qajar, were engaged in murderous internecine fighting on the death of their grandfather, the shah, when one of them had the idea of appealing to England. Accompanied by their faithful translator, they make an incredible winter journey to Beirut, where a 'fire ship' is waiting. From the moment they step on the steamship they are in another world, beset with unimaginable dangers of which the sea itself is quite the most terrifying. On the voyage from Malta they run out of coal and the captain, with what seems to be remarkable insouciance, calculates that it will take them three months to drift to Gibraltar – by which time they will all be dead anyway. Happily, a passing English ship supplies them with sufficient coal to get to Gibraltar.

From here on, all is wonder. Outside Gibraltar they see HMS *Caledonia*: 'It is the largest ship in the world and the English emperor by having such a ship

Falmouth, dominated by Pendennis Castle. The Persian princes arrived here after their terrifying crossing of the Bay of Biscay.

takes the pre-eminence over all the shahs of Europe. He can in a moment destroy all the kingdoms of Europe and of Roum [Roum = Rome = Turkey] with this ship alone.' They marvel at the rigours of quarantine, which they assume to have something to do with the Christian religion and the penalty for transgression of which is death. But they marvel even more at the great fortress of Gibraltar, bristling with guns, sewn with mines, heaped high with cannon-balls – but plentifully supplied, too, with the most achingly beautiful ladies in the world. The three brothers succumb totally to the charm of these ladies, henceforth a more or less routine reaction.

They cross the terrible Bay of Biscay, so deep that only the Creator has ever plumbed its depths, and suffer again the indescribable torments of sea-sickness until their arrival at Falmouth. But all is made good when they are put up in a stupendous mansion, a place seemingly out of the Arabian Nights, 'most splendidly furnished and fine looking houris serving in it'. It is only with some difficulty that the reader realizes that this supernatural palace is the Green

Bank Hotel which, a generation or so later, will shelter Kenneth Grahame and so act as midwife for the *Wind in the Willows*.

They leave Falmouth for Bath. And throughout his travels in England Prince Najaf's narrative bears a remarkably close resemblance to the science-fiction of the late twentieth century, where the writer is trying to convey the impression of an alien universe, trying to describe technological marvels in a language that has no words for them. The high road is never dark but lit day and night by incredible lanterns that do not burn oil, but a ghostly substance, the 'spirits of coal' which is made in vast bottles on the edge of towns. They travel in marvellous machines that might have been designed for djinn. 'All that seems to draw these coaches is a box of iron in which they put water to boil. When the steam rises up the coach spreads its wings and the travellers become like birds.' Again, it takes a moment's reflection to realize that he is describing a railway. Along the sides of the road there are great herds and flocks of 'partridges, gazelle, deer and other game'. The princes ask for guns and are astonished to be told that these huge herds of game all belong to somebody. Prince Najaf's mathematics are, to say the least, hit-or-miss. There are at least two million carriages on the road. At Bath, 10,000 people besiege their house all agog to see these exotic visitors, and when their servant goes out 20,000 crowd round him, drinking in his Oriental finery.

The Prince sends one of his younger brothers to London to sound out the government but he and his other brother are obliged to remain in Bath for some weeks (vagueness about time is an outstanding characteristic of the Journal: almost everything happens 'about the Asser', i.e. 3 p.m., the equivalent of saying such and such a thing happened 'at Vespers'). They were, in fact, purposely kept kicking their heels while the wily Lord Palmerston found out, through his labyrinthine Foreign Office, just what was the situation in distant Persia. Occasionally, through his ecstatic hyperboles regarding the 'moon-like women', the 'incredible palaces', and 'sumptuous banquets', occasionally Prince Najaf lets fall an insight into the cool English brains behind the smiles and the welcomes. He quotes Palmerston uttering the usual bland inanities: 'As to your case, I would say that if it be according to the convenience and policy of the government' the English would help, but warning: 'If you have any other views I must tell you that we never like disturbance in Persia', quelling the hopeful young man's vision of the mighty English army, whose soldiers are 'naked from knee to thigh', placing him on the Peacock Throne.

While awaiting a decision, they threw themselves into sightseeing and the Prince's narrative takes on the appearance of a phantasmagoria. The trivial and the portentous, the permanent and the ephemeral jostle side by side, all

While their fate was being decided, the Persian princes were kept quiet with sightseeing trips. Above is Regent's Park Zoo, where Prince Najaf saw an elephant 'with a proboscis 40 feet long'. Other diversions were the Opera (opposite below) and the waxworks in Baker Street (opposite above).

equal in wonder to his bemused eye. They visit an astronomer, marvelling at the moon brought to within a handsbreadth of them, accepting his assurance that the planets are inhabited. They visit the waxworks, where Najaf's brothers play a practical joke upon him so that he thinks all the waxen figures are real people, 'so wonderful are the arts of the Franks'. They visit a flea circus ('one large flea was a soothsayer, telling fortunes and future events'). They visit the Zoo and see an elephant '24 feet high with a proboscis 40 feet long'. They see monkeys playing chess with men and not infrequently beating them: on the day of their visit one beat a Jew, 'who felt exceedingly ashamed and left immediately'.

There are innumerable social occasions, balls and dinners and tea parties in private houses for the three young princes in their gorgeous costume, who with an aura of not very clearly defined royalty around them are definitely the catch of the season. They go to the opera, and Najaf's description of the

scenery is, again, something that would not be out of place in the Thousand and One Nights. But even these wonders pale before the massed beauty of the 'thousands' of young ladies. 'My whole soul cried out to leave my body that it might go near these houris.' The three young men seem to have spent much of their time in a state of sexual excitement. One would not guess that the 'fine-looking women with arms like jasmine and faces like shining mirrors' were, in fact, waitresses in the supper room.

The wonders continue to pour in. Najaf is particularly fascinated by a recently invented 'wonderful art for making things to keep out water' and describes at length the process of making waterproof cloth. There are no flies or mosquitoes or other noxious insects in the land. The cities have no government or need of civil laws because the people are of such high morals. There is no distinction between the classes in dress. 'Their houses are like the palaces of heaven, their houris resemble those of paradise.' All shops are magnificently made of marble.

King George IV graciously receives them at Windsor and if London and Bath and Falmouth have taxed Prince Najaf Koolee Merza's vocabulary, it all but fails to do justice to the wonders of Windsor Castle. 'All the furniture was of gold and precious stones. Even in the smallest room there appeared to be an assemblage of all the jewels in the world.' All the great kings of England in the past have had their palace in the castle: each has left his statue, adorned with jewels, upon a jewelled throne, each with his crown upon his head 'of a hundred mauns of pure solid gold'. Each sovereign has left a great library, one of which alone contains 50,000 volumes. The castle itself is set in a park fifty-two miles in circumference, blazing with roses, alive with gazelles and antelopes, the air sweet with the song of countless nightingales and goldfinches, the grass underfoot a beautiful green velvet: 'My pen tells me, do not proceed. I am incapable of describing it, it is paradise'.

'On Saturday 23rd of Jamad the first [that is the first of September 1836] an hour before noon we started from London' on the first leg of the long, overland journey back to Persia, laden with presents and vague political promises. They had spent four months in England, most of it in London: Prince Najaf's impressions are garbled, inconsequential and, at times, quite absurdly fantastic. But they do, in some manner, manage to convey the picture of an immensely inventive and energetic people, coiled as taut as a spring, on the brink of an unprecedented leap into the future.

II

THE IMPOSITION OF FORM

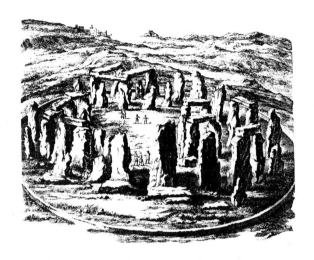

'Nothing is more delusive than to
suppose that every view which pleases in
nature will please in painting.'

William Gilpin, *Observations . . . relative
chiefly to Picturesque Beauty*

CHAPTER FIVE

In Search of the Picturesque

Some time about the year 1809, William Combe, confined within the 'rules' of the King's Bench Prison in Southwark for debt, pinned on the wall of his squalid chamber the latest drawing by the highly successful artist, Thomas Rowlandson. Combe, then in his late sixties, had been in the King's Bench for 21 years and would remain there for almost as long again. The peculiar laws affecting debtors, however, gave him a considerable degree of autonomy and when the fashionable publisher, Ackermann, was looking for a hack to put together some verses linking a series of plates to be provided by Rowlandson, he thought of Combe. In his time, Combe had rubbed shoulders with the wealthy as well as the fashionable, first at Eton, then at Oxford, where he had plunged into the dissipated society of his day, promptly squandering a legacy of £2,000. He had travelled on the Continent with Sterne and on his return to England set up his plate as a barrister. He earned much, but he spent far more: the King's Bench was an inevitable result of his life style.

Rowlandson had proposed to Ackermann a series of plates depicting the varying fortunes of a travelling schoolmaster, both he and Ackermann accurately calculating on the current obsession with 'Tours' and tour-writing. Combe, in an introduction to the second edition of the unexpectedly successful book, remarked truly enough that 'the following poem, if it may be allowed to serve the name, was written under circumstances whose peculiarity may be thought to justify a communication of them. . . . An etching or drawing was sent to me every month, and I composed a certain proportion of pages in verse in which, of course, the subject of the design was included. When the first print was sent to me, I did not know what would be the nature of the subject and in this manner the Artist continued designing, and I continued writing, every month for two years 'till a work containing near ten thousand lines was produced.'

Now the first plate was tacked on the wall before him. Entitled 'Doctor Syntax setting out on his Tour to the Lakes', it is set in a village. In the

Dr Syntax setting out on his tour of the Lakes.

background is Dr Syntax's parish church, in the foreground he, shabbily
dressed, is about to mount a sorry-looking nag held by a poverty-stricken
groom. Behind, the good Doctor's wife scolds and nags. Combe thought,
then began to scribble, line after line effortlessly pouring out on to paper. Dr
Syntax, a poor clergyman, reviewing his parlous financial state: no Church
preferment . . . barely 30 pounds a year . . . the boys in his humble school
eating him out of house and home . . . his wife endlessly scolding . . . what to
do. Suddenly, inspiration dawns:

> I'll make a TOUR and then I'LL WRITE IT
> I'll ride and write and sketch and print
> And thus create a real mint
> I'll prose it here, I'll verse it there
> And *picturesque* it everywhere
> I'll do what all have done before
> I think I shall and somewhat more
> At Dr Pompous give a look
> He made a fortune by his book
> And if my volume does not beat it
> When I return I'll fry and eat it.

Mrs Syntax eagerly assents to this means of making their fortune. He collects his sketching material, scrapes together £20, has Grizzle saddled, and off he goes on his Tour.

Ackermann published the successive parts of *The Tour of Dr Syntax in search of the Picturesque* originally in monthly parts. But so remarkably successful did it prove that not only did he issue it in book form (with a frontispiece showing the good Doctor at his moment of inspiration) but Rowlandson and Combe collaborated in sequels which – sure testimony of success – were promptly copied and plagiarized. But none equalled the success of that first *Tour*, for it came at the precise moment when the English public, thoroughly surfeited with the 'picturesque', were just in the mood for this astringent antidote.

Until the eighteenth century, 'the countryside' in general was that empty bit between towns which could be used to grow things on, or for armies to fight each other on. Mountainous country in particular was regarded with a kind of horror: the only person ever known to have climbed a mountain for the sake of doing so was the Italian scholar Francesco Petrarch who, in 1333, ascended Mount Ventoux in Provence, though dissuaded by an old shepherd who said that he had had to do so in his youth 'but had got nothing by it save toil and regret'. Even the English love of nature was highly selective: Chaucer's April landscape was simply the background along which his pilgrims made their way, the innumerable lyric poets who enthused over the chaunting of birds and the sweetness of flowers seemed to be thinking rather more of gardens and bowers than natural landscape. Celia Fiennes, different in this as in so much else, did indeed briefly respond to the wildness of Westmorland, hitching up her skirts to clamber up a fell where a waterfall 'gave a pleasing sound and murmuring noise.' But all she had to say of Windermere was that its potted char – 'big as a small trout, rather slenderer' – was excellent. And Defoe dismissed all of Westmorland as 'a country eminent only for being the wildest, most barren and frightful of any that I have passed over'.

But the change in viewpoint began in Defoe's own time. The exclusive interest in man and his works began to broaden out to include the landscape in which those works were situated and by which they were, of necessity, influenced. That early interest was purely analytical, like the Appendix which Thomas Pennant printed in one of his many Tours in 1769. It was a questionnaire compiled by the Society of Antiquaries and was designed to build up a picture of a parish: 'What is the appearance of the country, flat or hilly? . . . Do the lands consist of woods, arable, pasture, meadow or what? . . . Are they fenny or moorish? . . . . Are there any lakes . . . subterraneous rivers? . . .' So the questions run on, requiring only factual answers but, in

The Lake District cult getting into its stride: Upper Fall at Rydal, an engraving of 1801.

their sum, creating the profile of a locality in its own right and not simply describing its economic potential.

It was typical of Pennant to include such a document, for he was the kind of man of whom the Society of Antiquaries would undoubtedly approve. 'He's a Whig, Sir, a sad dog', boomed Samuel Johnson. 'But he's the best traveller I ever read: he observes more things than anyone else does.' Posterity is more inclined to agree with Boswell's lukewarm opinion: 'I could not help thinking that this was too high praise of a writer who traversed a wide section of country in such haste, that he could put together only curt, frittered fragments of his own.' Boswell is perfectly right: most of Pennant's observations *are* 'curt, frittered fragments', but – like the questionnaire – together they create the rudiments of a landscape.

This landscape none the less had no shape – until the Reverend William Gilpin came up with the idea of the 'picture-esque'. The word has suffered a sea-change in the intervening years. Today, it is probably a synonym for 'quaint', something vaguely romantic, applied to a situation or a person vaguely 'ethnic' or out-of-date. Gilpin and his followers meant it, absolutely literally, as something which was, or was not, fit to be placed in a picture. 'Nothing is more delusive than to suppose that every view which pleases in nature, will please in painting. In nature, the pleasure arises from the eye's roaming from one passage to another. In painting, it arises from seeing some select spot adorned agreeably to the rules of art.'

William Gilpin and his many followers (including those of the calibre of Horace Walpole and Paul Sandby) set about putting nature into a straitjacket. Their chosen instrument, the Claude-glass, perfectly illustrates their ideal. Thomas Gray used one during his Tour of the Lakes, reducing that tumultuous landscape to the proper proportions acceptable in a Georgian drawing room. It was a mirror, about four inches in diameter, 'on a black foil and bound up like a pocket-book'. The person using it turned his back on the landscape, holding the glass by the upper part of the case at eye level and slightly to the left or right. Instantaneously, the landscape was transformed into a picture, and the earnest seeker after the 'picturesque' was able immediately to ascertain whether or not it was worth his while actually to turn round and look at the landscape behind him with a view to painting it.

It is easy to smile at the Reverend William, and become increasingly irritated by the artificiality of his ideals. James Clarke, who sturdily described himself as a 'land surveyor', went for Gilpin with no holds barred. 'The whole of this outcry against regularity seems to me to have arisen from that cant style of writing which Gilpin and some others have introduced. Not a tree, not a shrub, not an old wall but these gentlemen take measure of by the painter's scale. A poor harmless cow can hardly go to drink, but they find fault with a want of grace in her attitude.' But there was much more to William Gilpin, both personally and in his contribution to the idea of England, than a foppish affectation.

Born in Scaleby Castle near Carlisle in 1724, Gilpin took his degree at Oxford and later ran a school in Cheam, Surrey, so successfully that he built up a reserve of £10,000. In his early fifties he accepted the living of Boldre in the New Forest. On the surface, he seemed the archetypal English country parson, dabbling in a little science, a little art, while comfortably living on his flock. The appearance is quite misleading. Boldre was a poverty-stricken parish whose inhabitants seemed to live largely by poaching, and Gilpin threw himself into the work of both reforming them morally and looking to their physical wellbeing. The genuine love in which he was held was admirably brought out in a poem, written by Caroline Bowles, who became the second wife of the poet Robert Southey. Entitled *The Birthday*, it describes a visit she made as a child to Gilpin in his vicarage – and, incidentally, gives an exquisite pen picture of that rural setting.

> Let me live again, in fond detail
> One of my happy visits. Leave obtained
> Methought the clock stood still: Four hours past noon
> And yet not started on our three mile walk!
> And *six* the vicarage tea-hour primitive
> And I should lose that precious hour most prized
> When in the old man's study, at his feet
> Or nestling close I might sit . . . . .
> [they set off]
> Like a fawn I bounded on before
> When lagging Jane came forth and off we went
> Sultry the hour, and hot the dusty way
> Though here and there by leafy skreen o'erarched
> And the long, broiling hill! And that last mile
> When the small frame waxed weary!
>
>   Lo! the well-known door
> Festooned about with garlands picturesque
> Of trailing evergreens
> One eager, forward spring
> And farewell to the glaring world without
> The glaring, bustling, noisy, parched-up world
> And hail repose and verdure, turf and flowers
> Perfume of lilies through the leafy gloom
> White gleaming; and the full, rich, mellow note
> Of song thrush, hidden in the tall thick bay
> Beside the study window!

Boldre lacked even a school and, in order to finance the founding of one, Gilpin put up his drawings for sale. In 1780 he had shown Horace Walpole his manuscript of a 'Tour to the Lakes' and Walpole had urged him to publish, but – concerned with what medium he could use for the drawings – advised him to use the new process of 'aquatinta' introduced by Paul Sandby, 'an easy and expeditious method for one that can draw well'. Essentially, Gilpin regarded his drawings as a means for illustrating his theory, rather than artistic works in their own right, and they had met with a somewhat mixed reception, Oliver Wendell Holmes describing them, curiously, as 'orange-juice landscapes'. But Gilpin was rather more popular than he thought, for an auction of some 2,000 drawings at Christies produced a total of £1,560 for his school.

Throughout his adult life, Gilpin had been casting a painterly, analytic eye on the world of nature. He wrote a solemn little treatise *On the Amusements of Clergymen*, in which he diffidently advanced the view that sketching was an activity that could be properly undertaken by a man of the cloth. Thereafter, 'The exercise of walking with a memorandum book in my hand hath ever been among the first pleasures of my life.' His first major tour, and one which was not only to start a cult but also contribute to his compatriots' changed view of nature, was down the Wye Valley. Out of this arose his *Picturesque Observations*, published in 1782. Suddenly, this remote valley, which hitherto had been known only to such dedicated travellers as John Byng, became the goal of scores of fashionable tourists, ladies as well as gentlemen, all bearing sketching blocks and Claude-glasses, intent on following the master. Had they previously thought that Tintern Abbey was the ultimate in romantic beauty? They were soon disabused. 'Though the parts are beautiful, the whole is ill-shaped. No ruins of the tower are left, which might give form and contrast to the walls. Instead of this, a number of gable ends hurt the eye with their regularity and disgust by the vulgarity of their shape.' However, he did allow that a close-up view showed 'a very inchanting piece of ruin'. He lays down the most precise rules for viewing the landscape in terms of a picture – no nonsense about admiring for its own sake: 'A hard edge of distance checking the view is exceedingly disgusting.' But is there no place for the casual, the spontaneous? Yes, indeed – 'Floats of timber are among the pleasing appendages of a river when the trunks are happily disposed. This disposition, I fear, must be the result of chance rather than that of art.' He holds some very modern, and salutary, views on conservation. He admits that the owner of an estate has a right 'to deform his ruin as he pleases. But though he fear no indictment in the King's Bench, he must expect a very severe prosecution in the court of taste. An elegant ruin is not a man's *property*, but a deposit of which he is only a guardian.'

But it was his instructions to the would-be painter on how to assemble a landscape that aroused the mockery of the sophisticated. It was permissible to move things around: 'Trees he may generally plant, or remove at pleasure. If a withered stump suit the purpose of his landscape better than the spreading oak which he finds in nature, he may make the change. He may certainly break an ill-formed hillock: he may pull up a piece of awkward paling: he may throw down a cottage: he may even turn the course of a road or river a few yards on this side or that. These trivial alterations may greatly add to the beauty of his composition, and yet they interfere not with the truth of the portrait.'

This was a gift to William Combe in his debtor's prison. He makes Dr Syntax lose his way within a few miles of leaving home and, coming to an

The imposition of form: a landscape composition by William Gilpin. The technique is satirized by William Combe below.

illegible signpost, he decides to rest till someone comes along. But instead of wasting time:

> I'll make a drawing of the post
> And, though your flimsy tastes may flout it
> There's something *picturesque* about it
> I've a right, who dare deny it
> To place yon group of asses by it
> And that same pond where Grizzle's drinking
> If hither brought would better seem
> And, faith, I'll turn it to a stream.
> I'll make this flat a shaggy ridge
> And o'er the water throw a bridge
> I'll do as other sketchers do
> Put anything into the view
> Thus I (which few, I think, can boast)
> *Have made a landscape of a Post.*

Combe sent Dr Syntax to the Lake District because, by the time he was writing, this once abhorred area had not only achieved the identity which we now recognize but the crowd of fashionable visitors to it was so great that they too had achieved an identity. Long before Wordsworth and friends had been labelled, somewhat pejoratively, 'the Lakers', the word was used to describe the thronging tourists. In 1798, indeed, a comic opera under that title was put on the London stage and though it was not particularly successful its producers reckoned, accurately enough, that their stock characters of wandering aesthetes would be recognizable to their fashionable audience. After being ignored, or dismissed as unprofitably barren, the mountainous region of Cumberland and Westmorland had become, as it were, a test-bed of English sensitivity, the place where the new view of nature was tried out.

It is possible to trace a kind of apostolic succession in the 'discovery' of the Lakes. Undoubtedly the first appreciation was an extraordinarily clumsily named 'poem' entitled *Descriptive Poem Addressed to Two Young Ladies at their Return from viewing the Mines near Whitehaven* by a certain Dr John Dalton, published in 1755, and a brisker, though scarcely less 'romantic' prose account, *Description of the Lake and Vale at Keswick* by a Dr John Brown, published in 1767. Dalton's verse is interesting in that it echoes something of Defoe's opinion of the savage, unproductive scenery, but also looks forward, if dimly and clumsily, to the 'poetics' of a generation later. Although he was certainly no Wordsworth, the good doctor deserves at least a passing salute for his pioneering spirit: he looked beyond the barrenness and saw beauty:

> Horrors like these at first alarm
> But soon with savage grandeur charm
> And raise to noblest thoughts the mind.

Both he and Brown shared the prevailing passion for romantic exaggeration. Even today, the fells of the Lake District can pose a savage threat, a most dangerous playground for the unwary and the unskilled: a sudden mist on Scafell on a June morning can constitute as great a danger as any climber would wish to encounter. But the fells and hills are not exactly Himalayan or even Alpine: nevertheless, that was the role in which they were cast by these two sincere but pedestrian writers, to be faithfully followed by others of a much higher calibre. Mountains 'frown' and have a 'horrid grandeur'; waterfalls dash themselves down, uniting 'beauty, horror and immensity'. 'On these dreadful heights the eagles build their nests: waterfalls are seen pouring from their summits, and tumbling in vast sheets from rock to rock in rude and terrible magnificence.' Thus Dr Dalton. Dr Brown dips his brush in an even gaudier paint:

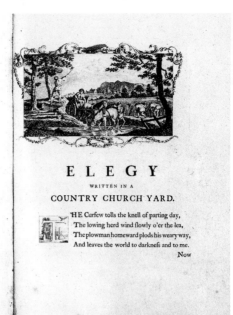

ELEGY

WRITTEN IN A

COUNTRY CHURCH YARD.

HE Curfew tolls the knell of parting day,
The lowing herd wind flowly o'er the lea,
The plowman homeward plods his weary way,
And leaves the world to darknefs and to me.

Now

Although the artist, Richard Bentley, took some liberties with the text, his illustrations
for Gray's Elegy *perfectly capture the atmosphere of this most evocative of*
English rural poems.

> The craggy cliff, impending wood
> Whose shadows mix o'er half the flood
> The gloomy clouds, which solemn sail
> Scarce lifted by the languid gale
> O'er the capp'd hill, the dark'ned vale
> The rav'ning kite, and bird of Jove
> Which round the aerial ocean rove. . . .

And so on and so on. But these two men paved the way for a greater, a man with a naturalist's eye and a poet's tongue who really would bring the two aspects of nature together and so create a third – the poet, Thomas Gray.

The one poem whose opening line, at least, is probably known to every speaker of the English language is 'Elegy in a Country Churchyard'. In 1935 the New Zealander Ian Donnelly recorded how, standing in Stoke Poges churchyard, he was told by a postcard seller: 'Where you're standing I suppose I've heard every language spoken. I've even seen Zulus.'

It was this ability to touch a common chord, to take an everyday, earthy experience and transmute it into one of universal significance and permanence that made of Thomas Gray's modest *Journal in the Lakes* a turning-point in his compatriots' view of nature – and, in so doing, 'opened up' the Lake District.

His journey took a little over six days, and the account of it was written and posted off, section by section, to a friend in order that he could have a vicarious experience. The *Journal* therefore has the immediacy of a genuine diary, and an almost total avoidance of stylistic flourishes and conventional expressions of horror and awe.

The very first line opens with that mixture of precision and poetry, of practicality and observation that makes it, in its modest way, epochal. Gray is at Brough, looking across the valley to where the great cattle fair is in its second day. The date is 30 September:

Wind at N.W. clouds and sunshine. A mile and a half from Brough on a hill lay a great army encamped. To the left, a fine valley with green meadows and hedgerows, a gentleman's house peeping forth from a grove of old trees. On a nearer approach appeared myriads of horses and cattle in the road itself and in all the fields around me, a brisk stream hurrying cross the way, thousands of clean, healthy people in their best party-coloured apparel, farmers and their families, esquires and their daughters hastening up from the dales and down the fells on every side, glittering in the sun and pressing forward to join the throng. While the dark hills, on many of whose tops the mists were yet hanging, served as a contrast to this gay and moving scene.

Each entry is preceded with a brief description of the climate for, of all places in England, the Lakeland landscape is modified by the weather, either with infinite subtlety or stark drama. It is in these brief, exact climatic descriptions that Gray's poetic precision is best displayed. Thus, at 7 o'clock of a frosty morning in Borrowdale, he notes that the hoar frost which thickly covered the grass 'melted and exhaled in a thin blueish smoke'. While he was ascending Crow-park, 'a little shower fell, red clouds came marching up the hill and part of a rainbow seemed to rise along the side of Castle Hill'. His descriptions are so clear that a modern traveller can follow his footsteps, as in the still perilous descent at Gordale Scar. He is a writer, a poet, but always his descriptions sound as though he were jotting down details for a visual composition – partly the result of trying to bring a scene alive for his distant friend. The 'Claude-glass' is never far from his hands: once, so intent is he, that he stumbles and falls, but happily the glass is unbroken and, though shaken, he stays on to see 'the sun set in all its glory'.

In general, unlike his predecessors, Gray is restrained. Only once does he really let himself go, and that is at Gowder Crag. 'The rocks atop, hanging loose and nodding forwards seem just starting from their base in shivers: the whole way down, and the road on both sides is strewed with the piles of fragments strangely thrown against each other and of a dreadful bulk.' He compares it to those Alpine passes where the guides urge total silence lest an

The reality of the 'romantic' Lake District: a working farm at Easedale. The background, charming on a summer's day, menacing and dangerous in winter.

avalanche be started off and quotes Dante's vision in *Inferno*: 'Let us not discuss them but look, and pass by.'

He was ecstatic about Grasmere: 'one of the sweetest landscapes that art ever attempted to imitate.' He was among the very last to see it in its virgin state: De Quincey, following in his footsteps some time later, sourly noted how: 'Thirty years ago, a gang of Vandals, for the sake of building a mail-coach road that never would be wanted, carried a horrid causeway of sheer granite right through the loveliest succession of secret forest dells and shy recesses of the lake.'

But Gray is also aware that this is a working country, a harsh, dangerous land where people are scraping together a living under enormous difficulties. He tells the story, vividly but with economy, of the farmer who raided an eagle's nest. Each year, he was told, this was necessary, for the eagles carried off a variety of game and lambs. The farmer 'was let down from the cliffs in ropes to the shelf of rock, on which the nest was built, the people above

Watercolour by Thomas Hearne, showing two 'Lakists' sketching a waterfall during a tour of the Lake District in 1777 (below).

(Opposite) Derwentwater.

shouting and hollowing to fright the old birds which flew screaming round'. On this occasion, they killed an eaglet: sometimes they also managed to shoot one or other of the parents, but the survivor usually found a mate (in Ireland, he believed, and even identified the species).

The locals are slow to share the ecstasies of southern aesthetes: 'They call the vale of Derwentwater the Devil's Chamberpot and pronounce the name of Skiddaw Fell with a sort of terror and aversion.' He makes practical notes that could almost have come from Cobbett or Defoe or Young: they mine lead at Keswick, which is pure, black and soft-grained and sells for thirty shillings a pound; oats is the main local crop; fell mutton has just come into season and will last six weeks; the lakes are full of excellent fish and he gives his friend's wife a mouth-watering recipe for cooking perch, known locally as bass.

The fact that Gray not only stayed at country inns in this remote area but was also pleased with them gives the clearest possible indication of the sudden popularity of the Lakes. For Thomas Gray was, if not exactly a

hypochondriac, of a 'delicate' constitution and very much alive to his creature comforts. His own *Journal* was to open the floodgates to southern tourists but was not, in fact, published until twelve years afterwards, in 1780, and then only as an appendix to the second edition of Thomas West's *Guide to the Lakes*. Whether or not West's is the first true English guidebook, it can safely be affirmed that to the Reverend Father Thomas may be credited (or, rather, debited) the invention of the pernicious concept of the 'beauty spot', the locality which has to be looked at from a certain place, at a certain angle and, preferably, at a certain time and in a certain mood. Father Thomas undoubtedly knew the Lake District like the back of his hand, for he lived there for nearly twenty years. On that bedrock of solid knowledge he erected a composition combining Gilpin's fussy directions and the luscious descriptions of Dalton and Brown: the fact that his *Guide* went through ten editions is testimony enough to its popularity. Year after year the tourists now came, carrying their Claude-glasses, their sketching blocks and their battered copy of the *Guide*, obediently seeking out 'the rock, on the left of the road [where] you have a general prospect of the lake upwards. This station is found by observing where you have a hanging rock over the road, on the east, and an ash tree on the west side of the road.' This particular direction applies to a 'viewing point' from which to see Lake Coniston, but the entire area was now spattered with these notional spots, direct ancestors of the 'view points' of today's Ordnance Surveys, lodestones for touring motorists.

And there occurred now in the Lake District what had already occurred on the Continent at a relatively few select points on the Grand Tour and would occur, increasingly, round the globe as well-heeled tourists, on pleasure bent, came into contact with poor natives in backward economies: mutual exploitation – the native viewing the tourist as milch cow, the tourist viewing the native as a source of entertainment, demand inevitably creating supply. The guide came into being who, for five shillings a day (at least double what he would earn in backbreaking toil), would lead the tourist to the fashionable views. In place of the occasional fisherman plying his boat in search of food and a little cash, there now appeared fleets of craft to take their palpitating misses, their sensitive young men, out on to the 'broad bosom' of the lakes. Derwentwater and Ullswater were particularly popular and here came into being one of the most bizarre of tourist attractions: the creation of echoes. Earlier travellers venturing out on to the lakes had been intrigued to find that a gun discharged produced the most extraordinary succession of echoes. In a

Drawing by Gainsborough showing an artist using a Claude-glass. This is the logical development of the 'picturesque' theory, where the artist does not allow reality to come between him and his picture. His back is turned to the landscape.

*Turner's dramatic view of Buttermere after a shower, based on a watercolour
executed during a trip to the Lakes in 1797. This is, perhaps, the visual equivalent
of Wordsworth's lyrical approach to the landscape.*

very little time, these impromptu firings gave place to highly organized broadsides: for a fee of 1s 6d, the tourist could hear let off a brass cannon, loaded with half a pound of powder. William Gilpin left a good description of them, recommending that not simply one, but preferably half a dozen cannon should be fired in quick succession. 'Such a variety of awful sounds, mixing and commixing and at the same moment heard from all sides, have a wonderful effect upon the mind: as if the very foundations of every rock on the lake were giving way.' As if this were not enough, an even greater treat was evolved with the substitution of French horns for cannon: their harmony 'was repeated from every recess which echo haunted on the borders of the Lake: – here the breathings of the organ were imitated, there the bassoon with clarinets – in this place from the harsher sounding cliffs the cornet: in that from the wood creek, among the caverns and the trilling water falls, you seemed to hear the soft-toned lute.'

And while on the lakes the boatmen were making the ancient silences hideous with noise, on land their fellows running inns and taverns were taking part in the most ancient of all travelling games: overcharging the traveller. The inns doubled and trebled their prices; the little villages grew into towns, the towns suddenly swelled with the villas of wealthy immigrants. Gray left a delightful description of Kendal, most of whose houses 'seemed as if they had been dancing a country-dance. There they stand back to back, corner to corner, some up hill some down without intent or meaning' – a description which would have fitted most of the little towns of Lakeland. Under the impetus of tourism they grew solider, staider. At Keswick Peter Crossthwaite, 'formerly Naval Commander in India', found it economically possible to run a museum. In 1792 he published a curious broadsheet lauding its treasures, cajoling the quality – and castigating his enemies: 'were it not for the low Cunning and mischievous Falsehoods continuously circulated against him by an ungrateful JUNTO of imposters it is thought few of the Gentry would pass him by'. But he seems to have been successful in attracting the gentry, for the following year, he claimed stridently, '1540 persons of rank and fashion' came to inspect his extraordinary collection which included, among much else, the hat of a sailor from Captain Bligh's *Bounty* and a lamb with claws, supposedly the product of a sheep and a raccoon. Two centuries later Peter Crossthwaite would have made a highly successful travel agent, for he was endlessly engaged in preparing stunts and entertainments for the delight of tourists. His most solid achievement, however, are his maps, which are now something of a collectors' item.

'It was well for the undisturbed pleasures of the poet [Gray] that he had no foreboding of the change which was soon to take place': thus the poet who, of all writers, is instantly associated with the Lake District. The fact that William Wordsworth wrote a *Guide to the Lakes*, a solid factual guide, comes as much as a surprise to the reader as if he discovered that William Shakespeare had written a room-by-room description of Elsinore Castle. It was precisely what it claimed to be: it went into five editions between 1810 and 1835 (and was thus responsible for the celebrated anecdote about the admiring Methodist parson who enquired if Mr Wordsworth had written anything else), but it was also more than a guide. It was an attempt to restore the idea of unity to this extraordinary area and Wordsworth illustrates his intention by comparing it to that model of the Alpine countryside which was currently a showpiece at Lucerne. It is interesting and delightful in itself, he says, 'but it supplies also a more substantial pleasure: for the sublime and beautiful region, with all its hidden treasures and their bearing and relations to each other, is thereby comprehended at once'.

VI Mill Gill and Tarn Crag in the Langdale Valley.

Overleaf
*VII Derwentwater veiled in mist: the 'picturesque' in
its modern connotation.*

The *Guide* is a remarkable compendium, at least a century in advance of its day. Singlehanded, Wordsworth takes on the work of the economist and the topographer, of the historian and the folklorist, to show all the factors which create a living, working human community, which could only come into existence in this particular place at this particular time. Let us imagine, he says, that we are sitting on a cloud floating between Great Gable and Scafell. From that vantage point he points out the great wheel of valleys below and then swoops down to examine the physical structure of the land: the mountains covered with soft turf or with their great bones still visible; the lakes which are of living water, not sullen stagnant pools, because of the sparkling streams that run into them; the native trees; the mists; the waterfalls – all creating one great stage.

Or, rather, one great symphony in which Man himself is an instrument. He backtracks into history to show how and why the native communities developed. He detects the moment of change as taking place in the mid-century. Sixty years ago, he says, there was no carriage road between the dales: everything was carried on packhorse along immemorial trails. Then, sixty years ago, 'travellers, instead of confining their observations to Towns, Manufacture or Mines began (a thing till then unheard of) to wander over the island in search of sequestred spots'.

And out of that unrest, change began to be wrought. He takes as text a remark of Gray's about Grasmere: 'Not a single red tile, no flaring gentleman's house or garden wall breaks in upon the repose of this little unsuspected paradise.' Alas, this is not the case now, Wordsworth says with a sigh, and devotes the third section of his book to a single theme: 'Changes, and rules of taste for preventing their bad effects.' There is much that is sensible and could, with value, be drawn to the attention of many a twentieth-century planning officer. He deplores the intrusion of foreign trees in the native woodlands, the larch in particular attracting his ire. He quotes Joshua Reynolds's dictum that the colour of a gentleman's house should match the colour of the soil in the locality. He inveighs at something called Ornamental Gardening . . . all very sensible and valuable.

But, irresistibly, the reader hears the voice of the writer to *The Times* protesting against this or that intrusion of modernity into a traditional

VIII–IX First regarded as a wild and savage land which the civilized traveller would do anything to avoid, the Lake District became an aesthetic attraction in the early nineteenth century. Windermere from Stickle Tarn (above); Ullswater from Hind Crag (below).

The camera replaces the sketchbook: a photograph of holiday makers looking over Grasmere which appeared in Our English Lakes, Mountains and Waterfalls as seen by W. Wordsworth *in 1864, some fourteen years after the poet's death.*

landscape. And in the final edition of the *Guide*, with its castigation of the Kendal and Westmorland railway, the cosmologist has almost wholly gone and in his place is a tired, rather querulous old man holding up his hands in despair as the modern world looms over him like a tidal wave:

> Is then no nook of English ground secure
> From rash assault? Schemes of retirement sown
> In youth, and 'midst the busy world kept pure
> As when their earliest flowers of hope were blown,
> Must perish – how can they this blight endure?

CHAPTER SIX

The Stately Homes of England

About the year 1730 Marcellus Laroon, a not otherwise particularly distinguished artist, painted a picture – *A Nobleman's Levee* – which exactly summed up the role of the English country house at its apogee. In the mid-ground the nobleman, coldly indifferent to the press of petitioners awaiting him, is leisurely putting the finishing touches to his attire. On the walls in the background is evidence of his family's lineage, wealth and power in the form of portraits, paintings and tapestries. The faces and characters of those awaiting his lordship's pleasure are all strongly individual. In the left foreground an elderly gentleman, swelling with indignation at his cavalier treatment, is being calmed by a flunkey. Next to him a young fop, accustomed to being kept waiting, is offering snuff to a fellow sufferer. Beside them, a swaggering braggadocio is glaring across at the cause of their humiliation. Resignation, or anger, are the predominant reactions to their indifferent reception. What Laroon has presented us with is an exact, though singularly unattractive, view of life: the great house, after it had ceased to be a fortress, became a reservoir of wealth, and in order to allow that wealth to be distributed throughout society, it was necessary to engage the attention, and the goodwill, of its owner.

In the 1980s, each of the handsome guidebooks to Woburn, Longleat and Beaulieu – acknowledged leaders of the 'stately homes industry' – bears a personal message from the house's owner. Each message is a variant on the theme that, without the public, the house could not continue to exist in its traditional form. At Longleat, the Marquess of Bath records: 'In these days of heavy taxation it would be impossible to maintain [the house] in the condition in which you see it but for your contributions.' At Beaulieu: 'Your visit helps to preserve a vital part of our national heritage.' At Woburn the Marquess of Tavistock says unequivocally: 'We have become custodians, no longer the owners.'

The difference between the subject of Laroon's painting and these sentiments, the shift in emphasis from the crowd appealing to the single figure

The English country house at its apogee: A Nobleman's Levee by Marcellus Laroon. In addition to his calling as a painter, Laroon was also a musician, singer, professional soldier and socialite, and well acquainted with such scenes as this.

to the single figure appealing to the crowd, measures the scale of the enormous, though bloodless revolution that has taken place in the interim in Britain.

The ambivalent way in which the English regard this vast section of their national heritage is well illustrated by the fact that they have no adequate name for this entire class of building, unlike their Continental equivalents – *schloss*, *château* or *palazzo*. The term 'country house' manages to be at once imprecise and misleading: imprecise, because any rurally situated house must obviously be a 'country house', misleading because it conveys a limited, Victorian atmosphere of expensive cigars, leather upholstery and political intrigue. The currently fashionable term 'stately home' received a new lease of life in the 1930s through Noël Coward's satirical ballad, but it was long before it was blessed by the *Oxford English Dictionary*. It is a very useful term, identifying adequately enough a richly varied class of residence which can be anything from a modest manor house to a full-scale castle. There is an ambivalence about the phrase, a kind of wry self-mockery that is very much a product of the twentieth century. On the one hand, there is undoubtedly something incongruous about a building which, created to demonstrate and preserve privilege and power, competes now with its peers for the pennies of the masses. On the other hand, an age which has elevated the concept of social equality to the status of a moral law is reluctant to recognize that privilege might have produced excellence, that Jack indeed might not have been as good as his master. So the half-mocking, half-envious phrase passes into general currency, faithfully reflecting a period of social fragmentation and unease.

But the stately home has always reflected social change, unlike its great companion the church, which rapidly found a final form and so journeyed down the centuries essentially unchanged. The changes can be detected in the name which the building uses to describe itself. 'Palace' is very rare indeed, apart from royal and ecclesiastic use; 'Castle' is a survivor from an older, more primitive form: Arundel, Berkeley, Warwick are all genuinely military structures which have, as it were absentmindedly, transformed themselves into homes. 'Manor' describes a once vital function, the great house as a generator and reservoir of rural wealth: it was only later, in the eighteenth century, that its role as consumer of wealth dominated the other two. 'Hall' is simply the description of a form or structure, the barn-like building which served as a kind of tribal meeting place, became a nucleus and then a fossil. 'Abbey' or 'Priory', as in Woburn Abbey, indicates the great monastic plunder of the Henrician years. 'House' marks that prudent English tendency to play down wealth so that the rich man will use the same term for his vast mansion as the poor man uses for his hovel.

There were two great waves of change, in the fifteenth, and again in the eighteenth centuries. The Battle of Bosworth, which brought the Wars of the Roses to an end in 1485, marked a moment of change in English history as precise, if not as dramatic, as the Battle of Hastings. The heroic period lay now in the past: the future would lie with statesmen and merchants and financiers rather than with soldiers. The new king, Henry VII, summed up the qualities of the new age in his person, preferring to fine rather than imprison, eager to invest in anything that showed a profit, parsimonious, avaricious – but also imaginative enough to finance a Cabot. The coming men resembled their monarch: suddenly a swarm of new families were pushing aside the old

Hardwick Hall, Derbyshire, seen from the south-west. Bess of Hardwick was in her late seventies before the great new mansion was completed in 1597.

aristocracy – Cavendish, Cecil, Russell, Thynne – making their fortunes through a skilful combination of commerce and political astuteness. They began to build new houses and not simply to adapt the old on a series of ad hoc decisions. Sir John Thynne's house at Longleat, architect-built in Elizabethan times, confidently sounded the new note, followed by Bess of Hardwick's great mansion in Derbyshire.

Architecture faithfully reflected the great social changes of the mid-seventeenth century. The great Elizabethan and Jacobean mansions – Hardwick, Burghley, Knole and the rest – though scarcely a generation old, were already old-fashioned. They had been built by immensely wealthy people to entertain and impress the monarch. Now, rising prices, less capital and the emergence of a new middle class led imperceptibly to the building of less ostentatious houses, compensating for the loss of size with an increased opulence in interior decoration.

Confidence and arrogance came back with a flourish in the eighteenth century when, among other factors, the products of the Enclosure Acts and West Indian plantations vastly increased the income of the country gentleman at a time when it was fashionable to be aesthetic. Throughout, the English aristocracy had prudently avoided the path which their French counterparts had taken. A figure like the sixth Duke of Somerset, with his almost pathological snobbery, his almost frantic attempts to avoid contacts with the lower classes, was an anomaly, a rarity. The Restoration dramatists had certainly treated the provincial landowner as a stock figure of fun, but outside the tiny, artificial world of the metropolis the English ruling classes boasted of their rural origins. Richard Rush, ambassador of the infant United States of America, perspicaciously put his finger of the strength of the aristocracy: 'The enthusiastic fondness of the English for the country is the effect of their laws. Primogeniture is at the root of it. Scarcely any persons who hold a leading place in the circles of their society live in London. They have *houses* in London, but their *homes* are in the country. Their turreted mansions are there with all that denotes perpetuity – heirlooms, family memorials, pictures, tombs. The permanent interests and affections of the most opulent classes centre almost universally in the country.'

The eighteenth-century injection of wealth brought about a kind of architectural megalomania in which the greater the acreage covered, the more esteemed was the architect. It is now that the park comes into its own – the product of the landscape gardener, gifted with the ability to see years or decades into the future and so convince his employer that an avenue of oaks or yews would enhance his splendour. The landscape gardener briefly shares the glamour of the architect and is identified by name. Henry Wise, who forced nature into patterns acceptable to the Frenchman Le Nôtre; William Kent, of whom Walpole said, 'He leaped the fence and saw that all nature was a garden.' And the doyen of them all, Lancelot Brown, who gained the slightly comic nickname of 'Capability' and attempted to dragoon all England, from the wilds of Northumbria to the tames of Hampshire, into a preconceived pattern of harmony.

And at the centre of these barbered parklands stood the new, square brick house carefully conforming to accepted proportions. Few shared the Hon. John Byng's regret at the way the aristocracy were busily pulling down their Norman or Elizabethan or Jacobean homes to transform them into the fashionable brick box. Most would have agreed with Walpole's damning verdict on Haddon Hall: 'It is low and can never have been a tolerable house. Within the court in a corner is a strange confusion of half arches and beams that imply the greatest ignorance in the art.' In the whirligig of fashion that

Haddon Hall, Derbyshire. Retaining its medieval characteristics, it aroused the scorn both of Celia Fiennes ('a good old house, but nothing very curious as the mode now is') and Horace Walpole ('can never have been a tolerable house').

'strange confusion' at Haddon was to be particularly prized by the twentieth century as showing 'honesty' of development. William Gilpin was, predictably, minatory: 'We are amused with looking into these mansions of antiquity as objects of curiosity but should never think of comparing them with the great houses of modern taste in which the hall and the saloon fill the eyes on our entrance.' He was particularly patronizing and condescending about Longleat, the first known example of a house in England that was planned overall, instead of growing almost organically. Even this evidence of an intellectual approach failed to make it acceptably picturesque: 'Longleat has nothing of the Grecian grandeur to recommend it. The whole is certainly a grand pile, but it has little beauty and I should suppose less convenience.'

Gilpin and Walpole were members of a new species of tourist, the afficionados of country houses, travelling from one to another, comparing this gallery with that, this façade, or gazebo, or vestibule with others of its kind. Country-house visiting was no new phenomenon. In the past, however, they had been regarded essentially as places in which to stay. The aristocracy, as a matter of course, expected to be entertained by their peers on their travels through the land, but as for looking objectively at the immense building that was sheltering them and making any kind of aesthetic judgment about it – this was a product of the new age. Celia Fiennes was perhaps the first 'stately home' visitor in the modern sense. She not only automatically expected, and was as automatically offered, hospitality on her journeys but that observant, critical, sardonic eye of hers would not ignore the building itself. Her aesthetic judgment might be limited but, when a place took her interest, she could give an excellent sketch of it. An outstanding example is her description of Burghley House. It had been built by Elizabeth I's formidable old councillor between 1553 and 1587, but shortly before Celia's visit it had been substantially altered by Talman and grandiosely decorated by Antonio Verrio. She was impressed by the architecture, in particular Tissot's gate – 'the finest I ever saw all sorts of leaves flowers figures beast wheate in the Carving' – but, as a good Puritan lady, she was decidedly shocked by Verrio's opulent, slightly draped women. In each room were 'very fine paint in pictures, but they were all without Garments or very little, that was the only fault, the immodesty of the pictures especially in my Lord's appartment.' Chatsworth, too, she describes at considerable length, being particularly taken with the

'*They were all without Garments or very little*', a shocked Celia Fiennes recorded
of Antonio Verrio's murals at Burghley House. This is a part of the
grandiloquent Heaven Room.

complicated waterworks in the grounds but, with her brisk preference for modernity, she dismisses Haddon Hall as 'a good old house, but nothing very curious as the mode now is' – much as she dismisses her own family seat of Broughton Castle.

Burghley and Chatsworth both attracted the attention and the pen of a rather more plebeian visitor, Daniel Defoe, clear evidence that 'stately homing' was well into its stride by the early eighteenth century. Burghley, he thought, more resembles a town than a house, with its multiplicity of turrets and pinnacles, and he hints at the scandalous life of the artist, Verrio. 'The character this gentleman left behind him at this town is that he deserved it for all his paintings, but for nothing else: his scandalous life and his unpaid debts causing him to be but very meanly spoken of in the town of Stamford.' Considering his dislike of the antique, he was surprisingly enthusiastic about Warwick Castle, though the recent improvements would undoubtedly have won his approval. He falls over himself in admiration of the Earl of Nottingham's house, also known as Burghley, and even appends a poem of indifferent talent to celebrate it. And as for Chatsworth, 'the Duke of Devonshire's noble House there, a real Wonder of the Peak' (as he describes it in his discursive index), this was 'indeed a palace for a Prince'. Was Defoe perhaps hoping for a few subscriptions from the gentry? Certainly he seems to go out of his way at least to refer to the country houses.

By the middle of the eighteenth century, stately-home visiting had developed into a pattern. And in a pattern, too, developed the complaints. Dominating all were complaints against the English vice of tipping. The Swiss Saussure said feelingly: 'if you take a meal with a person of rank, you must give every one of the five or six footmen a coin when leaving. Should you fail to do this you will be treated insolently next time.' Lord Southwell approached him in Hyde Park and reproached him for not visiting him again: '"In truth, my lord, I am not rich enough to take soup with you often." His Lordship understood my meaning and smiled.' If the personal guests of the owner could be treated like chickens to be plucked, how much more vulnerable were casual visitors wholly at the mercy of the staff. Blenheim seems to have been particularly heavily infested with rapacious servants. In 1781 Byng was recording, with commendable restraint: 'the expence of seeing Blenheim is very great: the servants of the poor D— of M being very attentive in gleaning money from rich travellers.' Arthur Young was rendered all but incandescent with rage at the 'excessive insolence' of the gate keepers. 'I was witness to their abusing a single gentleman in a very scurrilous manner for not feeing them after giving the house porter a half-a-crown for seeing it. The person abused complained aloud to several parties of the

A view of Blenheim Palace, engraved by James Maurer in 1745. The house rapidly acquired a reputation for the rapacity of its staff when showing visitors round the house.

insolence and observed that he had seen most of the great houses in the kingdom but never knew a park or yard locked up by gentry who formed such a gauntlet.' A handwritten, pencilled note in the London Library's 1769 copy of Young's *Tour* says: 'Extortion seems to have been a very ancient rule at Blenheim. In 1841 I was with a party from Oxford refused permission into the park until the gatekeeper had received a douceur.'

Most owners of great houses were quite happy to display their treasures to the crowd. Walpole recorded that Chatsworth was open two days a week, though 'it is the etiquette of the family to return no visits in the County'. At Burton Constable in Humberside, William Constable was so proud of the refurbishing to which he had submitted the old house that, on its completion in 1778, he actually had notices printed saying that the house was open to the public, probably the first such overt wooing of the masses. But the owners could also be remarkably highhanded even to others of their class. John Byng was turned away from Wroxton because his lordship had just arrived from London. 'Very rude, this', exploded the usually restrained Byng, 'and unlike an old courtly earl. Let him either forbid his place entirely, open it allways or else fix a time for admission. But, for shame, don't refuse travellers who may have come twenty miles out of their way for a sight of this place.' By an unpleasant coincidence the same thing happened to him at Sherborne Castle a few days later.

Arrangements for the reception of visitors varied greatly. At Holkham in Norfolk, in 1830, visitors were provided with a guidebook which exhorted them, 'When the Person who shews this house is engaged, the company is conducted into the vestibule. The curious visitor will not regret the time while contemplating the subjects in the room.' Certainly, only the most curmudgeonly would resent being asked to spend some time in William Kent's superb entrance hall, but sophisticated, knowledgeable tourists like Byng and Walpole were justifiably irritated to find themselves being taken round by some ignorant servant who knew little and cared less about the history of the objects he or she was so glibly describing. Frequently, the ignorance of the servant was finely matched by the indifference of the master. 'The wasteful, idle nobility does not know what they possess', was Byng's contemptuous verdict at Haddon when he had come across a collection of outstanding pictures dumped in one room after the house itself had been abandoned, a verdict to be echoed by more than one connoisseur in more than one house where the carefully garnered treasures of one generation were ignored by the next.

But if the visitor had complaints to make against the owner, the owner had placed himself in a vulnerable position by allowing these omniscient men into his home to price his paintings, calculate the value of his statuary and, in general, assess his place in the league table of culture. The two *Journals* of Horace Walpole convey the picture of the aesthete at his most insufferable. The *Journals* cover the years 1751 to 1784 and much of them reads like a bailiff's inventory of paintings. At Wimbledon – 'A woman in an old Dress. She is ugly and much dressed.' At St James's – 'Lady Frecteville, in Man's Cloathes'. Read aloud, the bailiff's list becomes the voice of the show-off, that ubiquitous man in every gallery who knows everything about every picture and yearns to tell the world. And at times, he contrives to sound like Mr Jingle: 'Holy Family, Rubens, coarse.' His judgment of the architecture of the houses themselves varies so greatly as to be capricious. Blenheim, the magnificence of which stunned almost the whole world, is dismissed in a line: 'Execrable within and without and almost all round', but the obscure house of Drayton has nearly three and a half pages.

But with all the irritations of the *Journals*, they do convey the impression that England is one vast country house, that the portraits Walpole discusses are either portraits of people he knows personally, or related to them. And the occasional anecdote brings the place to sudden life. At St James's Palace, 'He [the King] has never suffered the Queen's room to be touched since she died. I saw the wood lying on the hearth in this year 1758 which had been laid for her fire the day she died in 1737.' He gives a lively pen picture of the eccentrics at Medmenham Abbey: 'Now a ruinous and bad house. The Abbey is become remarkable by being hired by a set of gentlemen who have erected themselves

The marble entrance hall at Holkham Hall, Norfolk, modelled by William Kent on the design of a Roman basilica. Arthur Young took time off from his agricultural preoccupations to note caustically that it resembled a bath house of the utmost magnificence.

into a fraternity of Monks and pass two days in every month there. Each has his cell, in which indeed is little more than a bed. They meet to drink, the rule is pleasure, and each is to do whatever he pleases in his own cell, into which they carry women.' He has only one criticism. 'The habit is more like a waterman's than a Monk's.'

In April 1949 Longleat, the first architect-built great house, became the first 'stately home' to open its doors to the public on a commercial basis. The fee charged was 2s 6d – the noble 'half crown' coin which has itself vanished into history – and by the end of the year 135,000 people had trooped through John Thynne's house, now more than 400 years old. The stately home industry had been born.

The origins of that industry lay in the late nineteenth century. Until the 1880s, the majority of those who did not live in one of the chartered towns or cities lived on one of the estates of the nobility, contributing willy-nilly to the upkeep of the great house that formed the ganglion. The introduction of estate duty in 1894, coupled with the agricultural depression, began the great change. It accelerated after World War I (it has been calculated that about a quarter of the land changed hands between 1918 and 1922) and again immediately after World War II. The macabre guessing game of death duties introduced a new hazard: on an estate of £1 million some four-fifths could be demanded in tax unless the estate was passed over to the heir at some fixed period before the death of the donor. In 1947, for example, the Duke of Devonshire died unexpectedly just four months before the period expired, and the estate was taxed at eighty per cent.

In 1946 Henry Thynne, 6th Marquess of Bath, inherited Longleat and, with it, £700,000 in death duties. Although this was only a fraction of the amount which faced the Devonshire estate, Longleat had fewer reserves. As with most private houses, great and small, it was showing the effect of six years of wartime privation: cost of renovation would be enormous – additional to the £30,000 a year the house cost to run. The death duties were paid off by selling some thousands of acres of the estate, but that merely postponed the moment of decision. It looked as though Longleat, for all its beauty and history, would join the 500 country houses which, in just on a century, had become derelict.

There were, and are, a number of alternatives for houses of this nature. As early as 1910 the Inland Revenue had been prepared to accept property in lieu of taxes, but it was not until 1946, under a Socialist government, that a Land Fund was set up which compensated the Treasury for lost taxes and so allowed the nation itself to acquire houses while allowing families to continue to live in them. The Gowers Report, commissioned by the same government in 1948, emphasized that it was the presence of the family by and for whom the house was built that prevented a house becoming simply a museum. 'The owner of the house is almost always the best person to preserve it.' In return for public financial assistance, public access on a reasonable basis would have to be allowed. The National Trust was employed as the major piece of machinery to bring about the transfer. But the Trust provided only one way out of the dilemma and, in the eyes of many owners, by no means an ideal one: not only was an immense endowment necessary before the Trust would accept a property, there was also the fact that, superbly maintained though their houses might be, inevitably they became institutionalized. Bearing all these factors in mind, the Marquess of Bath decided to turn that centuries-old tradition of country-house visiting into the means of saving at least one great house. And he succeeded. Showmanship, unabashed showmanship, has continued to be the salvation of Longleat. In 1964 the impresario Jimmy Chipperfield suggested the establishment of a safari park, an unheard-of proposal in its day. Despite opposition both locally and nationally (*The Times* sternly adjured the Marquess that a Wiltshireman should stick to cattle, sheep and deer), the Marquess adopted the idea with such success that 'the Lions of Longleat' have

African lion, English oak. When the Longleat safari park was opened to help meet heavy death duties, The Times *sourly commented that cattle, sheep and deer were more appropriate for a Wiltshire estate. 'The lions of Longleat', however, have today taken their own curious place in the 'idea of England'.*

become a household phrase. Longleat publicity has maintained a frankly populist approach, appealing to the well-known tendency to love a lord: its exuberant publicity material shows the Marquess not only as owner but as enthusiastic promoter.

Longleat and the Marquess of Bath blazed a trail which others were to turn into a high road. And one man was to take it finally to its logical conclusion, making stately-homing truly a major branch of the entertainment industry. In 1954 Woburn Abbey, seat of the Dukes of Bedford, faced the same problem as had faced Longleat, but on an immeasurably greater scale: the sum that the taxman demanded there was £4.5 million. The Duke of Bedford set about raising it on a wholly unprecedented scale.

In his ironically titled autobiography, *A Silver-plated Spoon*, the Duke of Bedford charts the vast change that has taken place within living memory. Two vignettes sum up the crest and trough of this change. The first occurs some time between the world wars when, as a child, he is visiting his formidable grandfather, the splendidly named Herbrand, eleventh Duke. The vast dining room with its immense table; behind each diner a personal footman; at the head of the table – the Duke. In front of the Duke is his own private dumb waiter, containing a selection of choice appetisers for himself alone. On the table before him is a plate of consommé, made from exactly $9\frac{1}{2}$ pounds of best shin of beef, made by a kitchenmaid who is specially retained for just this task. The second vignette occurs some thirty years later, in the early 1950s when John, now himself the Duke of Bedford, stands with his wife in the long-abandoned house, contemplating an extraordinary medley of junk and treasures, in a chapter appropriately entitled 'Sèvres in the Sink'.

Early in the book, the Duke remarks that it was World War I which put an end to aristocratic magnificence. Nevertheless, there seems to have been enough energy and cash left over for a last flicker of eccentricity. The round of country-house parties ('one goes country-house visiting in the autumn') was still part of the social pattern. It took the young man, then penniless but with a potent title, to such places as the Moynes' home in Littlehampton – a house consisting, in effect, of two medieval houses joined by a tunnel, each separately staffed for husband and wife, the ground floor bleakly medieval, the upper floor replete with every luxury.

Even during World War II, Herbrand was living alone in Woburn Abbey with fifty indoor and two hundred outdoor servants, the six nurses who looked after him occupying ten rooms. And when a government unit, crammed uncomfortably into the stable block, asked permission to expand into the house, they were informed stiffly that its hundred rooms were occupied – by Herbrand, eleventh Duke of Bedford. But that marked the end

X *Longleat House, Wiltshire. The first of the great planned houses of England also became the first to enter the 'stately home business' in 1946.*

THE STATELY HOMES OF ENGLAND

*XI–XII The 'great house' in its two
extreme forms in Derbyshire.
Haddon Hall (above), ostensibly little changed since
its medieval origins – 'the English castle par
excellence', according to Sir Nikolaus Pevsner,
'. . . the large, rambling, safe, grey, loveable house of
the knights and their ladies'; and the formalized
Chatsworth House (right), seen from the Long
Canal – 'indeed a palace for a prince', observed
Daniel Defoe.*

*Overleaf
XIII–XIV Daniel Defoe thought that Burghley
House, built in Northamptonshire by William
Cecil, Lord Burghley, resembled a town, so
numerous were its turrets and steeples (above).
Beaulieu Palace House (below) was one of the
many results of the monastic plunder of the
sixteenth century.*

Decline and fall: the Rococo Room of Burwell Hall, Lincolnshire, used as a storeroom for sacks of grain.

of the days of extravagant glory. In 1953 the then duke, Herbrand's son and John's father, died accidentally and the Russells had lost the guessing game of death duties. He was killed in a shooting accident on 9 October: had he survived until the end of the year complex financial arrangements then in train would have been completed. As it was, the heir was faced with a vast sum to raise.

The new Duke found a dying house. It was by no means unusual for one generation of the English aristocracy to abandon the family home and for the next to resurrect it. In 1739 Longleat was shut up for fifteen years; in the nineteenth century Clandon Park in Surrey was also deserted for over forty years, while Haddon Hall in Derbyshire was abandoned, incredibly, for well over a century. But in each case the heirs had the financial resilience of their period; there were no such reserves in England during the austerity years of the early 1950s. To the contrary, the owners were regarded as the natural prey of the Chancellor of the Exchequer. Thirty years later, there would occur yet another change in the public view of these rural palaces, as they came to be seen as much part of the 'English heritage', as the current jargon had it, as Stonehenge or Westminster, and therefore deserving help – not least for their tourist potential. But in the immediate postwar years there was still the feeling that they were the private property of an already over-privileged caste whose assets were much overdue for stripping. Bedford, surveying the shambles of the interior of the great house on a freezing winter day in 1954, came to the conclusion that it had probably come to the end of its life.

In a lighthearted, but barbed, passage he sketches the history of the house. Discussing the family origins, he dismisses as nonsensical a historian's attempt to trace the Russells back to William the Conqueror and Central European kings, 'with gobbledegook names in medieval times. The plain fact is that we are of good lower-middle-class origin, though we did at least start on our way up five hundred years ago.' He points out that the Russell who acquired the Abbey on being created Earl 'never lived at Woburn and never saw it'. It had come to the family as property had come to so many of their contemporaries, for it had been a Cistercian Abbey until the abbot had been incautious enough to make an uncomplimentary remark about the King's proposed marriage to Anne Boleyn. After he was hanged, the Russells got the abbey, but it remained virtually derelict until the 1630s when the fourth Earl, using Inigo Jones as adviser, demolished much of the medieval building. There was a second major reconstruction by Flitcroft a century later, and this survived until 1950 when the entire eastern wing was pulled down because of dry rot.

What was to be the future now? Detailed inspection showed an astonishing situation, summed up by the Sèvres porcelain of the chapter title. This was an 800-piece set, given to the fourth Duke by the French king, valued even then at £28,374 and therefore today as near priceless as such a thing can be. It was found, in a filthy condition, packed loosely in hundreds of boxes in one of the stables. The very chaos showed the extraordinary range of objects that a family, securely ensconced in a major building, could acquire over the centuries. The pictures particularly attracted the heir's attention. They were stacked in rows, twelve feet deep from the wall, with their backs to the viewer. 'We had no idea what was what, whether it was my great aunt painted by her sister, or whether it was a Van Dyke.' The most logical decision would have been to sell the lot, pay off the Chancellor and retire on the by no means insignificant sum that would have remained. The new Duke's decision unconsciously echoed that opinion of the eighteenth-century American ambassador who remarked that the English aristocracy owed its stability to its rural roots: 'I do not know of any great family that has survived the loss of its house.'

The end was obvious, the means less evident. Other country houses had adopted the tactics of Longleat, and Bedford visited one or two of them, incognito. 'They were all doing it rather on the theory that the sooner the visitors were in the sooner they would be gone, and the quicker you got the

'Sèvres in the sink': the Duke and Duchess of Bedford inspecting the priceless Sèvres collection that had been dumped in one of the stables.

money the better and goodbye. That was not the way I intended to do it. I wanted to make people enjoy themselves, give them service and value for money and make sure they would come back again. If this enabled me to live in my ancestral home, everyone would be satisfied.'

In the event everyone *was* satisfied: the public who had found a fascinating new venue, the taxman who eventually collected his £4.5 million, and the Russells who again had a family home – though they shared it with a million or so people every year.

The wholehearted manner in which the Duke of Bedford and his son and heir, the Marquess of Tavistock, have thrown themselves into the 'stately homes industry' is again and again cited by purists as the fate worse than extinction awaiting great English houses. One wonders if the more vociferous critics have ever visited the place. On approaching the house from the village of Woburn there is no evidence whatever of the notorious fairground or its ancillaries. Humphrey Repton did his job well nearly 200 years ago, his gently undulating hills and carefully sited copses masking a wide range of tourist activities which would have astonished him.

The reception area of the house is low key. A much-thumbed copy of the Department of Employment's *Hours and Conditions of Work* hangs beneath stern portraits of the Russell family, but there is little else to show that the visitor has entered the headquarters of an organization that employs 250 people, spends at least £1 million a year in maintenance and has to cater for those one million visitors every year, each with two feet to wear out wood and fabric and stone, each with sanitary and culinary needs, each with different interests. Behind the velvet front is a very steely business, a not inappropriate symbol, one feels, for the English aristocracy itself.

CHAPTER SEVEN

The Mysterious Land

In 1756 the Reverend William Stukeley opened an address to the Society of Antiquaries with a remark which curiously echoes those made by both John Leland and Celia Fiennes. 'The love I had for my own country, in my younger days prompted me to visit many parts of it and to refuse great offers made me to go into foreign and fashionable tours. I was sensible we abounded at home with extraordinary curiosities.' And certainly no other traveller in England produced more, and more extraordinary curiosities than did this gentle Lincolnshire parson. William Warburton, Bishop of Gloucester and one of his warmest friends, described him as a mixture of 'simplicity, drollery, absurdity, ingenuity, superstition, and antiquarianism'. Edward Gibbon, who was not disposed to suffer fools kindly or otherwise, said: 'I have used his materials – and rejected most of his fanciful conjectures.' If any one person is responsible for the 'druidic' nonsense which twice annually takes place at Stonehenge today, it is William Stukeley. But our knowledge of the course of England's Roman roads is also heavily indebted to him. He actually walked the Fosse Way, from Lincoln to London, 'which perhaps has not been so scrupulously travelled upon for this thousand years. I resolved so far to imitate an ancient traveller as to dine and lie at a Roman town all the way if possible, and sometimes in danger of faring as meanly as a Roman.' In the eyes of the twentieth-century scholar, Glyn Daniel, he is 'the finest example of the romantic British archaeologist', no mean accolade from an archaeologist himself of international standing.

On the surface, Stukeley's background seems conventional enough: the middle-class origins (his father was an attorney at Holbeach), the Cambridge degree in medicine following which he later took Holy Orders, the distinguished memberships of the Royal Society and the Society of Antiquaries. But essentially he was an eccentric in a society which, happily, cherished its eccentrics. Once he postponed a church service for an hour in order that the congregation might witness an eclipse of the sun. In an

William Stukeley, antiquary: 'simplicity, drollery, absurdity, ingenuity, superstition, and antiquarianism' were all to be found in him. His depiction of the Picts' wall, Newcastle was one of the dozens of precise, accurate drawings he prepared for his major work.

autobiographical fragment, written in the third person, he betrays something of the paranoia which only too often besets the eccentric: 'He has traced the origin of astronomy from the first ages of the world. He has traced the origin of Architecture, with many designs of the Mosaic Tabernacle and an infinity of sacred antiquities, but the artifice of booksellers discorages authors from reaping the fruits of their labours.' Unsurprisingly, he was also a Freemason, believing it to be the 'remains of the mysterys of the antients'.

The bulk of Stukeley's work, and certainly the most valuable part of it, is contained in two handsome folio volumes, the *Itinerarium Curiosum*, each containing the account of a number of journeys, or itineraries, in various parts of England. His technique was to set out with a friend on an extended tour during the summer months, and then write up the result of that tour in the form of a lengthy letter either to another friend, or to an important patron like the Earl of Pembroke. He was an excellent draughtsman, and his volumes are a treasure house of antiquarian drawings. They are intended as illustrations, not decorations, and there is a curiously cold, surreal atmosphere about them, born perhaps of the hard clarity of the background, with some little human figures to give scale.

Stukeley marks, within himself, a point of change most clearly evident where he tries to reconcile the evidence of his eyes with his religious belief. The Deluge is, for him, as much a matter of historical fact as the arrival of

Julius Caesar or the Norman Conquest. When, therefore, near Lincoln, he uncovers a great quantity of seashells many miles from the sea-coast, this can have only one explanation: the Flood had carried shellfish from the Mediterranean right to England and, when it had retreated, the weight of their shells carried them to the bottom. At Bath he found even more intriguing evidence not only of the Flood itself, but of the exact time of the year it had occurred. He came across a great quantity of hazel-nuts, discovered when the springs were being cleaned out. 'These I doubt not to be the remains of the famous and universal Deluge which the Hebrew historian tells us was in autumn, Providence by that means securing the revival of the vegetable world.' Yet, side by side with the Christian still trying to interpret phenomena by means of The Book, was the nascent scientist extrapolating from the evidence of his eyes. Nearly two centuries before the invention of aerial photography had made the study of crop-marks a vital part of archaeology he had observed them, deduced their cause, and begun to employ them as an archaeological aid. Near Chesterford, 'the people promised to show me a wonderful thing in the corn which they observed every year with some sort of superstition. I found it to be the foundation of a Roman temple very apparent, it being almost harvest time. Here the poverty of the corn growing where the walls stood defines it to such nicety that I was able to measure it with exactness enough.' And, in passing, he recorded its development into a local superstition. 'The vulgar have a foolish story about it, as at other places, and say that Lady Kyneburg [an abbess] had cursed it.'

His investigation of the course of the Fosse Way uncovered a rich vein of these local superstitions, showing the pattern whereby half-remembered historical facts became transmuted, in the popular mind, into legend. At Brough he found the remnants of a Roman camp marked by ridges and furrows. 'The old landlady at the little alehouse says that the whole is fairy ground and lucky to live on. The country people have a notion that the Fosse Road is the oldest in England and that it was made by William the Conqueror. This is all that I could glean of this city which I thought no contemptible gleaning from the shipwreck of time.' He encountered the understandable puzzlement, and hence suspicion, of country people, who could not comprehend why this gentleman was poking around their muddy fields. He was particularly anxious to obtain examples of ancient coins 'called swine-pennies because these creatures sometimes root them up' and, although they had little value for the locals, he found it difficult to obtain any. 'Some that had coins would by no means let us see them, for fear that we were come from the Lord of the Manor.' His questions regarding local topography met with a similar blank wall: 'The country people had never heard of enquiries of this

Stukeley's depiction of the destruction of sarsens at Avebury by fire and water.

sort since any memory and were too apt to be morose upon that occasion, thinking that I had some designs upon their farms in my inquisitiveness.'

Stukeley could get carried away, particularly in anything that redounded to the credit of his admired Romans. Thus he is convinced that a continuation of the line of Watling Street on to the Continent would arrive at Rome. 'So the great founders had this satisfaction when they travelled upon it that they were ever going on the line that led to the Imperial Capitol.' In fact, a projection of the line goes on to Trieste, Lubljana and Belgrade. But Stukeley was remarkably agile in his deductions, particularly in the still unknown science of place names. Outside Aukborough he came upon an earthwork in the form of a maze (there is one still on the outskirts of Saffron Walden in Essex) known as Julian's Bower. The local lads had devised an elaborate game and from this 'I concluded that this is an ancient Roman game and it is admirable that both name and thing should have continued through such a diversity of people . . . as to the name *bower* it signifies not an arbor, but *borough* or any work made with ramparts of earth.'

His attitude towards preserving the monuments of the past strikes a very modern note and through the *Itinerarium* one can see clearly, for the first time, the depredation that was being visited on the remains of both Roman and prehistoric England. His description of the 'stonebreakers' of Avebury – how the locals subjected the stones to great heat by building fires in pits at their base – is justly famous. But he follows the trail of the vandals throughout England. In most cases, the destruction was wrought in order to obtain dressed stone and bricks. There were great holes in the Roman road near Stanford: at Ancaster 'the bowling green of the Red Lion is made in the ditch [i.e. the dry moat of the walled city] when they were levelling it they came to the old foundations'. He was appalled at the destruction which had taken place at Verulamium. 'Three years ago a good part of the [town] wall was standing, but ever since, out of wretched ignorance even of their own interest they have been pulling it up all round, even to the foundations, to mend the highway.' He said that he had counted hundreds of cartloads of Roman brick and made the commonsense point that it would have been cheaper and easier to have quarried stone 'because of the prodigious strength of the mortar so that they cannot get one whole brick in a thousand'. Christian memorials were not more secure. He records, with a kind of resigned despair, that the citizens of St Albans had just pulled down their Eleanor Cross and less than a month after he had sketched the north gatehouse of the Abbey, that, too, had been demolished. The destruction of Glastonbury was even worse: the stone of the Abbey vault had been used to build 'a sorry market house. Though I am no encourager of superstitious foppery, yet I think out of that vast estate somewhat might have been left, if only to preserve old monuments for the benefit of history.' Later, he entered the Swan Inn and saw a pile of mosaic fragments, part of a tessellated pavement that had been discovered only two days previously and had been promptly torn to pieces. 'I made the owner melancholy by informing him what profit he might have got by preserving it, to show to strangers', he said with relish.

The collection of antiquities was now in full swing, at no matter what cost to the monument. The civilized John Byng had had no hesitation about recording in his journal not only his bargaining for a piece of Shakespeare's chair, but also his readiness to undertake what he frankly knew to be 'plunder'. In one church he tried to screw himself up to remove some brasses, but there were people present ('I look'd around me but dared not plunder'); and he castigated the unknown vandal who had stolen some of the stained glass from the chapel at Haddon Hall. Stukeley's gentlemanly and aristocratic friends were as greedy, in their own way, as the untutored townsfolk who destroyed a thousand-year-old wall to make a midden. The Roman remains of Hereford had been throughly plundered. 'Colonel Dantsey has paved a cellar with square bricks dug up here: my lord Coningsby has judiciously adorned the floor of his evidence room with them.' And he ends one of his tours in the west with the thought: 'Riding along the road on the north side of Silchester I left with this reflection: now a person of moderate fortune may buy a whole Roman city, which half a kingdom could not do and a gentleman may be lord of the soil where formerly princes and emperors commanded.'

So, like a Roman himself, placing brick upon logical brick, the Reverend Dr William Stukeley built up a picture of the lost years of England. Reason rules him: he is by no means unemotional but he avoids exaggeration and, allowing for the fact that there are certain in-built barriers to full understanding (as, for instance, the need to fit in fossil evidence with the belief in a universal Deluge), his deductions would do credit to a modern archaeologist.

Until he comes to Stonehenge. There indeed he takes a flying leap into the unknown. And where he landed there sprang up one of the more preposterous legends of our own time, the birth of 'druidism'.

When Aurelius Ambrosius, son of Constantine, had defeated Hengist and became king of England and wanted to erect a worthy monument to commemorate the dead, he summoned Merlin the Wizard and asked his advice. 'Send for the Dance of Giants that is in Killare in Ireland', was the wizard's advice. 'For there is a structure of stone there that none of this age could arise, set up in a circle.' They had a special healing quality, he assured the king. 'Giants of old did carry them from the furthest ends of Africa and did set them up in Ireland. And unto this end they did it, that they might make them baths therein whensoever they ailed of any malady, for they did wash the stones and pour forth the water into the baths, whereby they that were wounded had healing.' Persuaded, Aurelius sends an immense army into Ireland, captained by his brother Uther Pendragon. They defeat the Irish in a great battle and Merlin, by his magic arts, transports the Dance of Giants to Salisbury Plain for a monument to the great dead. And there, in due course, were buried Aurelius and Uther and their father Constantine.

So, via the ever memorable *History* of Geoffrey of Monmouth, the first full account of the origins of Stonehenge enters the national consciousness. Buried in the extraordinary melange of legends and half-truths, of historical figures and mythical ones, is a shadowy awareness of the origins of the great monument: the fact that the stones, despite their titanic size, came from a distant place; the fact that they had to be placed in a certain order; the fact, above all, that there was something strange about them. The belief has persisted, in documentary form, for over eight hundred years. On 28 June 1978 *The Times* carried a letter unusual both in its provenance and its substance for that august publication. It was from a Mr Sid Rawl, a self-described squatters' leader, defending the current development of Stonehenge as a hippy centre. 'The evidence is indisputable that Stonehenge and its surrounding area is one of the most powerful spiritual centres in Europe. It is right that we should meekly stand in the presence of God, but it is proper that

Stonehenge in the twentieth century, the barbed wire epitomizing the almost hopeless attempt to regulate the pressure of mass tourism.

we should sing and dance and shout for joy for the love and mercy that he shows us.' Other, more extreme devotees of what was becoming known as the 'occult' picked up the hint relating to Merlin as the transporting agent, but transformed him into an extra-terrestrial intelligence. In 1984 the publishers of Penguin Books, who have gained an enviable and deserved reputation for their pictorial covers, adorned an anthology of 'horror' and 'supernatural' stories with a representation of Stonehenge.

Geoffrey of Monmouth had planted the seed of a remarkably luxuriant growth. Even those who took his stories with a substantial grain of salt, found it difficult to resist this one, relating as it did to a very real, very massive but utterly enigmatic structure raised so far from human habitation. John Leland, usually so meticulous in recording only what he saw, referred to the story of the stones' transportation by Merlin and, given that authoritative lead, few of the antiquaries who were beginning to explore the mysterious land that had come into being before the Norman Conquest, before even the rule of the Romans, could resist some version of the story. Stonehenge came briefly to royal attention in October 1661 when Charles II, fleeing from the battle of Worcester, spent a day mooching among the stones, filling in his time with that task which would attract so many people, the 'telling' or the counting of them. 'The story is that none can count them twice, they stand confused and some single stones at a distance. But I have told them often and bring their number to 91', said Celia Fiennes complacently. But Daniel Defoe made the number 92, a certain Lieutenant Hammond recorded 90 and even the meticulous John Evelyn counted 95.

Whatever total Charles made is not recorded: had he but known it, indeed, an authoritative account of the monument – wholly erroneous but authoritative because produced by King James's favourite architect Inigo Jones – had laid down in terms which brooked no argument who built the monument, why and when. Sometime about 1620 the King had been staying in the splendid new home of the Earl of Pembroke at Wilton House and with that pedantic mind of his, wanted the mystery of Stonehenge cleared up once and for all. And who better to do this than Inigo Jones, the architect who had been trained in the clear, rational light of Italy and had already done such sterling work for his monarch in London, the Banqueting Hall in Whitehall, the Queen's Chapel in St James's and St Paul's at Covent Garden all standing as testimony to his skill and dedication to the art of architecture.

Jones's book, *Stone-henge Restored*, was not published until three years after his death in 1652 and it presents a fascinating picture of a mind at once rational, highly trained, but imaginative, groping in the dark, just missing its objective. As a good Renaissance man, viewing everything by that clear light of reason

Stonehenge in the eighteenth century, antiquaries engaged in the perennial problem of measuring and counting the stones.

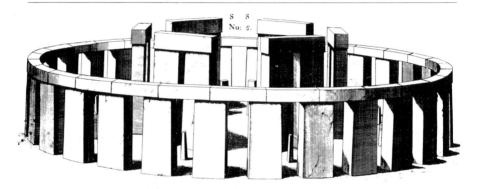

Stonehenge as actually seen and recorded by Inigo Jones and (below) his reconstruction intended to prove that it was a Roman monument based on the Vitruvian system.

and with excellent architectural models to follow, Inigo Jones had little difficulty in dismissing not only Merlin and all his supernatural helpers, but the very idea that this vast temple could have been built by the naked savages who had inhabited England before the coming of the Romans. 'The truth is, those ancient Times had no knowledge of publick works, either sacred or secular, for their own use or Honour of their Deities.' How was it possible, he demanded rhetorically, that a people 'destitute of the knowledge even to clothe themselves' would know how to build so vast and stately a structure? Who, then, built it? Why, it was obvious from its perfect Vitruvian geometry: it was a Roman building.

And after Jones's, Stonehenge theories come thick and fast. Dr Thomas Fuller mocked the story of Merlin's involvement: what did Merlin use as vehicle? The star cluster Charles' Wain? It was too ridiculous even to argue about and Fuller proposes his own solution, paying particular attention to the problem that engages archaeologists today. How were the great lintels raised? They were never raised at all, Dr Fuller insists, for they were made of artificial stone – 'consolidate sand': cement, in other words, that had been cast in situ, a solution which has at least the virtue of simplicity. Dr Walter Charlton scoffed, with fine impartiality, at Geoffrey of Monmouth, Inigo Jones, Thomas Fuller and all: it was plain to the meanest intelligence that the great monument could only be the work of those virile, inventive and industrious people who had conquered the Saxons – the Danes. The diarists, treading in the footsteps of the antiquaries, at least lacked their aggressive dogmatism: 'God knows what their use was' is Pepys's forthright comment, though he allowed that they were as 'prodigious' as rumoured. John Evelyn dropped by in July 1645 and subjected the supposed indestructibility of the stones to a pragmatic test. 'They were so exceeding hard that all my strength with a hammer could not break a fragment.' He had to bring his own hammer: later souvenir-hungry tourists could hire a massive hammer from a resident vandal to knock off fragments.

Throughout the Stonehenge story one is aware of a number of brilliant minds firing arrows, as it were, at a target all but obscured by thick and drifting mist. Most come quite close: some even hit the outer ring, but remain unaware of the fact. In the second half of the seventeenth century one of the most enthusiastic of these archers visited the site and so showered the target with missiles that some, at least, found a mark.

John Aubrey, born in Wiltshire in 1626, far more closely approximates to the popular picture of the antiquary than does Stukeley. He had the antiquary's undisciplined enthusiasm, the magpie tendency to gather up

Curious 'vandals' chipping off fragments of rock at Stonehenge. It was even possible to hire mallet and chisel for the purpose.

anything and everything relating to his immediate subject, no matter how remote, throwing them down pell-mell. This, added to misfortunes both in finance and in love, ensured that the only book he ever finished and published in his lifetime was his *Miscellanies* – and this related, significantly enough, to the supernatural or the 'occult': dreams, omens, ghost stories and the rest. At the age of twenty-five he inherited a considerable property from his father but a mixture of bad luck and bad judgment embroiled him in a series of lawsuits that rapidly reduced him to near penury.

But he had good friends who admired him both as man and as antiquary. No less a person than Christopher Wren 'contrived an employment for him' in secret. But even this came to nothing financially. John Ogilby, who was to give to the traveller the incalculable benefit of his road maps, commissioned him to make a 'peregrination' of Surrey for a fine new history of England he was going to publish. Despite his splendid title of 'King's Cosmographer and Geographer', Ogilby – that 'cunning Scot' – was a far from dependable man. Poor Aubrey threw himself into the task with his customary enthusiasm, amassing a vast amount of material, paying his own heavy expenses. Then, in October 1673, 'On Sunday night Mr Og. told me he hath altered his mind & he would now make no more use of me but get what scraps he can out of bookes or by hear say. I asked him then for some consideration of my expenses in towne all this time on this account', but he got not a farthing out of Ogilby. The notes for his perambulation of Surrey gathered dust, like so much of his work, and were not published until nearly twenty years after his death – with John Evelyn's admiring letter as an introduction.

For John Aubrey was held in high regard by his peers – his work on Avebury alone would have ensured him a place in the annals of antiquarianism. Admittedly, his discovery of Avebury was a little akin to the discovery of America: the natives of both places could claim never to have been lost. Certainly, the villagers of Avebury had been doing their best to put to good use the great clumsy stones that littered the place. One of the grislier modern discoveries is of a medieval skeleton lying there beneath a fallen stone: quite evidently some incautious villager had miscalculated the angle and speed of fall of the stone he was undermining. But in the sense of bringing this great monument to the attention of the learned, Aubrey's claim stands undisputed. Later generations, for whom these ancient monuments have now been wholly overlaid with theories, superstitions and calculations, and their appearance made commonplace through innumerable paintings and engravings and photographs, can only envy the 22-year-old John Aubrey when, out fox-hunting in 1649, he first entered that enormous circle which he compared with Stonehenge, in that unforgetable phrase, as a cathedral to a parish church.

Avebury Stone circle somehow survived the treatment of fire and water recorded by Stukeley.

Aubrey's researches into Stonehenge were undertaken, it is said, at the direct behest of the King, presumably a belated fruit of the day Charles had spent counting the stones. But even royal patronage was unable to make Aubrey overcome his constitutional procrastination: the book for which it was intended, *Monumenta Britannica*, was never completed and *Templa Druidum*, part I of that book, was never published, but remains to this day in Oxford's Bodleian Library in manuscript form. But in the small world that was seventeenth-century scholarship enough of its details would have become common knowledge. Its title is sufficient indication of its theme. Much of what Aubrey discovered was solid and of lasting value: the Aubrey Holes, now part of the Stonehenge nomenclature, were, after all, named in his honour, for he had been the first to record them. He gives a good survey of the mythology of Stonehenge, including its transportation by Merlin, but then adds his own by deducing the monument's druidic origins, bypassing Inigo Jones to go back to an earlier, though now badly garbled, belief. He was bolstered in this by the oddly named Aylett Sammes who, in his own book *Britannia Antiqua Illustrata*, not only picked up the story of druidic foundation, but added yet another twist to it. And here again posterity can only marvel at the deductive powers of the seventeenth-century antiquaries and feel a vicarious regret at the closeness by which they missed their target. Over two centuries before a photographer recorded the outline of a supposed 'Mycenaean axe' upon Stone 53 of the Trilithon, Sammes postulated a Mediterranean influence in the construction of Stonehenge – not Mycenaean, but Phoenician. . . .

The study of Stonehenge had reached this point when William Stukeley arrived and bound the whole together in one splendid, rational, wholly erroneous form in *Stonehenge: a Temple Restor'd to the Druids*. The Index to the handsome, massive folio outlines his theme in a stately procession of ideas:

Stonehenge the latest of the Druid temples
Older than the time of the Saxons and Danes
Older than the time of the Roman Britons
Older than the times of the Belgae, who
preceded the Roman invasion
The stones of Stonehenge are from the gray weathers on
Marlborough Downs
Of their nature, magnitude, weight
Of their number . . .

So the entries proceed, squashing under their great weight of scholarship all earlier, erroneous ascriptions, coming at length to:

The Druids came with an oriental colony
The colony were Phoenicians or Arabians
They found out our tin mines
The Druids came here about Abraham's time or soon after
Stonehenge prov'd the work of the Druids from the infinite
number of the like, all over the Britannic isles.

By 1799, when this engraving was executed, Stukeley's theory of the 'Druidic' origins of stone circles was firmly rooted. This is an illustration to a once enormously popular, now forgotten, epic poem on Caractacus. The hero, in retreat among Welsh druids, receives British soldiers.

The 'Druidic' theory of Stonehenge's origin in its lushest form: march of the druids in 1905.

Stukeley provided a similar set of arguments, in yet another massive, handsome book, for Avebury. Backed with this authority the druidic theory proved indestructible even though, parallel with it, there developed the theory that modern scholarship has now accepted: that the great complex was some form of observatory. This view had been put forward as early as 1771 by a Dr John Smith, who accepted Stukeley's belief that Stonehenge was druidic in origin but insisted that it was not 'a cathedral of the Arch-Druid' (as Stukeley would have it) but an 'orrery'.

The two strands – the mythological and the scientific – were by no means mutually exclusive. In the twentieth century, in particular, their cross-fertilization created one of the most exuberant and fantastic of all growths. Devotees of 'ufology' (as students of supposed extraterrestrial objects termed their discipline) transformed Merlin into an extraterrestrial, a being of enormous but mortal powers, transporting matter by means of 'cosmic rays' or adapted flying saucers. And meanwhile, twentieth-century 'druids' quietly went about their pageants at the solstices, ignoring alike the caterwauling of the vulgar who turned up in thousands to mock, the scientists who argued in vain that the structures were in existence some thousands of years before the druidic orders came into being, and the ufologists who argued as passionately in favour of their own gods.

It was all very odd. But even odder things were happening at Glastonbury, some fifty miles to the south-west.

On 3 January 1908 Frederick Bligh Bond, the Bristol architect entrusted by the Somerset Archaeological Society with the excavation of Glastonbury Abbey ruins, sat with an unidentified companion in a house in Glastonbury. The companion was a spiritualist medium who specialized in automatic writing and on that bitterly cold winter's evening a few lines of garbled Latin began to emerge. Over the following months of patient sittings, the writings became more fluent and copious, the Latin being gradually superseded by a form of medieval English. Bond was particularly interested in the existence, or otherwise, of a supposed chapel dedicated to St Edgar, which Leland described as extending from the east end of the great church, but whose every trace had long since disappeared.

The town plan of modern Glastonbury tells the history of the place at a glance. An immense green space, dotted with ruins and approximately square in shape, is lightly fringed with houses on three sides, the houses thickening on the north side to form the present High Street. The square space contains the abbey ruins, and the abbot's kitchen is, ironically, the only structure to survive intact. Despite its purely practical function (even today it could be used as a kitchen, so efficient are its vents and funnels), visitors tend to talk in hushed voices in the massive building, for it still carries something of its ancient ambience. Elsewhere, all is ruin: two of the vast pillars of the crossing tower up from a greensward; the enormous crypt is open to the sky. This was a titanic church, bigger than most of our cathedrals – longer than St Paul's, taller than Winchester. The tranquillity of the ruins is deceptive, for there must have been a great degree of local hatred to have brought about so total a destruction. In 1539 Henry VIII decreed, but it was the townsfolk who demolished after the last abbot, Whiting, had been hanged on the Tor.

The abbey was begun some time in the late fifth century, the first certain date for the town. As to what happened before, who can say? The story of Christ's adolescence spent here; the coming of Joseph of Arimathea with his miraculous staff which rooted itself and became the 'Glastonbury thorn'; the burial of King Arthur in the abbey ruins; the Chalice Well with its miraculous cures; the Celtic goddess with her labyrinth on the Tor – each of these legends disappears, as evanescent as a soap bubble, as it is traced to its source. But together they tell of something very odd that happened here during the opening centuries of our era.

The long-drawn controversy over the supposed burial place of Arthur is exemplary in its mixture of fact and fiction and, not least, in the heated

Glastonbury Abbey. Ironically, the only section which survived intact was the Abbot's kitchen, seen here through ruined arches.

passions it arouses. There is firm documentary evidence that, in 1191, the monks uncovered a very deep grave marked with a leaden cross whose crude Latin legend, 'Here lies buried the renowned King Arthur in the Isle of Avalon', could indeed belong to some period before the sixth century. The monks built an immense marble tomb for the remains in front of the high altar; in 1278 they displayed its contents to King Edward I, who certainly accepted them for what they were purported to be. The bones disappeared after the Dissolution but a modest memorial marked the spot – not of the original grave but of the ornate tomb. Stukeley saw it and was disposed to accept it at face value. Opponents claimed simply that the monks had invented the whole operation. Monkish deceptions were by no means unknown, but it would have required archaeological and historical knowledge of a high order to have faked a pre-sixth-century inhumation in the twelfth century. No fragments remain, so there is no means of bringing modern science and scholarship to bear on the problem.

Less dramatic, but historically even more interesting were the problems relating to the abbey's own ruins, the position of the supposed Edgar Chapel in particular. Apart from Leland's unequivocal reference and a few other fugitive ones, all that the twentieth-century archaeologists had to go on was a drawing which Stukeley had preserved and identified. But even here there were doubts as to the precise location. And it was at this stage that Bligh Bond decided to have recourse to 'supernatural' aid. It was not quite as bizarre a decision as might, perhaps, appear today. The Society for Psychical Research had come into being in 1882, and its first steering committee included men of unquestioned academic standing, among them Henry Sedgwick, Frederick Myers and the physicist William Crookes, inventor of the 'Crookes Tube'. Reading their first publications, one can only be impressed by, and envious of, their immense self-confidence, the attitude of men rolling up their sleeves preparatory to disposing, once for all, of a problem that had plagued human imagination since the beginning of humanity. It is worth noting that Bligh Bond's first book, *The Gate of Remembrance*, was published by a firm of unimpeachable academic standing, B. H. Blackwell of Oxford; indeed, one of the sessions or seances was attended by Basil Blackwell himself and somebody described as 'Miss D. Sayers', presumably the formidable bluestocking, Dorothy L. Sayers.

The sittings were random, spread over a number of years. No indication is given of the character or even the sex of the medium, identified simply by the initials J.A. But whoever he or she was, and whatever reservations one might have about his or her command of medieval English and Latin, there is no disputing the medium's literary skill. A number of distinct entities emerged to give their recollections of the abbey in its prime. Outstanding among them is a figure called Johannes, 'whose body once lay in the cemetery hard by the East side of the Chapel of St Michael', described by one of his brethren as 'Simple he was, but as a dog loveth his Master so loved he his Howse with a greater love than any of they that builded it. . . . Being earthbound by that love, his spirit clings in dreams to the vanished vision which his spirit eyes even still see. . . . Even as old he wandered by the mere and saw the sunset shining on her far off towers and now in dreams the earth-love part of him strives to picture the vanished glories.'

Whatever the source of J.A.'s revelations he, or she, was able to build up so detailed a picture of the abbey that, in due course, the vanished Edgar Chapel was uncovered. In March 1917, the Hon. Everard Fielding, at that time Secretary for the now greatly influential Society for Psychical Research, wrote to Bond, saying, unequivocally: 'There is no question but that the writing about the Edgar Chapel preceded the discovery of it by many months.' Cause and effect? Or coincidence? The dean and chapter of Wells Cathedral, who were now responsible for the abbey, had no doubt. The discovery that the architect responsible for the restoration of one of the most potent of Christian shrines in England was dabbling in the occult caused very considerable consternation in the claustrophobic ecclesiastical world. Four years after Bond had published his book, he was dismissed as director. He

Glastonbury, the evocative Tor. The building on the summit is the tower of a medieval church, but the hill itself is deeply scarred with a prehistoric field system.

continued further spiritualistic 'communications' concerned with the abbey – but it is significant that these later writings were published not by Basil Blackwell but by one of the 'psychic' societies which mushroomed during the 1920s – the British College of Psychic Science. He died in 1948, his reputation wholly shredded by his quondam colleagues in the architectural and archaeological professions. But, in a manner that might well have pleased him, he has subsequently become a major figure in a new cult. Since World War II, Glastonbury has seen more than its fair share of the eccentric, or purely lunatic fringe, for with the decline of formal religion and the rise of a pseudo-occultry the little Somerset town has become a natural target. People seeking the Holy Grail; people who have found the Holy Grail and want to enshrine it here; people convinced of the reality of Arthur's tomb, or the shrine of the Earth Goddess, or a nodal point for UFOs – all have flocked here over the past few decades. It is a testimony to the town's toughness of identity that, instead of becoming transformed into a kind of psychic Disneyland, it remains solidly rooted, a workaday Somerset town whose major industry was, until recently, the preparation of sheep skins.

The development of Glastonbury as a supposed psychic centre is paralleled by similar developments across the whole country, the hesitant occultry adumbrated by seventeenth-century antiquaries flowering lushly in the supposedly scientific atmosphere of the twentieth century. Much of it is the product of wishful thinking, the means whereby inadequate personalities bolster self-approval by laying claims to vast powers and unique experiences. But much, too, gives the observer pause to account for its nature. And predominant among them is the discovery of so-called 'ley-lines'.

Ley-lines enter recorded history in an unhappily dramatic manner – unhappily, that is, for those who feel that one mystery at a time is quite enough for any one phenomenon. The discoverer of the lines was Alfred Watkins, an amateur archaeologist and solid businessman (a flour miller by trade) – a gentle, learned man with very strong convictions but certainly no fanatic. Some time in the 1920s Watkins, then in his mid-sixties, was riding on horseback in his native county of Herefordshire. He and his mount were ascending a gentle hill when he received what can only be described as a vision – the vision of a network of glowing lines apparently superimposed on the landscape before him. The experience was only momentary but so powerful that he was to spend the rest of his life determining the reality of the lines on a scientific basis.

In his book *The Old Straight Track* he assumed that they were trackways, their course being either determined or identified by not less than five ancient monuments in a straight line. Subsequent students of his theory put this to an

Alfred Watkins, discoverer of the ley system. He argued only that ley-lines may have been traders' tracks. Subsequent 'investigators' make rather more ambitious claims for them, including their identification as guide-lines (and or power sources) for extraterrestrial vehicles.

interesting statistical test: of forty-nine marks made at random on a sheet of paper, three would produce no particular form but five would produce the required straight line. Considering some of the fantastic theories that have subsequently been evolved to account for the lines, it is astonishing that Watkins's argument should have aroused such rage among professional archaeologists. He argued that primitive man, moving around a literally trackless landscape, needed to create a series of guidelines to get him home again. The ley-lines were created for this purpose, based upon distinctive natural points which would subsequently become 'sacred' and the site of structures.

The study of the lines was taken a considerable step forward, and the mystery was considerably deepened, half a century later with the posthumous publication of Guy Underwood's book *Patterns of the Past*. Like Watkins, Underwood's professional background was impeccably sober and respectable: he was a curator with the British Museum, not an institution disposed to give shelter to the lunatic. But he was also a dowser, and at some stage began to investigate a theory that the great monuments of the prehistoric past were located near underground water; thence his theory expanded into realms where academic colleagues, fearful for their professional reputations, refused to follow. He came to the conclusion that he was detecting something hidden deep below the earth's surface – an 'earth force' which 'appeared to cause wave motion perpendicular to the earth's surface and with great penetrative power'. This force formed spiral patterns which 'could be detected by the nerve cells of animals'.

Both Underwood and Watkins postulated an ultimately natural cause of the phenomena – Underwood thought in terms of magnetism, Watkins of topography. But this was by no means sufficient for the 'students' of the occult who began to proliferate in the 1960s and who pounced on these intangible but apparently real emanations. For some they were the nerve system of a living organism, the planet Earth itself, for others the channels of a force from which a long-dead civilization had drawn its industrial power. Guidelines for visiting spaceships, interplanetary signalling devices – interpretations of the significance of the lines grow ever wider and wilder even while their charting seems to be settling down to a codified discipline.

Travellers in this parallel 'occult' realm of England have been led, in the main, by some remarkably weird characters for whom Warburton's description of Stukeley would be very mild indeed. But among them are some of a stature to ensure that the questions they pose are, at the very least, left open instead of being dismissed with a contemptuous or pitying smile. Towering among them is T. C. Lethbridge, who combined the role of academic and man of action. Three times he took part in Arctic explorations; twice he went to sea in square-rigged ships. But he was also Director of Excavations for the Cambridge Antiquarian Society and for the University Museum of Archaeology and Ethnology. His popular publications frankly discussed the reality of ghosts, the possible visitation of extraterrestrials to the planet and advanced a theory for the function of the stone circles that litter northern Europe as a form of reservoir or accumulator of psychic energy. He was dowsing, with a pendulum, the circle known as the Merry Maidens in Cornwall and happened to touch one of the stones. Whereupon 'a strange thing happened. The hand resting on the stone received a strong tingling sensation and the pendulum itself shot out until it was circling nearly horizontal to the ground. The stone itself, which must have weighed over a ton, felt as if it were rocking and dancing about' – a curious reminder of Geoffrey of Monmouth's description of Stonehenge as the 'Dance of Giants'.

Lethbridge was well aware of the basic problems of communicating the unprecedented to the unconvinced. 'The reader is perfectly at liberty to believe I imagined all this, but if so there is no point in reading this book. It is for people with wider knowledge of what anthropologists call "the odd". It ranges from "couvade", where the father of an unborn child feels ill before its birth, to the "pointing bone" of the witch doctor who by this kills his enemy. Those who have had any dealings with the odd are not interested in the disbelief of those who have not.' And to this chastisement and dismissal, the would-be scoffer can only retort, perhaps, with the cautious Scottish verdict of 'Not Proven'.

III

BRAVE NEW WORLD

'After all these bloody wars and
vindictive animosities we still have an unspeakable
yearning towards England.'

Nathaniel Hawthorne, *Our Old Home*

CHAPTER EIGHT

Kissing Cousins

Early in the nineteenth century, there began to arrive on the shores of England a class of visitor equipped with a unique vision of the island. Technically, legally, they were 'foreigners' – that is, owing allegiance to a foreign government. Genetically, they were intimately related; linguistically, they spoke the identical language. The American visitors to England were (and are) uniquely capable of objective but literally sympathetic assessment of their Old World relatives.

And they made excellent use of their opportunities. In her immense compilation of American memoirs of English visits (appropriately entitled *The Passionate Pilgrim*) Alison Lockwood lists nearly 400 books in the bibliography, and refers to another hundred or so in passing. The bulk of these appeared between about 1820 and the end of the century: in some years, half a dozen fat books about England rolled off the presses in America. And the American hunger for information about the land many of them still referred to as the 'mother country' is demonstrated not only by the high quantity but also by the remarkably low quality of many. Most of them are on the 'Dear diary' level. Even so polished a writer as Oliver Wendell Holmes, that transatlantically famous 'autocrat of the breakfast table', feels it important to tell his readers how he shaved with a patent razor, how he coped with asthma, what he had for afternoon tea. The accounts written before the mid-century are, for the most part, the result of several months (in some cases even several years) stay in England. After the mid-century, when Thomas Cook took the wandering pilgrims in hand, whisking them from New York to London to Paris and back, full-length books about England could be based on an acquaintance of a matter of days, putting Count Smorltork in the shade.

Even by the 1850s an American writer, himself intent on unloading yet another travel book on to the market, observed: 'Books of travel have multiplied of late with fearful rapidity, but still the vast amount of readers in our country create a steady demand.' Such demand favoured a species of cannibalization, or recycling of material. Another writer gives a sour description of a fellow American's technique in amassing material. 'He scarcely arrived at a town before, with the dust of the road still upon him, he would start out, purchase a book and map of the place and run, without intermission, to every spot named. Worn out, scarcely able to sit up, he would return at nightfall for all the world as if his thirst for information would be his quietus. In this half alive condition he would take notes of what he had seen.' And, in due course, these notes would spawn another book, to be used as guide and source material for other visitors as they hared around. But, bad literature though most of these were, their very artlessness makes them priceless social history, even their mistakes showing what was the contemporary idea of England held by the booming young republic.

The span of time covered by the American discovery of England is neatly and dramatically illustrated by the change in the method of transatlantic travel, from the squalid discomforts of the sailing ships in the early part of the nineteenth century, to the great liners of the first decades of the twentieth century in which it was perfectly possible to cross the Atlantic without being obliged actually to see the ocean. The change, in fact, took place within a single lifetime. On his first visit in 1833 Oliver Wendell Holmes took twenty-one days to make the crossing: his return home after his second visit in 1886, took him not quite nine days.

The Americans' changing view of England faithfully reflects this technological change. At the beginning, the giant stride made as a result of the Industrial Revolution arouses the admiration (and sometimes the horror) of the transatlantic country cousins. At the end of the period the Americans, having won the technological race, are now looking for roots, and it is England's antiquity and quaintness which they seek out and extol.

Transport was the first thing noticed at the beginning of the nineteenth century. English stage coaches 'proceed at a tearing rate over hill and valley: the road was as smooth as if laid with rails and nothing impeded the rocket-like rapidity of our course', Alexander McKenzie noted in the 1830s. English inns met with universal approval. 'The English inn is as close an imitation as it can be of the private house.' The railway, that supreme example and medium of technological change, fascinated the visitors. 'England has 300 miles of railway,' said Isaac Jewett in 1836, 'and has 500 more contemplated. As an American, I am anxious to see converts made to a railway system. In our country it will be an agent well able to facilitate our very distant communities.' This precedence in English technology lasted until, and was most dramatically illustrated by, the Great Exhibition of 1851 and, above all, by the Crystal Palace itself – 'The wonder of the world, worth a voyage across

England's technical achievement is summed up by the Crystal Palace: 'The wonder of the world, worth a voyage across the Atlantic to behold.'

the Atlantic to behold.' But warning voices were raised from inhabitants of a land still rural in its roots. 'I have noticed how many of my fellow countrymen are now sighing and longing to have manufactories erected in the United States. . . . Let us be careful how we foster a snake in our bosom and translate to our fertile regions and happy shores the depravities of such places as Manchester and Birmingham.'

The Americans' first sight of England was Liverpool, which offered, for most of them, an almost arrogant display of technological skills. 'What docks are these, my countrymen. Substantial, spacious, well-covered and well paved. What a contrast to those in New York,' said George Putnam in 1836. But, again, words of envy and exhortations to emulate were balanced a little later by warnings, as what had been a moderate-sized port suddenly exploded into a major maritime city. In 1877 a visitor from Kansas was comparing the brightness and openness of America with 'the inner and outer darkness' of Liverpool.

Liverpool was naturally the place where Nathaniel Hawthorne was posted as consul in 1853. From here he got his first glimpse not only of England and the English but of his fellow republicans. He would see them arrive; only too often he would see them depart, considerably the worse for wear, a few weeks later. His consul's office was a 'dusty and stifled chamber', containing little more than a barometer and an out-of-date map of the USA in a smoke-stained office block on the corner of Brunswick Street, and from here he would see his fellow citizens come and go, the hopeful, the innocent, the arrogant and the plain mad. Such was the destitute American who had named his children after Albert and Victoria and, after sending their photographs to the Queen, had received the usual bland acknowledgment from a private secretary. 'Like a great many other Americans he had long cherished a fantastic notion that he was one of the rightful heirs to a rich English estate and, on the strength of Her Majesty's letter and the hopes of royal patronage it had inspired, he had shut up his little country store and come over to claim his inheritance.' Hawthorne met him after he had been conned out of his money and approached the US consul – not for aid to return home but for money to get a new suit to visit the Queen. Far more formidable was the New England lady who turned up with a vast bundle of documents laying claim to all the principal business parts of Liverpool and 'with considerable peremptoriness signified her expectation that I should take charge of her suit'.

Liverpool was not only the first, but the first modern city the visitors encountered. The first traditional city was Chester. Even so courtly a visitor as Wendell Holmes shared Defoe's view of the ancient city: 'It has a mouldy old cathedral . . . too highly flavoured for antiquity. I could not help comparing some of the ancient cathedrals and abbey churches to old cheeses. They have a tough grey rind and a rich interior which find food and lodging for numerous tenants.' But he was certainly in a minority in those early years. For Nathaniel Hawthorne, 'It was long before I outgrew this Americanism, the love of an old thing for sake of its age', and he declared that an American would venerate even an English turnip field 'when he thinks how long that small space of ground has been known and recognized'.

Liverpool was the first English city, Chester the first antique city and Eaton Hall, just outside Chester, the seat of the Duke of Westminster, was the Americans' first encounter with the English aristocracy. These citizens of a new republic had a somewhat uneasy, ambivalent view of the whole English class structure. Joshua White compared English servants with American slaves very favourably indeed, apparently quite unaware of any moral issue. Royalty hunting became a major preoccupation. The resoundingly named Sarah Maria Aloisa Britton Spottiswoode Mackin, who had no hesitation in

Harriet Beecher Stowe, author of Uncle
Tom's Cabin, *was fêted on her arrival in
England, but hastened to identify herself
with the aristocracy.*

entitling her book *A Society Woman in Two Worlds*, all but swooned with
delight on being taken to a reception where she was able to bow before the
King, Queen and Prince of Wales. Referring to Harriet Beecher Stowe's
grotesque grovelling before her aristocratic patrons, the Duke and Duchess of
Sutherland, Charles Mitchell observed sadly, 'I fear the American love of a
lord is not exaggerated, if even Mrs Stowe was blinded by it.' He, certainly,
did not exaggerate. All England was ringing with condemnation of the
Sutherlands for their brutal action in the so-called Highland Clearance, when
they were literally burning the wretched hovels of their peasantry in order to
make way for sheep on their enormous estates. This was necessary, said Mrs
Stowe, champion of the downtrodden American Negro, because of 'the
advancing process of civilization'. But not all Americans were bowled over by
the aristocracy. Henry Colman, an agriculturist, was contemptuous of the
technique of driving game on shoots at country estates. You might as well, he
said, 'have an armchair placed in the poultry yard and then hens and chickens
tied by the legs and shot at leisure'.

The tourists followed a clearly defined route, not much extended from
Thomas Platter's day. Inescapably, London was the first and major goal. Then
Stratford-on-Avon, Warwick Castle, Kenilworth, the Lake District, North
across the Border for a brief view of 'Scott-land', then back down via
Chatsworth and Haddon Hall. London, the largest city in the world,
overwhelmed by its size, its impersonality, its fogs and its bustle. 'Londoners

walk much faster than New Yorkers.' They were fascinated and impressed by the great city's internal transport, in particular the hansom cab ('the gondola of London'), and, later, shared the future G. K. Chesterton's opinion that the only way to see the city was from the top deck of an omnibus. In the 1860s American visitors were reporting a custom only too well revived a little over a century later, the examining of baggage in such places as the Palace of Westminster and the British Museum during the 'Fenian' dynamite scare. 'They shiver and call police when an Irishman passes with a lunch or tin can.' For the literary, London was a place of pilgrimage. 'I can scarcely believe that Paternoster Row is only a minute's walk from my hotel: that Cheapside, Haymarket, Piccadilly and the Old Bailey are within half an hour's ride: that Temple Bar, London Bridge and Old Westminster Bridge may be seen tomorrow', enthused the Reverend John Edward. Oliver Wendell Holmes was, predictably, ecstatic about the British Museum. The only way to come to terms with it, he said, was to get lodgings next door and pass the rest of your life in it.

London as seen by the first wave of American visitors: entrance to the Strand, 1842, by Thomas Shotter Boys.

It was Washington Irving who put Stratford-on-Avon on the map for Americans. Indeed, one gets the impression that they were far more eager to tread in his steps than actually to worship at the Shakespearean shrine. He had stayed at the Red Horse Inn and the walls of his bedroom there became covered with the signatures of visitors. The landlady there made a good thing out of the famous 'sceptre'. In his *Sketchbook*, which had made his name, Irving described his solitary evenings in the inn with 'the armchair his throne, the poke his sceptre, and the little parlour, some 12 feet square, his undoubted kingdom'. The poker (or, one suspects, its successor) was reverently kept in an American flag for display to visitors.

Until the mid-century, the overall American view of England was surprisingly warm and friendly when compared with the English view of America. Sydney Smith had set the tone with his slashing attack in 1820: 'Who reads an American book? Or goes to an American play? What does the world yet owe to an American physician? Under which of the old, tyrannical governments of Europe is every sixth man a slave, whom his fellow creatures could torture and sell?' Such an attack invited, and in due course received, a response at the same level. The American Samuel Young attacked the English, who 'got their notions of America from Marryat the tippler, [Mrs] Trollope the bawd, Fanny Kemble the female rowdy and Dickens toad-eater to the aristocracy'.

But relations between the two peoples were considerably warmer than those portrayed by the professional image-makers. 'An American is always favoured. They hardly look on him as a foreigner. I have frequently heard this phrase, "O, there were two or three Americans there and half a dozen foreigners".' Almost until the end of the century, those citizens from a land still engaged in finding an identity, still creating its institutions, were impressed by the solidity, the durability, the imperturbable certainty of English customs and institutions, and the buildings that reflected them. 'All seem to carry an air of stability; iron lamp, bridge, gallery, piazza and almost everything for which we use heavy timber is there substituted by iron.' Even English draught horses were praised as 'young mastodons'. Looking at the merchants' houses in Liverpool, Noble Prentice remarked on 'the big knockers on the door which would break in an American door'. Another transatlantic visitor reflected that 'the houses are built to shelter the heads of generations to come'. There was an almost uncritical admiration of the 'mother country' as 'the headspring of the life of our own nation' (as a Professor Popper put it), or, even more dramatically, in Nathaniel Hawthorne's words: 'After all these bloody wars and vindictive animosities we still have an unspeakable yearning towards England.'

XV Storm clouds over Stonehenge.

THE ENGLISH HEARTLAND

*XVI–XVIII Part of the nineteenth century tourists'
circuit. Warwick Castle (left) – 'the most perfect
piece of castellated antiquity in the kingdom',
according to an earlier observer; and the greatest
attraction of all: Shakespeare's birthplace in Henley
Street and his gravestone in the chancel of Holy
Trinity Church, Stratford-upon-Avon.*

Overleaf
*XIX Seaside England: deckchairs waiting for
occupants: stage waiting for players.*

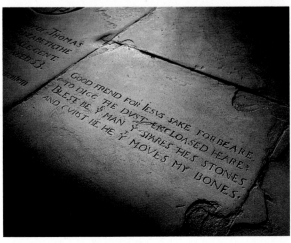

That yearning was undoubtedly muted during the long anti-slavery debate and was almost wholly smothered during the bitterness of the American Civil War of the 1860s when, according to a visiting American, Phoebe Palmer: 'Newsboys, by way of ensuring a more ready sale for their papers cry "War with America! War with America!"' But the wounds, though deep, were not mortal: far more lasting in its effect was the birth of mass tourism.

In 1873 Thomas Cook, who had already transformed the aristocratic Grand Tour of the Continent into a demotic circus, turned his attention to Americans. Hitherto, Americans in England had either been working here (like Nathaniel Hawthorne) or, like Oliver Wendell Holmes, were rich enough to be able to spend three or four months in the country and were sufficiently cultured to wish to do so. Now they came in regimented parties, covering the country in a matter of days, establishing that pattern of tourism which aroused the easy mockery of the English cousins until well into the twentieth century when they, too, could afford to take part in the frenetic dance of mass tourism. And from the 1870s onward a change in the way visitors regarded their involuntary hosts becomes painfully evident. The new breed of visitor was the forerunner of that which has now penetrated into every part of the globe – the tourist who regards the country visited not as host but virtually as prey.

Prototype of the 'Ugly Tourist' was a certain William Falkner. Mocking the accents of natives such as the official at Windsor Castle ('Hi beg pardon, Hi ham not hallowed to haccept fees for hexhibiting 'er Majesty's hapartments'), offering another attendant a shilling to dance on Henry VIII's grave and being surprised when the man indignantly refused, Falkner regarded England simply as an intricate piece of clockwork set into motion for his especial amusement. His compatriot and equal, Henry Morford, infuriated by an ostler's traditional cry ('Please Sir, remember the ostler') deliberately ran him down and drove off congratulating himself that, after seeing how one tyrant had been treated at Runnymede, 'I had been the humble means of teaching one milder lesson to the new and worse tyranny of all Great Britain, *servant begging*'. These were, perhaps, the ordinary run of globe-trotting louts, but Sophia Hawthorne, wife of the cultured and sympathetic Nathaniel, ought really to have known better. She and her son openly stole flowers and plants from Byron's old home of Newstead Abbey, and complacently described how she contrived to drive out would-be occupants of her railway carriage, leaving it for herself and her family.

Mrs Hawthorne's plunder of Newstead Abbey gardens marked the start of a remarkable outburst of relic stealing. The English themselves had never been averse to plundering their own monuments but their American cousins now

The lodestone for all visitors with literary interests: Shakespeare's birthplace at Stratford-upon-Avon. Both English and foreign visitors regarded it as a triumph if they could detach any part of the building as a souvenir.

extended the activities with a total lack of scruples. Falkner did his best to come away with something from Stratford. He succeeded in wrenching off a wooden button from a door in Shakespeare's birthplace and was quite unabashed when the custodian told him, sharply, to put it back. (Not the least remarkable aspect of Falkner's revelations is the self-admiring tone in which he describes his vandalism.) But even his depredations pale beside those of his compatriot Morford, the same who had run down an ostler. He actually adopted, and recommended, a 'low-crowned tourist hat of felt as the ideal place to hide one's plunder'. In Westminster Abbey, 'the vandal was as strong within me as it is in most Americans and the desire to knock off the nose of an alabaster cherub or the toe of an oaken baron of the Crusades overpowered me'. He attacked the Tower of London with a pen-knife, prising out a substantial chunk of stone, and at Chester stole a section of Roman tile. Charles Butler complained that one of his English friends had bitterly told him that 'the Yankees would carry away all England if it was possible' and certainly it was about now that one of the great myths of the early twentieth century had its roots – the story of the rich American who loved Europe so much that he tried to buy it to take back to America. The custodian of Stonehenge told Clifton Johnson that an American had offered a million dollars for the stones 'if he could get the privilege of moving them. He planned to set them up on American soil in or near some large city, charge admission and advertise it as the 8th Wonder of the World.'

But the crude, brash American was as much an object of embarrassment to his more cultured fellows as he was to his reluctant hosts. 'The European observer, particularly if he be English, picks out the least attractive of our people and then concludes that Americans are the vulgarest and the most ostentatious,' said Kate Field sadly. Her own sex came in for an ungallant trouncing from American males. William Dean Howells wistfully compared 'the cat-bird twang of so many of our women' with the 'soft and gentle cadences of English women'. Accents figured large in American estimations. The American girl 'may be pretty, have a dazzling complexion, bright eyes, handsome figure', but all was spoiled, according to her fellow American Dr Rodney Glissan, by her 'nasal twang'.

American womanhood had a doughty champion in Nathaniel Hawthorne, in particular in his vivid portrait of 'An English lady of fifty'. This truly terrifying woman 'has an awful ponderosity of frame, not pulpy like the lesser development of our few fat women, but massive with solid beef and streaky tallow so that (though struggling manfully against the idea) you inevitably think of her as made up with steaks and sirloins. When she walks, her advance is elephantine. When she sits down it is on a great round space of her Maker's footstool, where she looks as if nothing would ever move her. She imposes awe and respect by the muchness of her personality. . . . Her visage is usually grim and stern . . . she has the effect of a seventy-four-gun ship in time of peace. . . . She certainly looks tenfold – nay, a hundred fold – better able to take care of herself than our slender-framed and haggard womankind.' And he ends with a tacit warning to those of his fellow countrymen who compared English maidens so very favourably with American: 'It is a pity that the English violet should grow into such an outrageously developed peony as I have attempted to describe.'

The difference between their womenkind was much on the minds of American males. More than one noted wistfully how, in England, it was the woman who – in working-class households at least – waited on the man, pouring out his tea, buttering his bread, and not the other way round as 'back home'. But they noted, too, the almost universal courtesy of English males, comparing it, again most favourably, with the manners of their compatriots, some of whom seemed to go round 'with the Declaration of Independence in their pockets' in order to prove that they were as good as the next man.

Hawthorne remarked on that pronounced English ability to turn defeat into victory – on paper at least – to their own complete satisfaction. 'They have caught from the old Romans (whom they resemble in so many characteristics) this excellent method of keeping the national glory intact by sweeping all defeats and humiliations clean out of their memory' – this remark being occasioned by the fact that a young English officer had no idea of the identity of General Jackson whose bust stood in Hawthorne's office. Charles Williams believed that the Press deliberately manufactured a distorted view of events, being 'generally under the control and servilely devoted to the interests of the aristocracy'. But Harriet Beecher Stowe received an entirely opposite impression of English newspapers. They were, she thought, brutally indifferent to anything except sales and thus 'tell a vast deal about people's concerns which is not our custom to print in America'. She had cause to be upset, for the London Press had pilloried her, the supposed champion of slaves, for having her dress made in a sweatshop.

But by the end of a century of at times abrasive contact, the two peoples had gained a deep insight into each other. Oliver Wendell Holmes, writing after his second visit in 1887, summed up the long journey they had made, sometimes in harness, sometimes in bloody opposition. 'My parents, full-blooded Americans, were both born subjects of King George III. Both learned in their early years to look upon Britons as enemy of their country. A good deal of the old hostility lingered through my boyhood and this was largely intensified by the war of 1812. After nearly a century this had subsided when the War of Secession called forth expressions of sympathy for the slave-owning South and deeply wounded the lovers of liberty and England in the Northern States. A new generation is outgrowing that alienation.'

Alan Mulgan, a New Zealand journalist who came to England in 1926, was of Irish descent and was at pains to make his origins clear in the introduction to his book recording his experiences. 'I have no English blood in me that I ever heard of. Had I been brought up in a different atmosphere, I might have grown to manhood filled with the hatred of England which used to grow with such bitter luxuriance in the land of all her territories England most deeply wronged.' But the power exerted by that country on a people domiciled on the other side of the planet is shown by the title he chose for his book: *Home: a New Zealand Adventure*.

The overwhelming flood of books by American visitors to England is in stark contrast to the tiny handful of books by Antipodeans, of all the quondam colonies those closest to England in culture. The cause is, probably, a simple question of distance. By the 1880s it was taking Oliver Wendell Holmes a

Nineteenth-century tourists at the Tower of London, one of the high spots of a foreign tourist's circuit.

mere seven days to cross the Atlantic: even as late as 1926 it took Alan Mulgan five weeks to make the journey from New Zealand. A round trip occupying nearly three months, plus the heavy expenses necessary, eliminated automatically the ordinary Antipodean visitor. Not until the mass air transport that began in the 1960s did Australians and New Zealanders come to England in the same proportion as Americans had come a century before. But even allowing for this, it is still puzzling why fellow members of the British Empire, people who until well into the twentieth century regarded themselves, and were regarded, as distant members of the same community, failed to record their views of the heartland as had those citizens of the USA who had divorced themselves from that heartland nearly two centuries before. Alan Mulgan's book and that of his fellow New Zealander Ian Donnelly, published nine years later, have at the very least a rarity value. But both are the records, too, of trained journalists viewing their point of origin with an objective if affectionate eye.

Mulgan's book brings home a most vivid sense of England (not Britain) as the gravitational centre of an immense seaborne empire. He makes the point quite specifically in a passage reminiscent of a third-century citizen of Rome: Trafalgar Square and Whitehall are 'still, in spite of the buffetings of England, the centre of the whole world. London remains the world's most important city.' And a colonial's unconscious recognition of the fact that his civilization is wave-borne is brought out by the analogy he uses to explain New Zealand's old-fashioned taste in art and culture: 'My own country is like a village at the top of a long inlet: the tide is later there than at the mouth.'

Alan Mulgan's arrival in England had a touch of magic. After five weeks at sea, weeks during which it seemed that time itself had ceased and the universe been reduced to air and water, his ship entered the Channel – to find that an April rainstorm had thrown an impenetrable veil over land and sea and sky. The travellers who had eagerly come up on deck to get their first impression of 'home' were about to descend resignedly into the bowels of the ship when a sudden wind swept the rain-mist away like some vast curtain. And 'there was the patterned landscape, fields of green grass and crops and of warm red soil, groups of white houses and on the skyline all by itself an old, square-towered church enfolding we know not how many centuries. In a cleft of the hills running down to the sea nestled a comfortable little village. A door had been opened and England was before us – old, gracious, lovely.' He and his companion travelled on to London by way of Winchester, breaking their journey for a simple meal which seemed to have an almost sacramental quality for him – tea and toast in an ancient inn, in a room 'with rafters and panels of black oak, logs burning on an open hearth', and so onward through a rich and wet April. Throughout his stay in England he was fascinated by the colouring produced by an endlessly damp climate. Standing on Box Hill in the pouring rain he looked out, entranced, on the landscape beneath him. 'Rain is your most skilful colour maker . . . the deep valleys were drenched in colour . . . the woods were blue and the fields green and the villages red. The blue of Surrey struck home that afternoon like a spear.'

Like all those whose trade was in words, Alan Mulgan was vividly aware of the enormous, binding power of English, a linguistic commonwealth in which all partakers were equal, even though its practitioners might be in an indestructible hierarchy of talent. He knew Kipling's poems on Sussex by heart: 'Will English people believe that lines like these, read on the other side

---

No tender-hearted garden crowns
No bosomed woods adorn
Our blunt, bow-headed, whale-backed Downs
But gnarled and writhen thorn
                    Rudyard Kipling, Sussex

of the world by one who had never seen Sussex, brought tears to the eyes?' Like the Americans before him, he was fascinated by London's literary associations, by the discovery, for instance, 'that Lestrade and his associates in stupidity must have had quite a long and expensive journey when they dashed in hansoms from Scotland Yard to seek Holmes' advice'. Like most other non-English visitors before him, throughout the centuries, he was overwhelmed by the enormous size of London, by the knowledge that he was in the heart of what was still the largest city on the planet. Yet here, too, the English preference for the restrained, for the unstated, was admirably demonstrated in Downing Street. He was astonished by the humble appearance of Number 10, comparing it with the baroque splendours of the Quirinale, the classic majesty of the White House. He was amused and impressed by the English habit of putting up statues to determined ex-enemies like George Washington and Abraham Lincoln, and was deeply moved by the fact that men removed their hats on passing the Cenotaph in Whitehall. And in Westminster Abbey he, as a visiting New Zealander, had a unique opportunity to make an historical prophecy come partly true when he stood by Lord Macaulay's grave. 'Here was a New Zealander standing not on London Bridge and surveying the ruins of St Paul's, but by Macaulay's own grave, in the London he loved, a London far greater in his day and far mightier than he would have believed possible.'

Mulgan regarded himself as a member of a world community, using such adjectives as 'colonial' and 'imperial' with pride. It is doubtful if the English returned the compliment, and again and again he was astonished, or appalled, or simply resignedly amused, at the ignorance of the people at the heart of this great empire about conditions at its periphery. 'We get letters addressed New Zealand, Australia. We find a Manchester merchant enquiring about the extent to which the English language is used. I myself was asked by an English lady if there were any places at which she could stay if she came to New Zealand.' He sent a holiday photograph of himself, showing him standing barefoot on a sandy beach at a summer camp, to this same lady – and she assumed that this was the normal costume and accommodation in New Zealand.

Although Alan Mulgan gives no overt indication of his own social background, he was evidently moving through an upper-middle-class society in England, for he falls into one of those traps that lie in wait for the short-term visitor to a country – the assumption that the particular is also the general. In this instance, he takes for granted that all English society was underpinned by servants. 'The number of things that may be obtained in England by pushing a bell is surprising – and possibly delightful'; and, like the Americans of a century before, he compared English servants with those at home to the decided advantage of the former: in New Zealand, the attitude to servants was stiffer and more regimented ('more summoning of servants and giving instructions'), whereas in England the machinery worked smoothly, silently and frequently invisibly. He was uneasily aware of the class system, especially in a small village he visited where the villagers curtseyed to the colonial guest at the vicarage, but rejected the prevailing opinion that much of English manners was founded on hypocrisy. It was not hypocrisy, he asserted, but simply a hatred of logic. 'During a Sinn Fein demonstration in Trafalgar Square an orator, turning his stream of denunciation on to a bluejacket in the crowd, referred to him as the minion of a tyrannical government. When the incensed sailor tried to get at his insulter, the Irishman appealed to a policeman for protection.'

Mulgan was unfortunate – or fortunate – in arriving just before the General Strike of 1926. 'It was rather like seeing a man jump overboard in mid-ocean and cheering him vociferously for keeping himself afloat.' He was upset by the number of beggars in the street and so-called 'street musicians': 'to a colonial these street entertainments are a new aspect of poverty's straits'. But though he was shocked by the slums he thought that England's poverty was not as bad as he had expected and that, on the whole, 'the condition of ordinary people was steadily improving'. This was certainly not the impression received by his fellow journalist and compatriot Ian Donnelly nine years later. Donnelly came to England with a long list of important people he wanted to interview, among them J. H. Thomas, at that time Secretary of State for the Dominions. Thomas granted him an interview, 'but I was bewildered to find that it was Mr Thomas' intention to interview me'. He gave a polite, non-committal reply to Thomas's question as to how he found England, but this was not good enough for the Secretary of State. 'He wanted to embellish my eulogy. "There's another thing about England. You see no poverty in the streets even though we have two million unemployed. We've been able to save them from that here."' The bland assurance all but left Donnelly speechless. Later that day, outside the House of Lords, he saw a grim little procession of eight one-legged men, all wearing war medals, begging. 'Was it really their sad need to "beg bitter bread in realms their valour saved"?'

Although Donnelly's book is crisper, less overtly romantic than Mulgan's, the title he chose again illustrates that idea of England as a lodestone for the colonial: *The Joyous Pilgrimage: a record of months that realised a dream.* He, too, arrived up-Channel: his first vision of England, too, was almost that of a picture postcard: 'A stone village fitted so exactly into the scene that it caused no surprise.' And his impression of London as the hub of empire, an enormous, roaring, infinitely fertile centre was, if anything, even stronger

Stoke Poges Churchyard: a haven for visitors from all over the world.

than Mulgan's. He confirmed Mulgan's picture of a substantial cultural time-lag between hub and periphery, noting rather sadly that, after having been immersed in live music, on his return to New Zealand it would be back to a regime of gramophone records. And as for art, 'there would be a commotion if Cézanne or Van Gogh or their like were to be introduced into New Zealand galleries'.

Donnelly made the cultural circuit. Kipling refused to be interviewed, but he netted G. K. Chesterton, then at the height of his fame. He made that visit to Stoke Poges when the postcard seller told him of hearing every language spoken in the graveyard, and noticed that it was possible to have one's ashes buried there for a mere £90. Like Thomas Platter nearly four centuries earlier he, too, attended a sumptuous feast in London. On this occasion he was a guest at the banquet of a Livery Company and was at once impressed, amused but, in the end, somewhat disgusted by the institutionalized gluttony. 'Englishmen were about to feast ceremonially and they approached the laden board with seemly gravity. Conversation could not develop when such trencherman's labour had to be done. . . . Turtle soup, fillets of sole, *foie gras*, saddle of mutton, roast partridge, ham in champagne, sweets and caviare were consumed. With them were the proper accompaniment of wine. Then port and brandy. When an opportunity for talk came, the impulse was deadened.' He casts as cold an eye on the ritualized begging of servants, known as 'tipping', as any of the Continental visitors of the eighteenth century. The class system puzzled and irritated him: here, certainly, New Zealand descendants had parted company with their origins. 'The incessant peppering of "sirs" was unfamiliar to me.'

But in 1935 the shadow of the war that would be known as World War II was beginning to grow, emerging as a dominant theme in the book. He visited the Royal Air Force display at Hendon and received an ominous glimpse of the future. 'Those who would wish to see what war in the air would be like had two terrifying demonstrations. I hope to be far away if the air armadas of Europe have more than make-believe fighting to do.' But even that, he was told, would not save him, for distance was no longer a protection. On a visit to the offices of *The Observer* newspaper its editor, J. L. Garvin, told him – with, it would seem, a touch of relish – 'You must not think the Dominions will be out of trouble. Australia and New Zealand are three days away from Europe now.'

But was there not, perhaps, an alternative to suicidal conflict in Europe? Did not England belong to part of a larger community whose parts could work together in mutual assistance, instead of rending each other in mutual hostility? There was, apparently, no alternative: the offshore island must continue in the isolation imposed upon it over a thousand years before. He attended a meeting of the Royal Empire Society and recorded the speech of a politician which summed up the islanders' viewpoint. 'The day Europe is united under one power our island is doomed.'

CHAPTER NINE

Into the Abyss

At 9.20 p.m. of a bitterly cold February evening in 1926, Mrs Cecil Chesterton, a handsome middle-class woman in her thirties, stood outside London's Euston Station dressed in clothes 'which were shabby but not ragged, with water-tight shoes and a raincoat, and not one penny in my pocket'. A few nights earlier, in the company of a group of people which included her brother-in-law, the writer G. K. Chesterton, she had attacked the comfortable middle-class notion 'that for a woman who is willing to work employment can always be found'. In order to prove her assertion that society was rigged against the single, destitute woman she had agreed to live for two weeks in London on no other money than that which could be picked up by a down-and-out. She succeeded in doing so, and out of that experience came her book *In Darkest London*.

Ever since the middle of the nineteenth century, troubled members of the middle classes had been conducting forays down into the underworld of the destitute. Until the 1920s these explorers (as, with justice, they regarded themselves) were volunteers. In the twenties and thirties they were joined by a new breed of 'involuntary' explorers, those who had benefited from universal education, and then found themselves precipitated into the underworld by a collapsing economic system. In seeking titles for their books, both classes of explorers chose concepts which either reflected the idea of descending into a subterranean hell, or of venturing into some dark and ferocious jungle. Jack London, the tough American chronicler of the outdoors, entitled his foray into London's slums published in 1903 *People of the Abyss*; Mary Higgs, the daughter of a non-conformist clergyman who explored the world of destitute women in 1906, chose a similar title – *Glimpses into the Abyss*. General Booth's classic of 1890, *In Darkest England*, built up an elaborate analogy of exploration in an enormous lethal jungle on the model of Henry Stanley's immensely popular account of exploration in Africa. Motives for undertaking the journey varied from the simple, uncomplicated Christianity of Mary

Mrs Cecil Chesterton at the time of her 1920s journey In Darkest London.

Higgs to a straightforward desire to obtain good copy by the working journalists. Nineteenth-century newspaper readers, in particular, liked their reading strong and hot; editors were swift to oblige, free of the limitations later imposed by law.

Even Mrs Chesterton was a professional journalist, at the time of her experience working for the *Daily Express*. But whatever their original motivations, the experience left an indelible mark upon the most hardened observer. It is impossible to read *In Darkest London* without becoming aware of a burning indignation. Nobody would have put up with the humiliations Mrs Chesterton endured simply for the sake of a newspaper article. In many ways her record is among the most impressive, for she was begging her way in an area where she was well known. On one occasion friends met her while she was trying to sell matches in Piccadilly and urged her to come and have a meal with them. She refused, though she was wet and cold and had not eaten that day. Most of the accounts produced by these writers are what is known to librarians as 'ephemera': certainly few copies of their work exist today outside specialist libraries. But together, they chart a picture of England that none had ever attempted before, and very few since.

It was a journalist, James Greenwood, who was probably the first voluntary explorer of the abyss. His brother, Frederick, was the editor of the recently founded *Pall Mall Gazette* and it was in an unabashed attempt to give a much needed fillip to its circulation that James agreed to spend a night in a 'spike' or

A dosshouse of the 1880s, of the kind encountered by the first middle-class venturers into the abyss.

the casual ward of a workhouse set aside for vagrants, as opposed to the workhouse proper intended for parish paupers. It is an indication both of Greenwood's skill as a writer, and the degree of public interest in the underworld so close to their comfortable lives, that his report, 'A Night in a Workhouse', resulted immediately in a doubling of the magazine's circulation. The report is little more than a lengthy essay, a straightforward piece of popular journalism, but it embodied all the elements which writers as widely separated as Mary Higgs and George Orwell were to experience until the abolition of the workhouse, and with it the spike, in 1946.

Greenwood arrived in Lambeth spike on a January night in 1866 – so late that he missed the issue of 'skilly' – 'the first night of skilly under the new act', as the Tramp Major (the pauper placed in charge of vagrants) proudly informed him. Later, he had some of the sought-after brew and was both revolted by it and puzzled by the esteem in which it was held by tramps: 'a weak decoction of oatmeal and water without even a pinch of salt to flavour it'. He was subjected then to the ritual search. In theory, this was supposed to establish that no vagrant had sufficient money to pay for a 'kip' elsewhere: in practice, it was one of the small, mean humiliations intended to create a general reluctance to use a workhouse. Canny tramps learned to empty their pockets, burying the contents in recognized 'graveyards' outside the entrance. And it was not unknown for locals to prey upon these wretched treasures, marking down the graveyard to dig up the buried tobacco, or copper coins, as soon as the tramps were inside.

After the admission and the search came the bath. Again, in theory this was an admirable precaution: in practice it became yet another weapon to deter. Greenwood was shown a bathroom 'where there were ranged three great baths, each one containing a liquid disgustingly like a weak mutton broth'. More than half a century later George Orwell encountered a similar horror, when fifty naked men struggled for possession of two baths and two filthy towels under the malign gaze of a porter who cursed Orwell when he requested permission to swill out the grime-streaked tub.

After the bath, inmates were issued with nightshirts which may, or may not, have been clean and, if clean, may or may not have been dry. For Mary Higgs, who had stoically endured the horrors of the bath, 'the using of other people's dirty night gowns was the most revolting feature of our tramp'. Clothes were bundled up, the owners being given a wooden tag in exchange. In theory again they were supposed to be fumigated – an excellent social precaution. In practice, the bundles were simply chucked into one big container, a ripe ground for cross-infection.

The mockery of the bath was followed by the mockery of 'supper'. Vagrants were fed at a far lower level than criminals: food allowance per man per day in a spike was 5d, as opposed to 1s 6d for a man in custody in the local police station. And, as a matter of course, vagrants in the casual ward were fed at an even lower level than the paupers in the workhouse itself. Orwell was given work in the kitchen of the workhouse and found himself being obliged to throw away great quantities of perfectly edible and varied food while the tramps were all but starving on a bread and margarine diet.

Margarine achieves a kind of mystique of horror in the minds of most middle-class writers. Orwell returns to it again and again as the symbol not only of utter poverty, but of the debilitation made by that poverty. Speaking of an Irish tramp known simply as Paddy, he says: 'He was probably capable of work if he had been well fed for a few months. But two years of bread and margarine had lowered his standards hopelessly. He had lived on this filthy imitation of food till his own mind and body were compounded of inferior stuff.' Mrs Chesterton was even more outspoken: 'Margarine – that substitution for generosity beloved of the meagre, raises false hopes. How eagerly you take the first bite, with what satisfaction you proceed to masticate and then – that sickly, salty, rancid flavour overcomes you and in a violent physical revulsion you spit it out.' No means of spreading the stuff was provided, fingers instead being used, a fact which distressed Mary Higgs. And, like Greenwood, she too was puzzled by the popularity of skilly. 'The gruel was perfectly saltless. A salt box on the table into which many fingers had been dipped, was brought to us. But we had no spoons. It was impossible to mix the salt properly in the ocean of nauseous food.'

After bath and supper vagrants were locked up for the night. Mary Higgs, for one, keenly felt the humiliation of this, being sent to bed at 6.30 in the evening like naughty children. Sleeping quarters varied. Most spikes had cells – literal prison cells complete with spyholes in the door. The dormitory in Lambeth spike was a shed open on three sides: Greenwood slept there on a stone floor on that January night. Sixty years later Frank Gray – an Oxford magistrate who took to the road – slept in a kind of wooden coffin in a country spike. And in the morning was the mockery of work. The fiction was maintained that all users of spikes were itinerants seeking work. In practice they were kept at meaningless tasks (Mrs Chesterton polished the same door knob over and over for nearly three hours) until about 11 a.m. – far too late to get a job for the day. The compulsory work in the spike was a grotesque waste of labour which favoured the layabout against the industrious man or woman who was anxious to get outside and get a job of work.

On leaving the spike, the vagrant was issued with a meal ticket – another opportunity to practise humiliations. Frank Gray found that the Oxford spike deliberately issued tickets on an out-of-the-way café, obliging the tramps to walk an extra five miles. They were robbed as a matter of course, invariably receiving four pennyworth of bread and margarine and tea instead of the six pennyworth of the ticket's face value.

Mary Higgs and Mrs Chesterton were subjected to an additional hazard created by their sex. At Southwark spike, Mrs Chesterton discovered that women had the dregs of the men's tea an hour after the men had been served. Even the usually perspicacious and humane Frank Gray remarked of provisions in the spikes: 'Usually women's requirements are fewer than men's.' Mary Higgs discovered that the Tramp Major of one spike practised a species of *droit de seigneur*: 'He took my age and, finding I was a married woman (I must use his exact words) he said "Just the right age for a bit of funning. Come down to me later in the evening". I was too horror struck to reply: besides, I was in his power.' Orwell introduced that theory of love as a function of economics which he was to develop fully in *Keep The Aspidistra Flying* in one of his infuriating generalizations: 'No woman goes with a man poorer than she, or similar.' Mrs Chesterton remarked matter-of-factly that girls could at least sell themselves for food, and Terence Horsley, an out-of-work artisan in the thirties, emphasized that pairing off was the only means by which a woman could hope to survive. But the filthy food and general privation seems to have damped down libido, certainly among the vagrants themselves. Mrs Chesterton never had advances made to her, though she was a remarkably good-looking woman. General debilitation eroded even ordinary human contact. John Bentley, another working-class wanderer in the 1930s, emphasized the sense of isolation that slowly, inexorably developed. 'I was getting very bitter keeping myself to myself, always playing a lone hand.'

A major, and curious, difference between men and women was their attitude to clothing. Both Mrs Chesterton and Mary Higgs wore their ordinary clothes – and bearing in mind the fashion for skirts that actually swept the ground when Mary Higgs took to the road in 1906, one can only record with admiration her stoicism in filthy lodging houses where the floors were alive with vermin. Middle-class men who went 'on the toby', by contrast, adopted what can only be described as fancy dress. Both Jack London and George Orwell went to an old clothes shop and bought what they thought were appropriate garments for slumming. Both were resoundingly cheated – and Orwell's experience throws a curious light on his character and motivation. He wanted to exchange his good, if shabby, clothes for something less distinctive. 'I explained I wanted some older clothes and as much money as he could spare. He thought for a moment, then collected some dirty-looking rags and threw them on to the counter. "What about the money?" I said, hoping for a pound. He pursed his lips and produced *a shilling*' (Orwell's italics). There was no reason whatever why he should not have taken his clothes to another dealer and got at least ten shillings for them.

In any case, both he and Jack London were profoundly in error in thinking that a pauper willingly and consciously adopted a species of uniform. It is painfully evident, from the press photos which became common from the 1920s onward, that the down-and-out clung to the respectability of shirt-collar-tie-and-waistcoat for as long as they retained the faintest resemblance to their original shape. Bearing in mind Malcolm Muggeridge's description of the carefully casual dress of young people in the 1980s as 'proletarian fancy dress', it is deeply poignant to see how the 1930s proletariat clung to middle-class respectability at all costs. Orwell himself describes how the tramp, Paddy, who wore a pair of evening-dress trousers, meticulously repaired the braid upon it when it wore loose.

But gradually the clothes would disintegrate, losing all shape, evolving indeed into a kind of uniform which consisted of ankle-length, shapeless coat, hat crammed down over ears, sack and 'drum' for boiling up tea. Beneath that shapeless coat could be anything. Frank Jennings, the self-styled 'Tramps' Parson', described an old tramp reluctantly stripping for a bath. 'He peeled off a torn mackintosh, two old coats, two frowsty waistcoats, a grease-thick pair of trousers, a long pair of pants shredded with many holes, a lady's vest, a wide belt of blanket that covered his middle, and underneath that a thick wad of brown paper. On his legs were the remains of women's stockings, and on the soles of his feet were dirt-grimed toe-rags.' These last were virtually epaulets of the profession. Orwell refers to them, with patrician disgust, as 'horrid greasy little clouts called toe-rags'. Terence Horsley gives a common-sense explanation for them: 'They are rags, picked up off rubbish heaps, which are wrapped round the feet to ease chafing.' All writers, male and female alike, were impressed by the immediate social difference made by shabby clothes. Jack London noted that 'all servility vanished from the demeanour of the common people . . . I was one of them.' Change of clothes cancelled out the supposed difference created by upper-class accents. Both Orwell and Mrs Chesterton had feared that this would give them away but, as Mrs Chesterton put it: 'It is, I think, testimony to the part externals play that I was never once challenged as to my bona fides. I was accepted at face value.'

Some of the voluntary 'descenders' tried to study beforehand the world into which they were about to enter, as did Frank Gray. He was both a

'HEART OF THE EMPIRE . . . looking for anything. When the shops put out their rubbish there are bargains to be snapped up.' So reads the caption to the original picture, dated 22 October 1938.

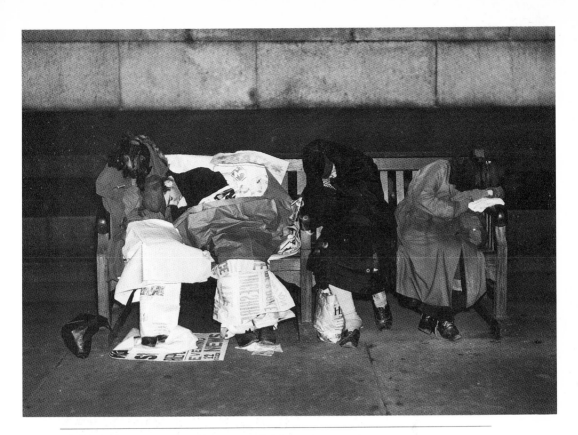

Vagrants of both sexes sleeping rough, 29 October 1930.

Member of Parliament and a magistrate, and his single book *The Tramp* is virtually the definitive work on a species which came to full flowering between the World Wars. The tramp was as different from the ordinary urban vagrant as the seaman is from the farmer. By law, no vagrant could spend more than one night in any given spike and they were set a day's march apart – an elastic measurement which allowed an interpretation ranging anywhere between two and twenty miles. Gray first gained his knowledge of the tramps' world by benevolently kidnapping specimens – plying them with food and drink in his car while questioning them. Only when he had a clear idea of the world awaiting him did he take to the road dressed as one of the brethren. Other descenders simply precipitated themselves into the abyss: Jack London took a cab into the East End, Mrs Chesterton took a train to Euston Station. The abyss opened at anyone's feet, in any part of England's green and pleasant land: all that was necessary to enter it was to ensure an empty pocket or purse.

But whatever the mental preparation nothing – but nothing – prepared the ordinary visitor, whether middle class or failed working class, for the first horrific impact of the dosshouse or spike, or even the poorer class of lodging house. On her very first night, Mrs Chesterton had had to walk for mile after mile from central London to the East End borough of Hackney, the only place where a free bed was available. 'I think I went a little mad, then. I felt that London ought to be burned down, that fire and brimstone should rain down on a city in which a decent woman could not find a bed.' Worse, far worse, was to follow. All writers referred to the awful restlessness which prevailed in the dormitories. 'Not for one moment was there peace,' said Mrs Chesterton of a Salvation Army Hostel; 'there was a stirring as of the leaves in a dense forest, to a continual accompaniment of coughing. No one slept kindly: no one found rest. When the continual stirring of leaves was still, there was the sound of the wind over the sea and once a voice cried out in agony "I can't breathe – I can't breathe".' All, too, referred to the stench of the dormitories. For Orwell, 'it had a sweetish reek of foul linen and paregoric . . . the sheets stank so horribly of sweat that I could not bear them near my nose'. Mrs Chesterton's hostel had central heating, a fact which should have been welcome on that bitter February night, but 'the warm air, heavy with the strong stench of humanity, and the odour of stale clothes – hot, acrid, sickly – made me feel faint.' Mary Higgs, with her customary stoicism, remarked on the number and variety of insect pests that invaded her bed during the night, so many that it took her a good half an hour to cleanse her clothes of them in the morning.

'Today is being opened up a new and grim field of sociological studies – the study of the psychopathology of human communities affected by profound disturbances of the basis of their economic life.' So, somewhat ponderously, the editors of *Memoirs of the Unemployed* introduced their book, published in 1934. The sudden experience of poverty in the thirties was totally different from anything that had come before. Prior to the Depression, poverty had been encountered either by a middle-class person, voluntarily, for purposes of research or reform or, if involuntary, by a member of the vast and usually inarticulate mass. In the 1930s, almost anyone could find himself precipitated without his volition into total poverty – among these *Memoirs of the Unemployed*, for example, were accounts written by an ex-officer and a professional accountant.

The stories told by the voluntary descenders change, subtly, in style. A different, rather uneasy note can be detected in them: they no longer convey quite the feeling that the writer is engaged in sympathetic but essentially anthropological research. They are writing about the people next door – or with the even more traumatic idea in mind: it's happened to them – could it happen to me?

Newspapers had again become interested in poverty and were sending out their reporters who, in due course, produced their work in hard covers. Outstanding among them was a certain William Teeling of *The Times*, who undertook a two-month journey, dressed as a tramp but prudently carrying two sovereigns with him, through the dosshouses of the north of England. *The Times* evidently thought highly of their special correspondent in the field. 'Much has been learned by writers who, like Mr George Orwell, have known tramping at firsthand. But we come nearer to Mr Teeling's kind of vagrancy with King Louis XI of France and the Caliph Haroun Al Raschid.' Teeling's viewpoint, and that of the newspaper he represented, was summed up by the remarkable opinion he advances on the very first page of his book: 'The miners in the north have in recent years trusted only two people: A. J. Cook, now dead, and the Prince of Wales. The rest of the unemployed of England, and those that dread unemployment at any moment, look to the Prince of Wales as the one disinterested man going amongst them and understanding them.' It ill behoves hindsight to crow over honest errors of judgment and William Teeling's casting of the future Duke of Windsor as the last hope of two million unemployed men was no more bizarre, for example, than *The Times*'s own current opinion of the then Chancellor of the Third Reich.

But William Teeling does seem to go out of his way to make a rod for his own back. In Darlington he discarded his tramp's outfit and thankfully spent the weekend at the home of a wealthy Conservative MP. 'To see men in dinner jackets, women well-dressed and then on to a tray beside the fire, some cold pheasant and whisky, and then to hear a conversation about hunting and the Hunt Ball . . . I knew these people well and, like everyone else they were doing their bit to keep things going in the country in the manner of the old days, and even if the Socialist objects the ordinary working man would understand and for fifty miles around there is no more popular family.' The idea that unemployed miners would think the world well lost as long as the inhabitants of the Big House had their whisky and cold pheasant and hunt balls must rank, for value, with Marie Antoinette's economic philosophy. Yet William Teeling's blinkered vision probably reflects accurately enough that of the class for which he was writing.

Frank Jennings, the self-styled Tramps' Parson, was another conscious slummer. His first book, *Tramping with Tramps*, has something of Mrs Chesterton's passion about it and it contains invaluable clues to the tramps' life style. But he does rather seem to have enjoyed the resultant publicity and his

The Two Englands. Great Howard Street, Liverpool, April 1924. Luncheon party,
Ascot, June 1921.

The conscience of England: George Orwell giving a wartime broadcast. (But why did he go 'on the toby' in 1931?)

autobiography, published in 1958, with its carefully posed photographs showing him 'with a typical New York Vagrant', leaves one somewhat doubtful as to his motivation.* George Orwell's *Down and Out in Paris and London* presents its own problem. On the one hand it bears the stamp of an almost unbearable verisimilitude: he undoubtedly experienced what he said he experienced and he seems to have suffered the physical horrors (in particular that relating to stenches) far more even than Mary Higgs or Mrs Chesterton. But it is difficult to gauge to what degree this was a genuine, unsought deprivation or that hankering for martyrdom which was a hallmark of his life. He arrived in England after his squalid experience as a *plongeur* in Paris only to discover that he had a month to wait for a job, and only thirty shillings to live on. He gives no real reason why he went 'on the toby' instead of seeking help from others of his class, and his account of how he sold his good clothes for virtually nothing does raise the suspicion of play-acting. But whatever the motivation for enduring the horrors that he did, the power of his language, fuelled by a raging indignation, makes *Down and Out* a touchstone and measure of poverty.

But with John Bentley's *The Submerged Tenth* and Terence Horsley's *The Odyssey of an Out-of-work*, one is hurled into the real world of sudden destitution. The publishers did not think it worthwhile to provide any hint as to the authors' identities, which have to be puzzled out from the texts. Both men were casualties of peace – ex-soldiers who had returned to the land fit for

*Nevertheless, Frank Jennings' contribution was recognized with the award of the MBE in 1984.

heroes to find that no job awaited them – but, this apart, their characters were quite different. Bentley was scarcely literate, the text of his book is stilted and bald, though for that very reason carrying with it a terrible urgency. For an unspecified period – probably for over a year – he travelled aimlessly back and forward between London and Manchester, sometimes starving for days on end, picking up odd jobs, selling matches, but usually dependent on handouts. His account ends abruptly with his marriage. Terence Horsley is a different proposition. He was, to begin with, a member of the new aristocracy of labour, a skilled electrician who was earning the very substantial wage of £3 5s a week in 1911 at the age of seventeen or eighteen. He joined the Gordon Highlanders in 1915 (he was a Scotsman), was wounded at Passchendaele and discharged in February 1919. Sharing in the national euphoria of the boom he started his own little electrical business and, when this collapsed through lack of capital, found a job easily enough in a Clyde shipyard. His periods of employment came to an end in 1928 and after two years' hopeless search for work in Scotland he undertook his 'odyssey'. Between November 1929 and the middle of February 1930 he walked a distance of some 748 miles between Glasgow and London and back, and in the whole of that period found one job, lasting perhaps three hours, which paid him 7s 6d. Apart from that sum, and an occasional handout of coppers, he lived on a total of £3 12s: in other words, his means worked out at between four and five shillings a week.

The view of England presented by all these writers in the thirties, by the near-criminal as well as the honest artisan, by the old Etonian Orwell and *The Times* reporter hobnobbing with the gentry, as well as the semi-literate Bentley – the 'idea of England' – is of a land overwhelmed by some cataclysm. As in all natural catastrophes many escaped and looked on with self-congratulation or puzzlement or occasional compassion on those struggling to come to the surface (the title of Bentley's book obviously came from the heart). Teeling was shocked to find that members of his own class were as vulnerable as any from the working class. In the common room of a lodging house in London's Camden Town, 'I was again struck by the variety of the types – men in plus fours and well-dressed, one of whom I was told was a doctor still in practice, foreigners, and what looked like university students.' In a spike, Frank Jennings encountered two holders of Military Crosses as well as an ex-naval officer. 'In Huntingdon "spike" I chummed up with the son of a Devonshire vicar who a few years ago owned extensive orange groves in Florida, USA. A cyclone ruined his groves, a bank smashed his fortunes and eventually he found himself back in England seeking any odd job that was going.' One of the press photographs which Jennings used for his book shows

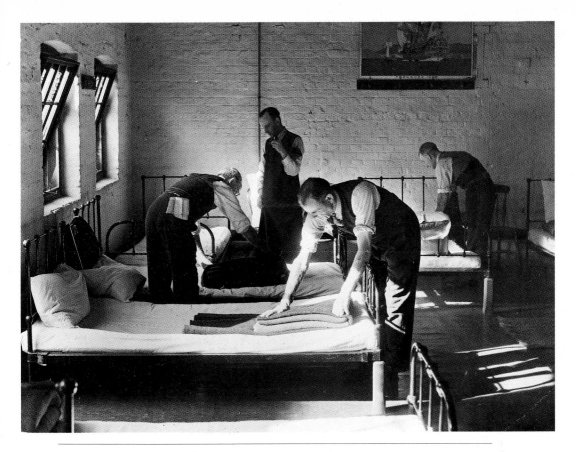

Embankment Fellowship Centre, established for the homeless unemployed, London, 1932.

an extraordinary range of down-and-outs sheltering in a London church. Among them are 'Old Bill' types in collarless shirts or chokers, and men who look as though they had just left the company's boardroom. Orwell found the attempt to maintain respectability particularly depressing and, for this reason, avoided Salvation Army hostels when possible.

The State's ordinary, niggardly provision for the destitute was enlarged by amateur organizations. Outstanding among them, and one which entered the vagrants' mythology, was the Silver Queen. Frank Gray describes it as 'a swift and silent motor van which is wont, at irregular but frequent intervals, to visit definite spots in London in the early hours. On arrival, the woman occupier of the van proceeds to dispense, free and gratis to those assembled round, hot coffee, sandwiches, cigarettes and sometimes even a silver sixpence. This done the van moves off silently, swiftly and unexplained.' Gray seems to have been writing, for once, from hearsay and garbled his sources a little, for it is evident that the title 'Silver Queen' was applied by the vagrants not to the car but the female occupant. Bentley, after eating and drinking in Trafalgar Square, says: 'I pulled at my mate's sleeve and enquired "Which is the Silver Lady?" "The blond, chum, and isn't she a pip?".' Horsley evidently met her on the Chelsea Embankment, though without giving her her title, and describes how she gave socks to a down-and-out who had obviously come by appointment.★

Organized religion came out badly by contrast with the spontaneous organizations. Jennings, himself a parson, recounts how a fellow parson went to ludicrous lengths to dodge him, believing him to be a genuine down-and-out. Teeling tells how Salvation Army officers marked him down for 'saving' – 'being tall, not too shabbily dressed and still holding myself reasonably straight I was fair game for the officials – obviously some one not quite gone yet, there must be a chance of saving me'. Orwell was enraged by the fact that 'people take it for granted that they have a right to preach at you and pray over you as soon as your income falls'.

The usual offering by small religious bodies was of tea and bread and margarine in exchange for an hour or so of extempore prayer and hymn-singing. Most of the vagrants accepted this, at one time or another, not only for the food but for the prospect of shelter and even transient companionship. Bentley's remark that isolation almost broke him applies to most, particularly those without intellectual reserves. Boredom was a destroyer. Teeling tells of a lodging house in Manchester where over 200 people sat on benches packed together in one large room. 'The men had nothing else to do but sit there every evening, after dark from five o'clock until they went to bed, about 9 or 10 o'clock. They sat there, just staring into space thinking of their bad luck and, if it rained in the day-time then unless they would get wet they must stay there too, all day. And if they stood in the passages that was loitering.' Orwell says that at a spike in Kent some 200 tramps sat packed elbow to elbow, locked in on a Sunday, staring at a blank wall for over ten hours almost mindless with boredom. It was during this period that so-called 'reading rooms' of public libraries – that is, rooms set aside for periodicals and newspapers – got a bad name with librarians for they became asylums for the down-and-out. Orwell remarks that his Irish tramp, Paddy, 'had a kind of loathing for books', but this seems to be most unusual, the English working classes certainly showing the same passion for reading even under these circumstances as the French and German observers had noted in the eighteenth and early nineteenth centuries.

★In 1983 the present writer wrote to *The Times* asking if it were possible to identify the Silver Queen and if she were still alive. Happily it was – and she is. She is Miss Betty Baxter who, after the War, established an annual Christmas dinner for tramps. The origin of the title is still in doubt. According to *The Times*, the term 'silver' applies to the coins she handed out.

According to Frank Gray, 'The genuine tramp never leaves a piece of newspaper behind him: he is fond of reading and paper or bits of paper are the only things he gets to read.' But even here Authority found ways of practising its institutionalized meanness. In the reading room of Sheffield public library Teeling found that the racing news in the papers had been blacked out.

Among the wanderers was a tough substratum which the Elizabethans described as 'sturdy vagabonds' and which somehow contrived to survive, century by century, in a kind of parallel universe. But of the scores of thousands of men and women roaming the roads and villages and towns of England in the 1930s the vast majority were bewildered exiles from the other, ordered universe, regarded by its fortunate inhabitants with contempt and suspicion. Frank Jennings met one of the latter near Kettering – as it happened, yet another parson. 'I called at the rectory to see if I could do an odd job and pick up a few coppers. The rector himself appeared. "Hullo, my man," he began pompously. "No, I've nothing for you. Do you honestly want a job? You know, I simply can't believe these tales. Lots of you chaps prefer to beg rather than work. Why don't you join the Army?"'

As it happened, there was to be ample opportunity, in the not too distant future, to solve the problems of the down-and-out by the means so heartily suggested. The Army – and the Air Force and the Navy – would indeed be welcoming men in their hundreds of thousands.

CHAPTER TEN

The Retreat from Empire

On Wednesday, 5 June 1940 those listeners to the wireless in the British Isles who had not switched off after the Nine O'clock News heard a comfortable Yorkshire voice asking the question, 'I wonder how many of you feel about this great battle and evacuation of Dunkirk?' The speaker was J. B. Priestley, and he went on to reflect in a relaxed, deceptively casual way on the significance of the armada of little ships that had taken part in the evacuation. The brief talk touched some chord of the national consciousness and, sensitive to that immediate response, the BBC shifted Priestley's *Postscripts* to the peak period of the week, that following the Nine O'clock News on Sunday. Thereafter the *Postscripts* were second only to the News in their ability to link the British together for a brief period of communal self-awareness.

Their overt subjects were, in the main, trivial and ephemeral – ducks in a park, a drunk singing *Rule Britannia* in an air raid, a clash with an official. Their delivery remained casual, the tone of voice one man might use when talking to another in a pub. But informing them was a deep unselfconscious love of country, unmarred by bombast, which precisely reflected the temper of the people themselves during the perilous months of 1940. A little over a year later the novelist Graham Greene, reviewing in *The Spectator* the published edition of the talks, summed up J. B. Priestley's contribution to the war effort. 'There were many of us who, before the war made such disagreements seem trivial, regarded Mr Priestley with some venom. We felt that, as a novelist, he represented a false attitude to the crumbling, untidy, depressing world. Then, after the disaster of Dunkirk, he became a voice – a slow, roughened voice without the French polish of the usual BBC speaker. We shall never know how much this country owed to Mr Priestley last summer, but at a time when many writers showed unmistakeable signs of panic, Mr Priestley took the lead. When the war is over we may again argue about his merits as a novelist: for those dangerous months, when the Gestapo arrived in Paris, he was unmistakeably a great man.' Nearly a generation later, when another novelist

– C. P. Snow – was asked what books a Russian should read to get an idea of England, he suggested the complete works of J. B. Priestley.

Although Priestley had published a number of books by 1940, his fame still rested largely upon *The Good Companions*, a rollicking novel whose relentless good cheer did indeed deserve the strictures directed at Priestley's craft by Graham Greene. There was, as it happened, a book of his which gave a far truer picture of England, though by the vagaries of fashion it had been almost wholly overlooked by the general public. Priestley undertook a long series of travels through England, which resulted in his book *English Journey* in 1933. That, incidentally, was the year Hitler came to power in Germany but, curiously, there is no reference at all to him. It was also the year in which both Orwell's *Down and Out in Paris and London* and William Teeling's *The Nearby Thing* were published – and the anthology *Memoirs of the Unemployed*. Priestley's book picks up the echoes and, at times indeed, amplifies them, in particular in bursts of rage directed against the brutally drab manufacturing towns of the Midlands. But, in general, he was like a traveller who, caught in a violent storm, is yet able to see better weather advancing on the distant hills. And throughout his sophisticated book, there is the same awareness of a country trembling on the brink of tremendous change as there was in the naive account by the Persian prince over a century earlier.

Priestley began his journey at Southampton by motor-coach, the first time he had ever ridden in one, and was amazed by its luxury. Other parts of his journey were undertaken in chauffeur-driven motor cars, and he makes a similar point about them that De Quincey had made about the railways: the speed and smoothness of car transport destroyed the sense of movement, of actually travelling. Work is the theme of *English Journey*, work for the most part in its positive, creative aspects: how things are made, who makes them, what they were thinking about while making them, who moves the products from place to place. He waxes almost lyrical on the great liners which imposed their enormous, graceful presence upon Southampton and compares them with the medieval cathedrals in the skill of their construction. Nevertheless, nearly half a century before it became fashionable to do so, he foresaw the end of Britain's heavy industries. As a native of the West Riding who knew 'what a proper factory looks like – a grim, blackened rectangle with a tall chimney at one corner', he found it difficult to take seriously the trim little factories, each set in lawns, along the Great West Road. Yet here, he suspected, the new industrial England was being born.

The hand of great change already lay heavy on Liverpool. In six years time, when the island kingdom was fighting for its life, the great docks would be booming again as they had done a century before. But in that year of 1933 was evidenced the beginning of the decline of the industry which had so impressed the visiting Americans. 'The warehouses we passed seemed empty of everything except shadows. A few men – far too few – came straggling along. . . . Something hooted, to break a silence that immediately closed up afterwards. I have rarely seen anything more spectral and melancholy.' What fascinated him in the great maritime city was its astonishingly rich racial mixture. 'The wooly curls of the negro, the smooth brown of the Malay, the diagonal eye of the Chinese, they were all there, crazily combined with features that had arrived in Lancashire by way of half a dozen European countries from Scandinavia to Italy.'

The Depression was most obvious in the cotton belt – one woman complained to him that the towns looked unnatural, they were now so clean. In his own home town of Bradford he encountered an unnerving phenomenon which, he believed, had contributed to the state of Britain. He found few of his schoolmates still in the town and of the group of particular friends he had known as a youth, 'there are, I think, only two of us left alive'.

'He speaks for Britain.' BBC
publicity shot of J. B. Priestley.

The Bradford which Priestley re-visited in 1933. A woollen mill closes the vista.

The rest had all been killed in the Great War. 'If they had been alive it is certain that I should be writing about another, and better England.' Most poignant of all was the fact that some of his old army comrades were unable to attend a reunion because their clothes were in rags.

Bradford formed, for him, a precise index of change: he was able to compare this town, of the 1930s, with the town he had known as a youth before the War. The richer merchants, he noticed, no longer lived in the city but – thanks to the motor car – were able to escape its dirt and gloom and live in the country – a trend he remarked elsewhere, particularly in the Potteries. On a wet Sunday night in what had been his home town he found that the only 'entertainment' available was drab public houses. Bradford had lost the concert hall he had known, and its theatre had been turned into a cinema: one of its lively newspapers had ceased publication.

Priestley turned again and again to the theme of mechanized, joyless entertainment. He went to Nottingham Goose Fair to find that not only were there no geese, not even on a menu, but that the whole fair 'was now simply an assembly of devices, chiefly mechanical, contrived to attract the largest number of pennies in the shortest possible time', a trend symbolized for him by a horrible machine that emitted recorded laughter. 'Even H. G. Wells, in his earlier and wildly imaginative days, never thought of machines that would laugh for us.' Time has a trick of turning truth into irony and the two media against which he particularly inveighed – the radio and the cinema – in the 1980s had become protected art forms. As a dramatist – above all, one who cherished the music-halls – he particularly loathed the cinema. In Leicester, he pointed out, with a population of nearly a quarter of a million people, there was only one live theatre. The future was to be very considerably worse, had he but known it, when the population – fragmented at last into households – would sit before the individual television screen.

Priestley found three Englands. 'There was first Old England' – the England of the tourist brochures and the patriotic songs, the England of cathedrals and manor houses and shaven lawns and quaint medieval towns. 'But we all know this England, which at its best cannot be improved on in this world – that is, as a country to lounge about in, for a tourist who can afford to pay a fairly stiff price for a poorish dinner, an inconvenient bedroom and lukewarm water in a small brass jug.' Side by side with this England lay that other whose beginnings Celia Fiennes and Daniel Defoe had so proudly charted, the England of the Industrial Revolution which had made it the most powerful country in the world, the heartland of the greatest empire in history – but which, too, had left an intolerable legacy of dirt and disease and squalor. And finally there was the third England, the England of bypasses and Woolworths and mass-production and motor cars and motor-coaches and wireless sets. It was, he thought, essentially a democratic England, not simply through the attainment of social equality, but in the fact that all classes were consuming the same mass-produced objects in necessarily the same kind of way.

And here J. B. Priestley differed wholly and emphatically from William Teeling (interestingly, their paths must have literally crossed, for Teeling was pursuing his investigation into the dosshouses of the North at the very same time that Priestley was driving round its industries and backstreets). Where Teeling felt that the miners were content in their deprivation so long as the squire and his relations had their traditional pleasures, speaking of the young, Priestley said emphatically: 'They do not live vicariously, enjoy life at second hand by telling one another what a wonderful time the young earl is having or how beautiful Lady Mary looked in her court dress.' He recognized the dangers of this new society, the knife-edge that must be trodden lest

Arrival of the Jarrow Marchers in London, 1935, by T. C. Dugdale. Sincere, but heavy-handed social comment typical of its period.

cornucopia turn into satiation, lest the wealth conferred by mass-production and mechanization should be paid for by an increasing anonymity. Yet he ended on a note of cautious optimism, for the first time in the book reflecting something of the ominous threat that gathered increasingly over Europe. 'I was not met in any town by the local representative of the secret police . . . the idea of liberty remained.'

J. B. Priestley's overwhelming obsession with the phenomenon of time rubs off onto the book so that, with *English Journey*, the reader is left with a desire to know 'what happened next'. What happened to the little chorus girl in that failing theatre in that dreary Midland town who so shone with her desire to please? What happened to the hopeless young man in Birmingham who carried his heavy suitcases for him, and was turned away like a dog by the hotel porter? What happened to the little girl sticking on labels in the chocolate factory? In the mind's eye one sees World War II, building up like a titanic tidal wave, ready to sweep these innocents into oblivion. What happened next?

Never before had there been such a mixing and a stirring of the population, such a confrontation of social mores. Typists from Kent found themselves manning lathes in Yorkshire factories; East End mothers, reluctantly 'evacuated', found themselves staring unhappily at Somerset fields; shop assistants from Putney struggled with fire-hoses in Bermondsey; tough eighteen-year-olds from the back streets of Liverpool shared pithead baths with public schoolboys from Surrey. Norfolk villagers, who looked on Suffolk villagers as effete foreigners, found themselves playing host to black men from Louisiana. Throughout the country, the monoglot British struggled to understand, or make themselves understood by, men from Poland, Denmark, Italy, France. Nicholas Bentley neatly summed up that aspect of the problem with his cartoon of the special policeman struggling to make head or tail of the polite request: 'Prosca Pane, ktora jest najbliszsa droga na Tottenham Court Road?' But the Geordie working on an East Anglian airfield, or the Welshman transported to Berkshire to make tanks, found it almost as difficult to communicate with the natives. And outside stood the 'foreign correspondents', the newspapermen from the 'free world' charged with the task of explaining the Briton's 'war effort' to nations still comfortably following a peacetime routine. 'Selling' the idea of England – or, rather, the 'image' of England – was now itself part of that 'war effort' and, to do this, the Ministry of Information came into being.

From its beginning, the Ministry was savaged by Press and public alike. The Press resented its powers of censorship and feared its potential as a rival. The public mocked it as a ramshackle ivory tower giving shelter to a very curious collection of literary refugees from the hard facts of wartime life. Shortly after the outbreak of war, Dylan Thomas tried to get a job with it, giving as his candid reason the fact that he wanted to avoid conscription 'because my one and only body I will not give'. His opinion of the Ministry probably summed up general opinion accurately at the time. 'I know that all the shysters of London are grovelling about the Ministry of Information, all the half-poets, the boiled newspapermen, submen from the island of crabs, dismissed advertisers, mass snoopers, and all I have managed to do is have my name on the crook list.' The extreme in criticism came with Evelyn Waugh's hilarious, corrosive, grossly unfair but satisfying portrait of the Ministry as a nest of lunatics, pansies and outright crooks, which he presented in *Put Out More Flags.*

England on the move. Children, wearing identification labels, at a London station during wartime evacuation.

The Ministry, of its nature, was a ragbag of people and objectives. Anything and everything could be classed as 'information', could be deemed able to accelerate or retard the successful prosecution of the war, whether it were promoting violin concerts in the Midlands or suppressing news about the sinking of the *Bismarck*. The left hand frequently had no idea what the right hand was doing. John Gunter, the American journalist, at that time a war correspondent in England, asked for the text of one of the leaflets dropped over Germany. His request was refused on the grounds that 'we are not allowed to disclose information which might be of value to the enemy'. Gunter then heavily pointed out that two million of these same leaflets had just been distributed to the Germans. 'The man blinked and said "Yes, there must be something wrong here".' Harold Nicolson, at that time Parliamentary Secretary of the Ministry, complained to the Naval Representative that there were no photographs of the sinking of the *Bismarck*.

Welcome to the strangers: a BEF soldier (centre) flanked by two Free French soldiers drinking a toast in hot milk, June 1940.

The reply was an English classic: 'Well you see, you *must* see, well upon my word, well after all an Englishman would not like to take snapshots of a fine vessel sinking.' In July 1941 the ebullient, red-haired 'Australian' Brendan Bracken, a personal friend of Winston Churchill's (and by no means averse to the wholly unfounded rumours that he was in fact rather closer related to the Prime Minister), took over the Ministry and gave it a more effective cutting edge in terms, at least, of wartime propaganda. The Ministry also acted as publisher, happily absolved from the paper rationing that affected the ordinary commercial publisher. It produced a considerable quantity of material in booklet form, highlighting such aspects of the 'war effort' as convoys, fire fighting, military campaigns and the like. But though many well-known names were commissioned to write the booklets, most remain curiously unreadable, with an unpleasing echo of bombast and lack of hard facts, an instructive demonstration of the fact that the State, for all its vast resources, does not necessarily make the best publisher.

There was a general expectation that the war poets and the war novelists would burst into song with the warbling of the first sirens. But they obstinately kept silent throughout the early part of the war, despite the literary weeklies asking, with a hint of pettishness, what had become of them. George Orwell spoke for most creative artists when he noted in his diary that it was impossible to write under prevailing conditions. But as compensation, if compensation it was, came the 'war books', the recounting of personal experiences, first coming as a trickle, then a gush and then a flood which threatened to overwhelm every other form of literature. A few, a very few, were destined to survive as literature in their own right, unique sparks struck off by unprecedented pressure on the individual: Richard Hillary's *The Last Enemy*, celebrating the brief reign of the fighter pilot, was one of this most rare breed. But the vast majority of them merely demonstrated that, while most people undoubtedly had a story in them, few could bring it out. Adventures of land girls and firemen, stories of soldiers on gun sites, and in tanks, of sailors in submarines and destroyers, of airmen in aircraft – in their sum they presented an unrivalled picture of a society under enormous stress, going through enormous changes, but individually the books are now as unreadable as the official publications. In a merciless passage in *The Spectator*, Simon Harcourt Smith summed up this vast class of book. 'The average warbook written by a serving combatant tends all too often towards the inarticulate or the two-dimensional. How well we know them now – the modest warrior who claps all his adventures into two classes, the "good show" and "bloody good show", or the type voluble in a strange language that has its roots in the road house era – "I pressed the tit and gave him a thirty-second burst. Then the glass-house bought one and so I had to do a brolly hop into the drink."'

It was, again, the Americans – sympathetically involved but geographically distant – who gave one of the best running commentaries on the island kingdom fighting for its life. There was probably a closer wartime affinity between the British and their Continental guests, despite the deep cultural differences, than between the British and their transatlantic cousins. The American authorities tacitly recognized the fact by publishing the admirable *Short Guide to Great Britain* for American soldiers bound for Britain. The book gave an excellent sketch of the British character as seen by a friendly, if slightly wary observer. The GIs were warned that the British really did prefer to sit in silence in trains and buses and restaurants and were likely to take umbrage if their privacy was invaded, no matter how great the goodwill. The booklet's glossary showed how far the two languages had drifted apart from their common origin: biscuits and pies were no longer the same thing in both languages and Americans should use great caution when referring to rubbers and suspenders. Above all, the GI was warned: 'KEEP OUT OF ARGUMENTS. You can rub a Britisher the wrong way by telling him "we came over and won the last one". Each nation did its share. But Britain remembers that nearly a million of her best manhood died in the last war. America lost 60,000 in action. In the pubs you will hear Britons openly criticizing their government and the conduct of the war. That isn't an occasion for you to put in your two cents' worth. It's their business, not yours.'

Among the American war correspondents based in London was a woman, Mollie Panter-Downes. She was a *New Yorker* staffer, cabling weekly or fortnightly 'Letters from London' which admirably trace the war on the 'Home Front' from its stumbling, reluctant beginning to its triumphant – almost ecstatic – ending. She was a sympathetic but by no means uncritical admirer of England (it is noticeable that she refers to her hosts as 'English' until Dunkirk, and then 'British' afterwards, a wholly unconscious change which only becomes evident when her cables are read as a narrative sequence). In the first part of the book, leading up to the trauma of June 1940, she seems to regard the islanders with an amiable mockery. Referring to the reverses in Norway, she remarked that it was probably a good thing, 'if only because it stopped people from chirping "Ah well, we always start badly" or "We English always lose every battle but the last."' She gave the obligatory pen pictures which continued the tradition of the English as cosily eccentric – the lady of the manor in her tweeds, the squire leading the hunt, the village wide-boy.

An American soldier pays a visit to his father's birthplace – only to find that the homestead has been bombed.

The two young women in the foreground are displaying the insouciance commented upon by Mollie Panter-Downes. The cloud in the background is the result of a flying bomb falling on Fleet Street.

Then, with the tremendous series of body blows which seemed to have ended the war in favour of the Germans in 1940, there is a change of pace in her records. 'It would be difficult,' she says in her balanced, measured style, 'for an impartial observer to decide today whether the British are the bravest or the most stupid people in the world. The way they are acting in the present situation could be used to support either claim.' Later in the war she was to return to that theme – insouciance or stupidity? – which engaged the attention of a number of foreigners, Adolf Hitler among them. Discussing the menace of flying bombs, she says: 'The behaviour of crowds is nonchalant to the point of idiocy. Housewives standing in queues glance up, when they hear a robot coming, with no more than the uneasy expression of a woman who has just discovered a wasp in the room.' But despite her irritation, by the end of 1940 she was aware that the islanders had closed ranks, presenting a united and determined front to a common enemy. The most dramatic demonstration, in her eyes, was the way they abandoned the passionate desire for privacy which had led the dwellers in a small, overcrowded island to erect individual barriers round themselves. Again and again she was to note how, in some great crisis, the British signalled their basic unity – by talking to each other. A habit which most other nationals adopt as a matter of course indicated, to this intelligent observer, a basic change in relationship produced under the enormous pressure of war. The average citizen found himself sustained as part of a purposive community, after perhaps spending a lifetime in social isolation. That camaraderie weakened with the ending of the great air raids and disappeared entirely, abruptly, with the coming of peace, but it left behind a profound and enduring sense of nostalgia, demonstrated and sustained by the endless postwar flood of books and films on the war.

Looking back down the turbulent perspective of the twentieth century, a perspective which, within living memory, had seen the country transformed from the gravitational centre of a world empire to, yet again, simply part of an offshore island complex, and seeking the point of change, the English invariably placed it at some point during World War II. 'Before the War' and 'After the War' became universally recognized points of chronology even

Their finest hour: Londoners using Piccadilly tube station as an air-raid shelter in September 1940.

*VE Day, May 1945, in London: an ecstatic scene repeated throughout the country.
Thereafter the British divided history into 'Before the War' and 'After the War'.*

when, in the receding passage of history, that war became one of many. In the popular mind, 1939–1945 drew a thick red line across the page of history.

But those who saw the country from outside did not so regard the point of change. The concept of 'England' formed a seamless web until well into the 1950s, so far as foreigners were concerned. The great change came later. Nirad Chaudhuri, who came to England for the first time in his life in 1955, was adamant about that. He had been warned by English friends of the great changes that had taken place. 'But I could not read or listen to this with full conviction. I asked myself "Are the changes so very thorough-going?" Why, to me it looks very much like what I had expected it to be, from reading and imagining. I thought today's England was very much like the England of history and perfectly consistent with it. I noticed the continuity more than the break.' A basic reason, as he recognized later, was that he was yet another non-Englishman who had taken in the English language with his mother's milk,

225

whose idea of England had been created and sustained and warmed by the great drum-roll of English literature. At Oxford, on catching sight of a low line of hills to the south, he asked his companion if they were the Cumnor Hills and if Bablock Hythe was in that direction. 'He looked at me and put a counter-question "Are you thinking of Matthew Arnold?"' When Chaudhuri agreed, he went on to say that an Indian had told him that his fellow countrymen came to England with too many literary associations and in consequence were deeply disappointed. '"I am not disappointed" was all that I said audibly, but my mental comment on this Indian was severe.'

Even as late as 1968 the Israeli diplomat, Hannoch Bartov, believed that the English gift for historical continuity was still strong. He arrived in England 'only days after Harold Wilson's second impressive victory' and so was able to observe the working of a Socialist monarchy. 'England has changed, they say, but tradition has not. Who would pretend that Ascot was *not* the event of the summer.' Class was still of immense – or predominant – importance: demonstrated unequivocally by the division in public houses, by the entrances to theatres, by the continued existence of tradesmen's entrances in houses. It was a two-way process, he found: tradesmen supplying his household were embarrassed to be told to use the main entrance. The aristocracy still had enormous influence and he, citizen of a socialist republic though he was, admitted that even he was impressed. 'I must in all honesty admit that I too felt greatly excited on being introduced to a real flesh and blood life peer. My knees shook when he actually addressed me.' He claimed that it was possible to tell a working man from the East End of London by his clothes. Clothes, generally, were still an index of class. 'You wear this on weekdays and that on weekends. You know in advance what to wear for dinner: it's formal, semi-formal or informal.'

But change, profound change was in the air. Unlike Chaudhuri, he had no common ground in the English language: for him, a Jew from what had been established as the Jewish National Home, evidence of the universal power of England was the Colonial Office, 'the centre of the universe, the seat of power'. He made a kind of pilgrimage to it and saw it in all its Victorian solidity and arrogance and overweening self-confidence. But scarcely had he got used to its new title of 'Commonwealth Affairs' when that, too, disappeared, subsumed into the Foreign Office. He describes a lunch at the Athenaeum as the guest of a very distinguished member. Outwardly, the concept of 'the club', that indestructible bastion of social – predominantly male – privilege, seemed as strong as ever. The abominable prep-school type food (his host made what was evidently a well-polished joke about the Athenaeum sheltering all the arts except gastronomy); the vast, shadowy rooms; the sensation of a frenetic world kept firmly at bay while the rulers of England planned their strategy. 'Inside the Athenaeum one has a peculiar sensation as though one has come at long last into physical contact with the Establishment, has actually seen the Holy of Holies. I came to learn that this is not the case. No longer is it the place where people who count decide on things which matter.' Nowadays, Bartov points out wryly, when somebody suggests 'lunch at the Club', it's likely to be the Playboy Club.

Looking back, this citizen of a country born under the wing of the British Empire identified the peak of that Empire as the coronation of King George V, 'when subjects and liegemen of the British crown gathered from every corner of the earth. That splendid hour looks to us today like a blind man's masque in a house on fire, not unlike the ironic opening scene of *King Lear*.' (Yet again, a non-Englishman draws on English literature to encapsulate some truth about the islanders.) In the postwar years, he identified the moment of change within the country itself, its inter-relationships, with the pompous *Declaration* issued in 1960 by the group of writers for whom the Press had coined the glib collective phrase Angry Young Men, a group of young men engaged in dismantling the society which had shaped them.

Hannoch Bartov identifies England's moment of change by hindsight, working up his notes some time afterwards in Israel, valid enough and accurate enough but still subject to the usual criticisms of the historical method, the placing of an imprint upon a period by an external agency. But his belief that the 1960s harbour the point of change is tacitly and unconsciously substantiated by two books wholly different from each other, as from Bartov's, in their style and provenance. One is by an Australian, Stuart Gore, who toured the country with his wife in a rattling little van, making a freelance film, in 1957; and the other is by an American, Paul Theroux, who travelled round the entire coastline in 1983. Allowing for personal differences, the contrast between the books charts a change in course of an entire society. Gore saw a charabanc load of holidaymakers spontaneously teaming up with natives in Stokesey to do a country dance: Theroux saw only bored 'holidaymakers' playing electronic games in dusty, dark halls. Gore fell enthusiastically upon the meal which every foreigner has been taught to recognize as 'the great English breakfast': Theroux swallowed with distaste the 'slimy, salty breakfasts'. Gore heard the clacking of clogs on cobbles in Lancashire: Theroux saw only mass-produced clothing. Gore enthused over Liverpool, still enjoying its wartime boom. For him, 'it exactly symbolized England. No Saxon tomb, no ruined Abbey, no ancient castle could crystallize the spirit of the Old Country in quite the same way' as this great maritime city, still proudly confident. Theroux saw only a city 'elderly, venerable, tough, somewhat neglected . . . shabby gentility mixed with unobtrusive ruin'. He had come there specifically, indeed, not to inspect what once had been the great gateway to the New World, but to see the results of the recent riots.

The title Gore chose for his book could not have better shown the shift away from the almost religious atmosphere in which his fellow Antipodeans had visited England in the 1920s. *Australians Go Home!* was his choice, at once perky, cheerfully aggressive, but also self-defensive. Even now, a generation after Mulgan and Donnelly had deplored the ignorance of the English about their distant cousins, a generation in which Australians and New Zealanders had fought side by side with the English and had lived for months on end in their country, Gore found the same deplorable attitude compounded at once of ignorance and contempt. 'We come from a country that everybody here seems to think is running neck and neck with the anthropoid apes, culturally speaking', and goes on to point out vigorously that the Aborigines were making their complex mystic designs when Britons were still fooling around with woad. He was in the vanguard of the great Australian invasion of England: over 15,000 of them had come to Britain that year, he remarked. 'This, for young Australians and New Zealanders, is a twentieth-century version of the nineteenth-century Grand Tour – the only difference being that they work their way round instead of loosening papa's purse strings.' He picked up again that picture of English indolence that had aroused the condemnation of Continentals nearly two centuries earlier, and was particularly fascinated by the English cult of lunch, the long ritual in the middle of what was supposed to be the working day, contrasting it with the sandwich hastily grabbed by the Australian.

The supposed English love of animals came as another revelation. He was puzzled at first by the sight, in every London suburb between the hours of 10 p.m. and midnight, of shadowy men, muffled up against the freezing fog, patiently waiting for someone or something. They turned out to be dog-owners 'exercizing' their pets – in other words, taking them on to public places in order to allow them to empty their bowels. He contrasts this almost slavish 'love' of one species of animal with brutality towards others, startled in particular by the 'gruesome-looking display of dead hares in glassless butchers' shop windows, the gaze of their bulging eyes seeming to horrifically survey their companions in misfortune – pathetic little bundles of feathers ticketed "pigeons for invalids".'

Gore enjoyed England, responding to the ancient pull of blood relationship, delighting in that Old World England which still survived. But the impression he received and conveyed was of a tired people still caught up

The beautiful little towns survive: the land remains. Although this poster illustration is intended, unequivocally, for publicity, it encapsulates an essential truth.

in sterile class distinctions, still engaged in drab activities. It was summed up for him in Lancashire where the 'decent' housewife not only still scrubbed her front doorstep, but also the pavement and the section of gutter adjoining – all this in the dead of an unusually severe winter. 'You have to be tough to survive in this country', was his conclusion. 'This is where all the pioneers live, not Canada or Australia or New Zealand.'

Paul Theroux is an American writer with a passion for trains and, though it may not be readily apparent from his book *The Kingdom by the Sea*, an admiration for England – certainly one strong enough to keep him here for more than a decade. His world, like that of so many longterm visitors to England, was the world of London. He wanted to go elsewhere and write of another England. But where? In what direction could he travel to find new ground in this ancient, overwritten, well-trodden country?

The answer proved to be obvious: England was, after all, part of an island surrounded by water. What better place to see the English and their Scots and Welsh relations than by the seaside with their hair down. And so off he went to explore this water-bound kingdom. But there was nothing royal about these people the American met in 1982: nothing of the confidence his forebears had met a century and a half before: nothing of the arrogance, the 'You be damned' that had enraged and impressed and made envious the Continentals in the eighteenth century. He begins, indeed, with invective against an effete, indolent, prejudiced, treacherous people that would not have been out of place in the charged atmosphere that prevailed in England during the American Civil War. And though it is 'Britain' which is his ostensible theme, it is England which again and again provides his examples. And horrific examples they are.

Theroux began his tour at Margate, finishing up three months later at Southend a few miles north of Margate. And if it is true, as he claims, that the essence of a people is to be found on its coast, then the English were in a very bad state indeed. The overwhelming impression conveyed in his book is of a people with badly fitting false teeth slurping up junk food and sour beer, drearily jingoistic (the Falklands War had just begun), mouthing third-rate opinions received at tenth hand through a gutter press. A people sadly taking their pleasure in dismal holiday camps, like the vast Butlin at Minehead whose population of 14,000 was double that of the host town, which he took as the very epitome of English life 'in its narrowness, its privacies, its pleasures. It was England without work.' Southend, where he completed his journey and his book, 'had that dirty, desecrated look which I thought of as English'. He made for the beach and the famous pier, but the tide was out. 'It was a sea of the filthiest mud. It was a fitting end to my trip.'

It is hardly England's fault that Southend beach is made of mud and not sand. And it is open to doubt whether a seaside population is really the best representative of an island people – at least a seaside population of the 1980s when 'pleasure' had taken over from the traditional industries. Gore, too, had been depressed by seaside 'resorts' which 'look like a vast amusement park into which someone had dumped a few truckloads of sand and shingle carefully bordered with a strip of mournful-looking sea'. It's fair to say that a very high proportion of English people also find themselves profoundly depressed by the 'seaside' cult and, far from spending three months exploring it, do their best to keep as far away from it as possible. But it also represents the Utopia of tens of thousands, the logical end-product of the process whose beginning J. B. Priestley recorded half a century before when he was shocked at the idea of a machine laughing for humans.

And much of what the American had to say about the English at the seaside in the 1980s is confirmed by the picture two native English writers present of their compatriots inland in the same decade. Richard West is a journalist, specifically a foreign correspondent, who had spent so much time abroad that he was able to see England with the objectivity of an outsider when he made an independent tour in 1981. 'And what I see frightens me.' Beryl Bainbridge retraced J. B. Priestley's journey with a television crew in 1983. Both writers chose the simple title *An English Journey* for their books. Both recorded, quite independently of each other, a vast new menace – the destruction of cities by the wave of greedy 'development' of the 1960s and 1970s. Richard West said forcefully that his experience of the Continent showed him that not all European countries have necessarily changed for the worse, as appears to have been the case with England. 'Cities destroyed in the second World War have been rebuilt and made attractive: in England, cities that have been untouched by war have been vandalized by crooks and property men.' Beryl Bainbridge, herself a native of Liverpool, turned to that great city – as so many before her had done – as a touchstone and index of change. It was no longer the proud, elegant city that the first American tourists had known: no longer the great symbol of English commercial power in which Gore had rejoiced; it was not even the melancholy, dying city that Theroux had seen. It was a dead city. 'All the landmarks I remembered gone without trace . . . no gunsmith with its velvet drapes and pheasants stuffed with sawdust . . . no ice warehouse, no Bears Paw Restaurant, no pet market' – a city scarred with unfinished projects and derelict sites. 'If I were an historian I could chart the reasons for all this chaos: decline of trade, loss of Empire, aeroplanes instead of ships . . . But it hardly matters now. It's too late. Someone's murdered Liverpool and got away with it.'

'*The Kingdom by the Sea': the unspoiled coast at Sansend, Yorkshire.*

Nearly thirty years before Beryl Bainbridge was moved to write her threnody over Liverpool, Nirad Chaudhuri – looking at the country which had been central to the lives of tens of millions of human beings of every possible tongue and every possible shade of skin – pronounced his mild and courteous judgment. 'They [it is the 'English' again, not the 'British'] give the appearance of thinking that they will come through if only they can hold on like Captain MacWhirr in Conrad's *Typhoon* (it is curious that it is a Pole, and not an Englishman, who has translated the national attitude into a personal story).' It is, perhaps, the alteration of attitude that is of importance – not the attitude of the observed, but the attitude of the observer. Perhaps the Honourable John Byng was right, if a trifle premature, when he considered, two hundred years ago, that speed had brought exploration to an end. Perhaps the new 'idea of England' will be born of the intensive, rather than the extensive – in the technique, for instance, which Melvyn Bragg used to

compose his picture of Wigton in Cumberland. At the opening of his book *Speak for England* he says: 'England has become fixed in a past which can no longer be placed . . . stuck in a part which is less and less meaningful. It is my hope that in the mirror of this book we can discover the outlines of a new appearance. To find the world in a grain of sand has been a sound method in art and science since men started looking for answers. And so it seemed a good idea to settle on one place for this book. Wigton . . . .'

It is as though the wheel has come full circle: 'a companye of sondry folk, by aventure y-falle', observed by one of their number, sympathetically but objectively, and so creating a picture of the society that created them, the idea of England.

Bibliography

CHAPTER 1 *Your Opulente and Ample Reaulme*
For general background to Chaucer see Derek Brewer's *Chaucer and his World* (1978). Jonathan Sumption's *Pilgrimage* (1967) puts the Canterbury pilgrims in an international context. J. J. Jusserand's *English Wayfaring Life in the Middle Ages* (1891) is still the best on its subject, despite its age and foreign authorship. Lucy Toulmin-Smith's edition (1907–10) of Leland's *Itinerary* is still, surprisingly, the only one generally available. Camden's *Britannia* has recently (1977) been re-issued with copious notes by Gordon J. Copley. There are many editions of Stow's *Survey of London*, including a very useful pocket edition (1923) with which one can follow him around. Harrison's book is available in Frederick J. Furnival's eccentrically edited version (1877), published under the title *Description of England in Shakespeare's Youth*.

CHAPTER 2 *Entry of the Clowns*
John Taylor's immense output has been made available through publications of the Spenser Society (1868, etc). Kemp's *Nine Daies Wonder* was published, with an introduction by A. Dyce, by the Camden Society in 1840.

CHAPTER 3 *The Idea of England*
Joan Parke's *Travel in England in the seventeenth century* (1925) provides an excellent general background for the period. Celia Fiennes's *Journeys*, edited by Christopher Morris, is now in an illustrated edition (1982). Daniel Defoe's *Tour through England*, edited by G. D. H. Cole, was re-issued in 1927. The Honourable John Byng's diaries were published under the title of *The Torrington Diaries*, with an introduction by C. Bruyn Andrews (1934–38). Arthur Young's *Tours* have never been reprinted: the reference here is to *A Six Weeks' Tour through the Southern Counties of England and Wales* (1769). There have been many editions of Cobbett's *Rural Rides*, the most recent being E. R. Chamberlin's abridgment (1982).

CHAPTER 4 *The Ambassadors*
The chapter is indebted to Francesca M. Wilson's superb anthology *Strange Island: Britain through foreign eyes 1395–1940* (1955). Individual publications which helped to flesh out the story include: *Chronicles of England, France, Spain* by Sir John Froissart, translated by Thomas Johnes (1849); *Thomas Platter's Travels in England*, rendered into English and with introductory matter by Clare Williams (1937); Rawdon Brown's *Four Years at the Court of Henry VIII*, containing translations of the Italian despatches (1857); W. B. Rye's *England as seen by foreigners in the days of Elizabeth and James I* (1865), with numerous translated selections. Najaf Koolee Merza's *Journal of a residence in England* was translated and privately printed without date. M. O'Rell's *John Bull and his Island* appeared in translation in 1883; H. Taine's *Notes sur l'Angleterre* was translated by W. F. Rae in 1872. G. M. A. Baretti brought out his own translation of *A Journey from London, to Genoa . . .* in 1772. Pückler-Muskau's *Tour in England . . . by a German prince*, translated by S. Austin (1832), has become a classic of its kind, as has Pastor Moritz's *Travels chiefly on foot through several parts of England* (1782).

CHAPTER 5 *In Search of the Picturesque*
William Combe's *The Tour of Doctor Syntax in Search of the Picturesque*, with Rowlandson's drawings, was published in book form in 1769. William Gilpin brought out a number of his *Observations* (on various parts of England) with his aquatints between 1770 and 1809 and was the subject of a major bibliography, *The Life and Work of William Gilpin, 1724–1804*, by William D. Templeman (Illinois Studies in Language and Literature, Vol. XXIV, 1939). Thomas Gray's *Journal*

234

subsequently appeared in his collected *Works*, edited by Edmund Gosse (1884), and the 5th edition of Wordsworth's *Guide to the Lakes* was published in 1906. Norman Nicholson's *The Lakers* (1955) traces the literary development of the cult, while the catalogue of the Victoria and Albert Museum's exhibition *The Discovery of the Lake District* (1984) illustrates its artistic development.

CHAPTER 6 *The Stately Homes of England*
Although books on the architectural and genealogical history of country houses are legion, ranging from the forelock-tugging accounts of the eighteenth and nineteenth centuries to the austere monographs of the twentieth, their social life had been largely ignored until Mark Girouard's *Life in the English Country House* (1980). The Duchess of Devonshire's *Chatsworth* (1982) gives an unusual insight into the running of a great house and incorporates substantial sections of the sixth Duke's *Handbook*, written in 1844. Two recent books on specific houses, Carol Kennedy's *Harewood* (1982) and David Burnett's *Longleat* (1978), place them in the context of today's rapidly changing social conditions, while Heather A. Clemenson's *English Country Houses and Landed Estates* (1982) illustrates the economic relationship between the houses and their estates. *A Silver-plated Spoon* by John, 13th Duke of Bedford (1959) is a refreshingly sardonic, inside view of the 'stately home business'.

CHAPTER 7 *The Mysterious Land*
William Stukeley's massive works have never appeared in popular form. *Itinerarium Curiosum or an account of the Antiquitys and Remarkable Curiositys in Nature or Art, Observ'd in Travels thro' Great Britain* remains in its handsome 1724 folio. Stuart Piggott's standard work has been republished in a revised edition, *William Stukeley: An Eighteenth-Century Antiquary* (1985). Geoffrey of Monmouth's *History of the Kings of Britain* has been re-issued (1958) in a translation by Sebastian Evans. In the vast number of books on Stonehenge, reference is perhaps best made to the official (HMSO) publication by R. J. C. Atkinson, *Stonehenge and Avebury and neighbouring monuments* (1968). Geoffrey Ashe's *Avalonian Quest* (1982) coolly surveys the lush growth of Glastonburian mythology, in contrast to Frederick Bligh Bond's *The Gate of Remembrance* (1918), which unabashedly embraces the supernatural.

CHAPTER 8 *Kissing Cousins*
Like Chapter 4, *Kissing Cousins* is indebted to a brilliant compilation, Alison Lockwood's *Passionate Pilgrim: the American traveller in Great Britain 1800–1914* (1981). Outstanding contemporary accounts by visiting or resident Americans in the nineteenth century include Nathaniel Hawthorne's *Our Old Home: a Series of English Sketches* (1863) and his wife Sophia's *Notes in England and Italy* (1870). Oliver Wendell Holmes's *Our Hundred Days in Europe* (1887) is the courtly American abroad, in contrast to the egregious Henry Morford's *Over-sea: or England, France and Scotland as seen by a live American* (1867). Orville Dewey's *The Old World and the New* (1836) is a thoughtful summary of the contrasts at the outset of the American 'discovery'. Washington Irving's seminal essay on Stratford-on-Avon appears in his *The Sketchbook of Geoffrey Crayon, Gentleman* (1854). The two New Zealand contributions to the chapter are *Home: a New Zealand Adventure* by Alan Mulgan (1927) and Ian Donnelly's *The Joyous Pilgrimage: a record of months that realised a dream* (1935).

CHAPTER 9 *Into the Abyss*
Of their nature, few copies of these autobiographies have survived outside specialist libraries. Among those which contributed to the chapter are: Jack London, *People of the Abyss* (1903); Mary Higgs, *Glimpses into the Abyss* (1906); James Greenwood, *How the Poor Live* (1876); Mrs Cecil Chesterton, *In Darkest London* (1926); Frank Jennings, *Tramping with Tramps* (1931); Terence Horsley, *Odyssey of a down and out* (1931); George Orwell, *Down and out in Paris and London* (1933); William Teeling, *The nearby thing* (1933); Beales and Lambert, *Memoirs of the unemployed* (1934); Frank Gray, *The Tramp* (1931).

CHAPTER 10 *The Retreat from Empire*
J. B. Priestley's *English Journey* (1934) has been re-issued in an illustrated format (1984). Mollie Panter-Downes's cables were edited by W. Shawn and published (1972) under the title of *London War Notes 1939–1945*. Stuart Gore's *Australian Go Home!* was published in 1954. Other sources for the chapter include Nirad C. Chaudhuri, *A Passage to England* (1959); Hannoch Bartov's *An Israeli at the Court of St James*, translated by Ruth Aronson (1971); Richard West, *An English Journey* (1981); Paul Theroux, *The Kingdom by the Sea* (1983); Beryl Bainbridge, *English Journey* (1984); and Melvyn Bragg's *Speak for England* (1976).

List of illustrations

Index